Text Databases and Document Management: Theory and Practice

Amita Goyal Chin
Virginia Commonwealth University, USA

IDEA GROUP PUBLISHING
Hershey • London • Melbourne • Singapore

Acquisition Editor:	Mehdi Khosrowpour
Managing Editor:	Jan Travers
Development Editor:	Michele Rossi
Copy Editor:	Elizabeth Arneson
Typesetter:	Tamara Gillis
Cover Design:	Deb Andree
Printed at:	Sheridan Books

Published in the United States of America by
Idea Group Publishing
1331 E. Chocolate Avenue
Hershey PA 17033-1117
Tel: 717-533-8845
Fax: 717-533-8661
E-mail: jtravers@idea-group.com
Web site: http://www.idea-group.com

and in the United Kingdom by
Idea Group Publishing
3 Henrietta Street
Covent Garden
London WC2E 8LU
Tel: 44 20 7240 0856
Fax: 44 20 7379 3313
Web site: http://www.eurospan.co.uk

Library of Congress Cataloging-in-Publication Data

Text databases and document management : theory and practice / Amita Goyal Chin [ed.].
p. cm.
ISBN 1-878289-93-4 (paper)
1. Text processing (Computer science) 2. Database management. I. Chin, Amita Goyal, 1968-

QA76.T48 T48 2001
005.74--dc21

00-054106

British Cataloguing in Publication Data
A Cataloguing in Publication record for this book is available from the British Library.

Text Databases and Document Management: Theory and Practice

Table of Contents

Preface

With modern word processors, interconnected global networks, gigahertz processors, and terabytes of database storage, we now enjoy unprecedented high speed access to data. Many futurists had predicted the demise a decade or so earlier of paper trails and the rise of the paperless office. The state of the art in electronic storage and communication of digital information, however, has thus far failed to fulfill the dream of the paperless office. While the explosive growth of the World Wide Web (WWW) has created an abundance of information dumping, effective cataloging and retrieval of the available information has become extremely difficult. Documents remain the backbone information carriers of most businesses. However, even in digital form, documents remain unwieldy constructs that are difficult to manipulate. The ubiquitous WWW has in fact exposed the boundaries of our ability to pragmatically categorize and efficiently utilize the required diversity and magnitude of electronic documents. The central issue in document management continues to be the handling of text.

The fundamental nature of digital text is deceptively simple. A continuous string of numbers, each number representing a character, provides the basic construct. If the requirements are simply to be able to digitally reproduce the printed word for storage, transmission, and finally human consumption, then this basic construct fulfills the needs. However, if the desire is to have the computer intelligently process text, the construct is insufficient. While our ability to handle digital text in the graphics and publishing arenas has revolutionized those industries, much of that text handling is intended for precise print layout. Unfortunately, these advances fail to aid in increasing the computer's information handling prowess. Tagged text, e.g., SGML and XML, enriches the basic construct with standardized means to add descriptive information to specific portions of text and provides a structured framework. The in-line nature of the tags, however, creates certain weaknesses; the difficulties in standardization of document structures, as well as other issues, clearly prove the inadequacies of current technology.

As the number of documents available on the Internet and on local storage devices increases, the urgency for sophisticated methodologies for the manipulation of required information increases. An examination of the movement of structured databases from flat files to the relational model clearly delineates the breadth of transformation necessary for the effective handling of text. The demands for concurrent access, version control, security, and volume demonstrate the tremendous necessity for innovation. The technologies that help explicate these issues will elevate productivity from computer systems.

This book provides a focal point for researchers and professionals endeavoring to formulate solutions for textual data management. The eight chapters of this book include discussions of multiple topics proven crucial in obtaining a comprehensive perspective on the intricate challenges of judiciously handling text.

The first chapter, *Markup Languages and Electronic Commerce* by Ingrid Fisher and Jagdish Gangolly, presents an introduction to the evolution of markup languages. The article further discusses database connectivity in generating hypertext documents, including the use of the Document Object Model (DOM). Finally, the article furnishes an electronic commerce application that dynamically generates Web pages from a database.

Most organizations face the increase of both the vicissitude and plenitude of electronic documents at a dramatic rate; good search engine technology is one fundamental mechanism for coping. *Search Engines, Relevancy, and the World Wide Web* by Wendy Lucas focuses on an essential tool used to find relevant documents across large collections. This chapter analyzes the various search engines currently in use on the WWW, focusing on the relevancy of the obtained search. The chapter also explores specific usage patterns of search engines and the results of using search engines in aggregation.

A mechanism used to increase the effectiveness of mining large text repositories is utilization of metadata, the data about the text. Documents are rarely created in isolation, and metadata is the information about the document not necessarily contained in the document. *Addressing the Metadata Gap: Ad Hoc Digital Documents in Organizations* by Lisa D. Murphy examines the issues surrounding metadata management, especially in complex, ad hoc situations.

Most search engines estimate search relevance through vectors of keyword frequencies, using logical operators to combine the search results of each keyword. Unfortunately, single keywords often do not provide sufficient semantics to narrow searches to a useful result set with both incorrect inclusion and exclusion. One possible enhancement is to pre-categorize documents. By selecting a certain category, a search may be more focussed.

A Learner-Independent Evaluation of the Usefulness of Statistical Phrases for Automated Text Categorization by Maria Fernanda Caropreso, Stan Matwin, and Fabrizio Sebastiani, examines phrase indexing for text categorization. Using multiple contiguous stems or *n*-grams can greatly increase the semantic accuracy of a search. Through the investigation of the use of bigrams, this chapter provides experimental results for automatic text categorization. The next chapter, *Interactive Query Expansion with Automatically Generated Category-Specific Thesauri* by Fabrizio Sebastiani, explores automatic text categorization using machine generation of associative thesauri.

To further increase the ability to manipulate collections of text, databases designed specifically to store the internal structure of documents are necessary. *Database Concepts for Marked-Up Textual Documents* by Arijit Sengupta presents a database language, similar to relational languages, that provides the basis for intelligent storage of documents by allowing structured access to document contents. Relational and query by template mechanisms using this language are also discussed.

Beyond the simple mechanics of the technologies in textual data management, the manner in which organizations employ textual data as knowledge bases and a means of communication provides the impetus for continual technological evolution. *Cooperative Document Management in Multidisciplinary Healthcare* by Mareike Schoop delves into the document management requirements in multidisciplinary healthcare to institute a concrete basis for understanding the myriad of predicaments in textual data management.

Finally, in a detailed study of a legal setting, *Supporting Access to Information Created in Interorganizational Processes* by Virpi Lyytikäinen, Pasi Tiitinen and Airi Salminen investigates the sharing of documents between organizations.

I would like to thank each of the authors for their high-quality chapter contribution to this volume. I am also grateful to the staff at Idea Group Publishing for all of their guidance and assistance during the arduous process of compiling this volume. Finally, I want to express my sincerest thanks to my husband, Bill, and my children, Brandon and Nikita, for all of their love, support, and patience during this project.

Amita Goyal Chin

Chapter I

Markup Languages and Electronic Commerce

Ingrid Fisher and Jagdish Gangolly
State University of New York at Albany, USA

INTRODUCTION

The developments in database connectivity, markup languages, Web server extensions, and the standardization efforts relating to such technologies are already revolutionizing the interactions between consumers and businesses as well as those between businesses. Theoretical advances in semi-structured data models are evolving and percolating through Web application software development in the integration of back end databases (and data warehouses) with front-end browsers to support decision-making, electronic commerce, and document management in all their glory (transaction management, concurrency control, versioning, document/information retrieval, security, etc.).

In this chapter, we provide a brief description of the development of markup languages, describe their role in the context of web application development and deployment, and finally provide an example of an XML application for a simple Web page displaying a typical sales invoice. Our objective in this example is to illustrate the relationship between the relational and XML representation of data that is required for the use of XML in the development of web-based applications in electronic commerce.

TEXT AS SEMISTRUCTURED DATA

Structured data such as those in relational (object, hierarchical or network) databases can be contrasted with text documents in that while the former have *schema*, the latter are *schema-less* or *self-describing* (see for example, Abiteboul et al., 2000). Since structured data has schema, there is a clear distinction between data and metadata; database stores only the data and the metadata describing the semantics of the data is embedded in the specification of the database (in, for example, the relational schemas in relational database systems). In case of text documents, on the other hand, the text content as well as the metadata pertaining to the document are stored together by serialization in byte-streams in the electronic text databases. While the model of data in relational (or other structured databases such as hierarchical, network, or object-oriented) is well understood, the study of modeling of text documents is more recent. Abiteboul et al., (2000) call such text-oriented data *semi-structured* in that there is no separate description of the structure and type of data.

The metadata describing the semantics of text documents consists of the form, structure and content of such documents, and the text document itself is a serialized byte-stream that contains data as well as such metadata. The metadata relating to form specifies the *format* of the text content and so governs the presentation of such content with respect to fonts (type, size, color, bold, italics, etc.), alignment, etc. The metadata relating to the *structure*, on the other hand, governs the presentation with respect to aspects such as headings (level), lists (ordered or unordered), etc. The metadata relating to the *content*, however, depends on the domain that the document originates and therefore requires an understanding of such underlying domain.

Early Markup Languages

During the early stages in the development of markup languages, the objective was to embed the metadata relating to the formatting of the document in such document itself. For example, in the earliest markup languages such as runoff, troff/nroff, and to a large extent in Donald Knuth's (1992) TeX typesetting system that supported formatting of text, the tags almost exclusively had to do with the formatting of documents. The distribution of troff with the unix systems made it popular in scientific publishing since, in those early days, the delivery platform for such documents was primarily the print medium. The cost-free availability of the TeX/LaTeX system on diverse platforms (with the associated utilities for browsing, postscript/HTML conversion) has made it, since then and to this day, the platform of choice for document preparation in computing, mathematical and natural sciences. However, neither troff nor TeX/LaTeX found acceptance in the commercial market (outside of technical publishing) because of their complexity and rather steep perceived learning curve.

In traditional paper-based publishing, the division of labor has been quite explicit: document formatting is the preserve of the typesetters, the document structure is that of the editors, and document content is that of the authors. When alternative media for the delivery of text documents (in formats such as on-line, CDs, floppy disks, etc.) became available, there arose a need for the same document to be stored once but delivered in various media from the same storage. This necessitated the specification of format as well as the structure of documents, and the separation of the document structure from the document content. The result was the evolution of style files and later stylesheets.

In the case of the TeX typesetting, for example, Lamport's macros in LaTeX (Lamport, 1994; Kopka & Daly, 1999) separated the logical design of the document from its physical design so that the structure could be specified in a document style given in a style file. The basic idea in the LaTeX system, which Lamport borrowed from Brian Reid's *scribe* text formatting system, was to incorporate the specification of the structure (and most of the formatting) of the document in style files. In the LaTeX system, the author of the document has to worry primarily about the *content* of the document, the development of which is what document authoring is really about.

Soon in word processing, stylesheets began to be used to accomplish the same objective, but with the author having full control over the entire document, specially the appearance of the documents. Referring to the visual document design features in the WYSIWYG word processors which were then coming into vogue, Lamport observed: "Logical design encourages sound typography, while visual design discourages it."

SGML and HTML

With the development of alternative delivery media there was a need to develop a tagging scheme that facilitated the storage of documents just once but their delivery on many different media. It is in this context that the markup language SGML was born and became popular. Not surprisingly, the early biggest users of SGML were the Department of Defense (technical manuals for equipment in the Armed Forces), the Internal Revenue Service (for delivery of tax documents and forms), and the large publishing houses. All three had much to gain by way of economies generated by "store-once-deliver-in many-forms" facilitated by the use of SGML (Travis & Waldt,

1995). The Department of Defense had a pressing need to provide on multiple media the relevant versions of technical manuals and specifications for sophisticated equipment systems in the Armed Forces. The Internal Revenue Service had the need to deliver tax documents and forms on alternative media. The large publishing houses had the need to develop systems to facilitate delivery on multiple media materials that needed to be revised often.

A very important aspect of SGML is the requirement that the rules of *grammar* that a document must conform to be specified in a *document type definition* (DTD). The grammar rules specified in the DTD along with the rules pertaining to certain other requirements can be used to test the correct formation and validity of the documents and thereby impose discipline on the way they are generated. However, every SGML document required the adoption or development of a DTD, thereby making it unsuitable for widespread use by users who can not be expected to be SGML specialists. SGML was therefore found to be too complex for widespread application and did not gain wide acceptance, especially in the business world. However, there was a pressing need for a simpler language that provided default DTD that would be supported by browsers for the World Wide Web.

The language HyperText Markup Language (HTML), a simpler SGML application with a standard DTD, was developed by the World Wide Web Consortium to meet that need. In the process of simplifying the language for use by novices, the HTML specifications froze, at least temporarily, the tags available to the users but in effect considerably restricted the document semantics. For example, it prevented an author from representing adequately the rich semantics that underlay the domain in which the document originated. Also, the forgiving nature of the DTD (for example, optionality of the end tags and quoting of tag attribute values) coupled with the forgiving nature of the HTML browsers spawned a culture of creative indiscipline in web document authorship.

The early versions of HTML consisted primarily of tags having to do with the document structure. For example, HTML 2.0 contained mostly structure tags (such as <TITLE>, <HEAD>, <BODY>, <H1>, <CITE>, and block structuring tags such as <P>, <PRE>, <ADDRESS>, <BLOCKQUOTE>, <OL>, <UL>, <MENU>, <LI>, <DL>, <DT>, <DD>, <FORM>, etc.) and a few format tags (such as <B>, <I>, <TT>, <BR>, <HR>, etc.). However, the ease of document generation in HTML and the fierce competition in the browser market led to addition of tags such as <TABLE>, <FONT> (specification of most attributes later deprecated in favor of relative sizes, font color specification in style sheets, etc.), <MAP> (for client-side image maps), <APPLET>, <FRAMESET>, <FRAME>, <SCRIPT> (later deprecated in favor of <OBJECT>), and so on.

Database Connectivity and Web server Extensions

With each new version, the HTML language became feature-rich in terms of document structure and format, but the need for the delivery of dynamic web content based on back-end databases was not met by HTML alone. This led to the development of three technologies: the technology to support server side delivery of dynamic data, the technology for interface with back end databases, and the technology for the Web servers to communicate with applications (programs) that work with back end databases. The development of Server Side Includes (SSI), Object/Java Database Connectivity (ODBC/JDBC), and the Common Gateway Interface (CGI) respectively fulfilled these needs.

The popularity of Server Side Includes (SSI) led to the development of specialized Server Side Markup Languages (SSML) such as Extended Server Side Includes (XSSI), popularized by the Apache project; SSMARKUP in MHonArc (for converting e-mail to HTML); and the ColdFusion Markup Language (CFML). For example, if you wanted the Web server to display the current time on an HTML page, you would include in case of SSI, in that page, markup such as

<!—#echo var=”DATE_LOCAL”—>

where echo is the SSI tag. Soon, server vendors were defining tags specific to their servers, leading to some extent the Babelization of server side markups.

The ODBC/JDBC technologies facilitated interfaces between back end databases (usually relational, object, hierarchical, or network) and the application logic implemented in middleware programs. While CGI-scripting and ODBC/JDBC enabled development of early e-commerce systems, the high resource requirements imposed by CGI (each HTTP-request spawned a server process) revealed a need for extensions to Web servers to manage such requests for dynamic pages. The Web server extensions implementing Server (or platform) APIs, such as NSAPI (Netscape), ISAPI (Microsoft), or Servlet API (Java platform), enabled separation of the presentation logic (in the HTML Web pages) from the application logic (in the form of, in Java for example, servlet code) was the result.

Once the back end databases could be connected to the web through applications, the latent demand for processing transactions through the web revealed the impediment posed by the statelessness of the HTTP protocol. But the HTTP protocol was designed to support document delivery through the Internet and not transactions processing. For transaction processing in electronic commerce, it is necessary to maintain the history of each session with a customer, which might consist of a number of connections until the customer commits to the transaction. A number of methods for session tracking such as

URL rewriting, hidden form fields, cookies and, ultimately Http Session objects in Java Servlet API were developed to satisfy this need (see Ayers et al., 1999; Callaway, 1999).

As at the time of writing, much activity is under way in the areas of developing APIs for integrating XML into e-commerce systems, the most recent being the publication of APIs by Sun Microsystems for parsing XML documents (see, Sun Microsystems, 2000) and the flurry of developments in newly announced XML-based languages for electronic commerce such as eXtensible Financial Reporting Language (XFRML), eXtensible Forms Description Language (XFRML), the schema libraries announced in Microsoft-initiated Biz Talk Framework, the Microsoft-Ariba Commerce XML (cXML), the XML version of Interactive Financial eXchange(IFX).

XML and the Document Object Model (DOM)

With the widespread use of ODBC/JDBC for database connectivity and CGI for generation of documents with dynamic content, there arose the need for the modeling of documents that alleviated the drawbacks of the fixed HTML tagset and the need for interfaces to those models and their manipulation.

HTML was a poor choice for presentation logic since it commingled the metadata relating to the formatting and content of the documents. It was also a poor choice for connectivity to back end databases since its tagset was fixed and content tagging, of necessity domain dependent, was lacking. The development of the meta-language XML, derived from SGML by eliminating the aspects that made SGML complex while retaining those features that provided flexibility, was a solution to both the problems. In fact, XML was originally christened "Web-SGML" (see Bosak, 1999) to suggest a modification of the language for the web.

In XML, the structure and content tags as well as the grammar rules are defined in a DTD, whereas the formatting information is defined in either a cascading stylesheet or an XSL file. In addition, XML also provides for a document object model (DOM), which is a formal model for the structure of a document. In the development of web application software, one can map the results of database queries to a document object model, and the DOM can be presented on the web browser by the use of a cascading stylesheet or an XSL (eXtensible Stylesheet Language) stylesheet corresponding to the document to be displayed. This separation of the document itself from the metadata relating to its format (in the stylesheet) and the structure and content (in the document type definition) made possible the parsing of the documents for their validity (in terms of the DOCTYPE declaration, the conformity of the document with the DTD in terms of the logical structure, etc.) and correct formation (in terms of the physical structure of the document).

An important aspect of these developments is a clearer view of the now popular "three-tier-architecture" of web applications. In a three-tier application, the database logic (in database schema and the queries to create and manipulate data), the application logic (in the mapping of the query results to the document content in DOM), and the presentation logic (in the CSS or XSL stylesheets) can be specified separately. This separation makes the development of web applications relatively easy.

The development of the Document Object Model (DOM), on the other hand, provides a platform and language-neutral interface that programs can use to dynamically access and update the content, structure and style of documents. In fact, DOM provides a model of the structure of the document to be displayed, into which data from the results of queries to the back end databases can be mapped.

Using the language bindings (for Java or ECMAScript) given in the DOM APIs issued by the World Wide Web Consortium, software developers can build programs that validate and test for correct formation any XML document, build a DOM tree model for the document and manipulate such DOM trees, extract desired information from DOM tree for display, and so on (Maruyama et al., 1999). Using ODBC/JDBC, it is possible to develop software to display database query results in XML conforming to stylesheets in XSLT as IBM has done using DB2XML APIs and Java servlets (International Business Machines, 2000). Oracle (2000), Sybase (2000), Informix and Software (2000) all have provided XML solutions to web application development in the context of their proprietary database systems.

With the development of database connectivity, XML, DOM, and web server extensions (specially with Java servlets), the software infrastructure for the development of web applications for supporting electronic commerce is substantially ready. In a sense, XML was one of the last building blocks in the infrastructure for electronic commerce.

In the next section, we will describe how some of the technologies described above are applied in the context of electronic commerce.

MARKUP LANGUAGES AND THE ARCHITECTURE OF WEB APPLICATIONS IN E-COMMERCE

Web applications in electronic commerce include storefronts, auctions, merchandising and coupons, shopping cart management, e-mail, catalogs and search, profiling, order processing, credit authorization, order tracking, electronic payments, customer relations management, credit authorization, content publishing, and event notification; and innovative new applications are introduced every day (see Fingar et al., 2000). Most of these applications involve interaction of web documents presented on client browser screens with structured as well as text back end databases.

While anecdotal evidence suggests that around 90% of corporate databases consist of text, until recently most of the efforts at theorizing and systems development have been concentrated in the area of structured databases (relational, object, hierarchical, and network). With the need to incorporate text, the database vendors provided facilities for incorporating text in traditional database systems by providing text as a native data type, and facility for indexing and retrieval of text from structured databases (such as the context cartridge in the Oracle database system). For the full support of web applications of the type mentioned earlier, it is necessary to provide facilities for the validating/storing/retrieving of marked-up documents as well as generating documents using the stylesheets for the presentation at the client end.

Figure 1 presents the architecture of a typical three-tier web application to support electronic commerce. It shows the separation of the database logic in the bottom tier (back-end databases), the presentation logic in the top tier (client browser), and the application logic in the middle tier (Web server). The presentation logic has to do with the semantics of the document as specified in the document type definitions, stylesheets, and the document instance. The application logic consists of the generation of database queries based on the documents, the interface with the database system via ODBC/JDBC and the interface with the presentation via servlets or CGI.

Most systems currently in use are based on the key value pairs received by the Web servers, on the client clicking the "submit" button on the Web pages, by the POST method (attribute in the <FORM> tag in the HTML pages at the client browser). Such key value pairs are used to create embedded SQL statements in Java servlet (or similar CGI-script) code using the interfaces and class implementations provided by the Java Servlet and JDBC APIs. Such applications generate Http responses by piece-by-piece assembly of the

HTML page to be displayed as response at the client browser. In this view of the world, the document model is not used.

Recently, however, attempts have been made, especially in DB2XML, to dynamically generate a DTD for the results of a query by mapping the relational tables into elements in the DTD and then generating the XML document containing the query results. The XML document so generated can be exported as structured objects using the document object model and finally as the document displayed on the client browser using XSLT or XSL stylesheets. This attempt in DB2XML can be considered prototypical of efforts that will be forthcoming in the mapping of back end relational databases into the document object model in order to automatically construct fragments of the DTDs for the dynamic generation of XML pages to display query results on browsers.

In the remainder of this chapter we will discuss the display of a sales invoice, a common document in business, to illustrate the mapping from the relational model to an XML Web page via the document object model.

THE SALES INVOICE EXAMPLE

We have chosen to use a commonly occurring accounting document, the sales invoice, as an illustration. Through the sales invoice example we will demonstrate how data is mapped as it moves from the database, in which it is stored, through the DOM tree to the XML document, displayed by the browser to the user. The DOM is employed to create, access and manipulate the internal structure of XML documents, resulting in the eventual presentation of the document, effected by XML, on the user's browser. Currently only

Figure 1. The Three-Tier Architecture

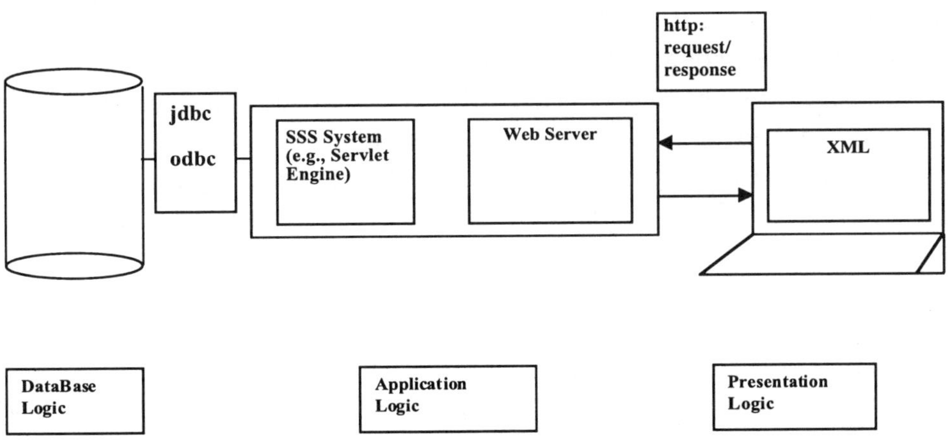

Microsoft's Internet Explorer 5 supports XML. We will then discuss the issues in the translation of the table structures into DOM trees in order to illustrate the differences between the relational and the DOM model of data.

The top portion of Figure 2, the data model (an entity relationship diagram, or ERD), presents the relational schema representation of the manner in which the data contained on the invoice is stored within a typical relational database. The rectangular structures represent tables (or entities) within which specific fields represented by the ovals (or attributes) store characteristics of the entities. The structures are linked through "relationships" (e.g., invoice "contains" an invoice line) designed so as to result in the simplest possible schema that captures all necessary data. Simplicity in data storage is important in that it promotes efficient access, reduces costly redundancies, and prevents errors. The arrowhead at the end of a relationship line indicates that the entity being pointed to can occur only once in the relationship. On the other hand, the absence of an arrowhead in a relation indicates that the entity can occur many times. For example, in the case of the invoice-invoice line relation: a specific invoice can contain many invoice lines, but a specific invoice line can be contained by only one invoice. Common data attributes (e.g., item number is common to both invoice line and item), shared by entities, provide a mechanism for navigating the relationships and accessing data.

A well designed data model (Figure 2) or ERD will result in a database comprised of entities (tables) containing the minimum number of attributes necessary. Smaller tables facilitate fast, and less costly, access to the data. The ERD is a flat representation that does not evidence an order or hierarchy of elements. In moving from the ERD to the DOM tree, a hierarchy must be imposed, since DOM is a tree model (hierarchical). If the sales invoice is generated by a query to the database, such query result must be translated to a DOM tree. The DOM tree for a particular document can be constructed from the DTD (in Appendix B) and the data content of the XML file (in Appendix A). In fact, a DOM tree can be constructed for any relational table given the table schema (see Abiteboul et al., 2000).

The sales invoice entity of the ERD becomes the root element of the DOM tree, the top of the hierarchy. The elements of the sales invoice branch out from the root. Those elements with substructure (e.g., invoice line, customer), in turn, have branching elements. The resulting hierarchical tree provides a structure that moves systematically from the most complex component to the simplest. The design can be used to control document organization and presentation. The ERD, in contrast, is unconcerned with presentation, focusing on access to the data. For example, access to the item description in the database (ERD) is easily effected by specifying the entity/

table: item, and the attribute/field: item description. In the DOM tree, it would be necessary to work through the hierarchy of sales invoice to invoice line to item and, finally, to item description, a significantly longer path. The models address and accomplish different objectives.

JDBC/ODBC enables data to be extracted from the database and Java servlets allow interaction between the data and external clients (Web applications). Java interfaces, defined by the DOM, can be used to extract the key value pairs from the XML document (parsing the document) and resulting in a hierarchically structured tree describing the document. The document itself is "pushed through" to the browser by reading the XML document, validating the document against its document type definition (DTD) and formatting the document according to the specifications provided by an XSL stylesheet. The DOM tree portion of Figure 2 illustrates the hierarchical structure of the XML document as represented in the DTD (Appendix B). The bottom portion of Figure 2 provides a screen shot of the browser display of the XML document (Appendix A) formatted according to the XSL stylesheet (Appendix C).

Relational Model and the Document Object Model

Most web applications in electronic commerce require interfaces between XML pages and back end relational databases. It is important to understand the limitations of both relational database technology and the XML technology as it is evolving. We will now compare the two to provide some insights to aid in mapping relational query responses to the DOM model in XML.

It is tempting to draw analogies between relations (and attributes) in a relational database and elements or tags (and attributes) in XML. However, such an analogy is inappropriate because of the nature of relational databases and XML. Relational databases were developed in the context of structured data, and the relational model reflects that pedigree in terms of the axiomatic development of the underlying theory and the data structures permitted. On the other hand, XML was developed from SGML mainly in the context of text, and that pedigree also is reflected in the hierarchical nature of the model and sparse data types available.

Firstly, in a traditional relational database, attributes of relations must be atomic datatypes (such as INT, VARCHAR, etc.) and can not be structures. This drawback of relational databases, however, has been eliminated substantially in most commercial database systems, since vendors have provided structures as native data types. Examples include DATE, BLOB, CLOB, etc. In XML, until the appearance of XML Schema, the types have been quite limited, in fact mainly strings (PCDATA). However, an element (tag) can have nesting of sub-elements (tags). Since a relation in a relational database can not have sub-relations, the analogy is not appropriate.

The importance of providing a rich set of types in XML is crucial for the support of electronic commerce, and this is currently an active area of development, with the recent activity at the World Wide Web Consortium (Biron & Malhotra, 2000) and elsewhere (Buck et al., 1999).

Secondly, the order of relations, the order of tuples in a relation, and the order of attributes in a relation can be permuted without altering the semantics of a relational database. In XML, on the other hand, the order of appearance of elements is important for the meaning of the document. It is possible to suitably define an element in a DTD by listing all the permutations of the sub-elements that can occur in the document, but this is too unwieldy and clumsy a solution.

With the support of a rich set of data types in XML, programming of e-commerce systems for client-side validation of customer input as well as type-checking in the application logic will be easier without having to resort to adhoc methods as at present.

CONCLUDING COMMENTS

The role of markup languages has changed dramatically since the early days when they were used to provide formatting information to aid typesetters. Today, they support publishing (where the objective is to store documents once, but deliver them on various media) as well as electronic commerce. In the future, they will help businesses seamlessly integrate their back end databases with the customers via a Web-based interface. For this to happen, research in the areas of modeling semi-structured data and interfacing relational databases with hierarchy-oriented document object models will be necessary.

Figure 2. Data Model-DOM Tree-Browser View (SalesInvoice Example)

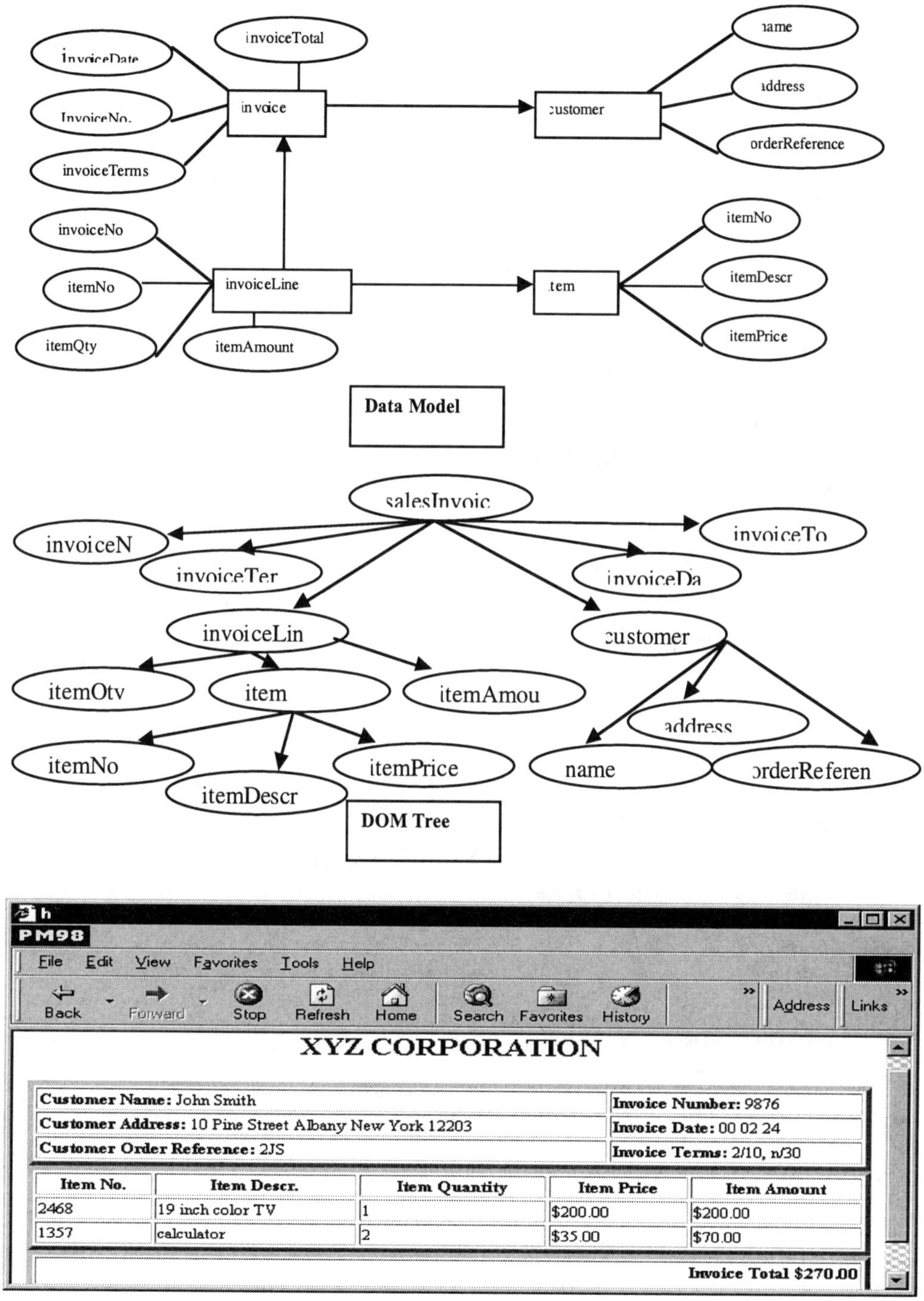

Appendix A: An XML Document for a Sales Invoice (invoice.xml)

```
<?xml version="1.0"?>
<?xml-stylesheet type="text/xsl" href="invoice.xsl"?>
<!DOCTYPE salesInvoice SYSTEM "invoice.dtd">

<salesInvoice>
 <customer>
  <name>
   <Fname>John</Fname>
   <Lname>Smith</Lname>
  </name>
  <address>
    <street>10 Pine Street</street>
   <city>Albany</city>
    <state>New York</state>
    <zipcode>12203</zipcode>
  </address>
  <orderReference>2JS</orderReference>
 </customer>

 <invoiceLine>
  <item>
    <itemNo>2468</itemNo>
    <itemDescr>19 inch color TV</itemDescr>
    <itemQty>1</itemQty>
    <itemPrice>$200.00</itemPrice>
    <itemAmount>$200.00</itemAmount>
  </item>
 </invoiceLine>

 <invoiceLine>
  <item>
    <itemNo>1357</itemNo>
    <itemDescr>calculator</itemDescr>
    <itemQty>2</itemQty>
    <itemPrice>$35.00</itemPrice>
    <itemAmount>$70.00</itemAmount>
```

```
   </item>
  </invoiceLine>

 <invoiceNumber>9876</invoiceNumber>
  <invoiceDate>
   <year>00</year>
   <month>02</month>
   <day>24</day>
  </invoiceDate>
 <invoiceTerms>2/10, n/30</invoiceTerms>
 <invoiceTotal>$270.00</invoiceTotal>

</salesInvoice>
```

Appendix B: A Document Type Definition (DTD) for a Sales Invoice (invoice.dtd)

```
    <!ELEMENT salesInvoice (customer, invoiceLine+, invoiceNumber,
invoiceDate, invoiceTerms, invoiceTotal)>
    <!ELEMENT customer (name,address,orderReference)>
    <!ELEMENT name (Fname,Lname)>
    <!ELEMENT Fname (#PCDATA)>
    <!ELEMENT Lname (#PCDATA)>
    <!ELEMENT address (street,city,state,zipcode)>
    <!ELEMENT street (#PCDATA)>
    <!ELEMENT city (#PCDATA)>
    <!ELEMENT state (#PCDATA)>
    <!ELEMENT zipcode (#PCDATA)>
    <!ELEMENT orderReference (#PCDATA)>

    <!ELEMENT invoiceLine (item+)>
    <!ELEMENT item
(itemNo,itemDescr,itemQty,itemPrice,itemAmount)>
    <!ELEMENT itemNo (#PCDATA)>
    <!ELEMENT itemDescr (#PCDATA)>
    <!ELEMENT itemQty (#PCDATA)>
    <!ELEMENT itemPrice (#PCDATA)>
    <!ELEMENT itemAmount (#PCDATA)>

    <!ELEMENT invoiceNumber (#PCDATA)>
    <!ELEMENT invoiceDate (year,month,day)>
    <!ELEMENT year (#PCDATA)>
    <!ELEMENT month (#PCDATA)>
    <!ELEMENT day (#PCDATA)>
    <!ELEMENT invoiceTerms (#PCDATA)>
    <!ELEMENT invoiceTotal (#PCDATA)>
```

Appendix C: An XSL Stylesheet for a Sales Invoice (invoice.xsl)

```
<xsl:stylesheet xmlns:xsl=”http://www.w3.org/TR/WD-xsl”
    xmlns:fo=”http://www.w3.org/TR/WD-xsl/FO”>

<xsl:template match=”/”>
 <HTML>
  <HEAD>
   <H1 align=”center”>XYZ CORPORATION</H1>
  </HEAD>

  <BODY>
   <TABLE border=”4" width=”100%”>
    <TBODY>
     <TR>
      <TD> <B>Customer Name:</B>
       <xsl:value-of
        select=”salesInvoice/customer/name/Fname”/>
       <xsl:value-of
        select=”salesInvoice/customer/name/Lname”/>
      </TD>
      <TD> <B>Invoice Number:</B>
       <xsl:value-of
        select=”salesInvoice/invoiceNumber”/>
      </TD>
     </TR>
     <TR>
      <TD> <B>Customer Address:</B>
       <xsl:value-of
        select=”salesInvoice/customer/address/street”/>
       <xsl:value-of
       select=”salesInvoice/customer/address/city”/>
       <xsl:value-of
        select=”salesInvoice/customer/address/state”/>
       <xsl:value-of
        select=”salesInvoice/customer/address/zipcode”/>
      </TD>
      <TD> <B>Invoice Date:</B>
       <xsl:value-of
```

```
     select="salesInvoice/invoiceDate/year"/>
    <xsl:value-of
     select="salesInvoice/invoiceDate/month"/>
    <xsl:value-of
     select="salesInvoice/invoiceDate/day"/>
   </TD>
  </TR>
  <TR>
   <TD> <B>Customer Order Reference:</B>
    <xsl:value-of
     select="salesInvoice/customer/orderReference"/>
   </TD>
   <TD> <B>Invoice Terms:</B>
   <xsl:value-of select="salesInvoice/invoiceTerms"/>
   </TD>
  </TR>
 </TBODY>
</TABLE>
<TABLE border="4" width="100%">
 <THEAD>
  <TR>
   <TH> Item No. </TH>
   <TH> Item Descr. </TH>
   <TH> Item Quantity </TH>
   <TH> Item Price </TH>
   <TH> Item Amount </TH>
  </TR>
 </THEAD>
 <TBODY>
<xsl:for-each select="salesInvoice/invoiceLine/item">
 <TR>
  <TD>
  <xsl:value-of select="itemNo"/>
  </TD>
  <TD>
  <xsl:value-of select="itemDescr"/>
  </TD>
  <TD>
  <xsl:value-of select="itemQty"/>
  </TD>
```

```
<TD>
<xsl:value-of select="itemPrice"/>
</TD>
<TD>
<xsl:value-of select="itemAmount"/>
</TD>
</TR>
</xsl:for-each>
</TBODY>
</TABLE>
<TABLE border="4" width="100%">
<TFOOT>
<TR>
<TD align="right">
<H3>
Invoice Total
<xsl:value-of select="salesInvoice/invoiceTotal"/>
</H3>
</TD>
</TR>
</TFOOT>
</TABLE>
</BODY>
</HTML>
</xsl:template>
</xsl:stylesheet>
```

REFERENCES

Abiteboul, S., Buneman, P. & Suciu, D. (2000). *Data on the Web: From Relations to Semistructured Data and XML*. San Francisco: Morgan Kaufmann Publishers.

Ayers, D et al. (1999). *Professional Java Server Programming*. Birmingham, UK: Wrox Press Ltd.

Biron, P. & Malhotra, A. (2000). XML Schema Part 2: Datatypes W3C Working Draft. World Wide Web Consortium retrieved on the World Wide Web: http://www.w3.org/TR/xmlschema-2/

Bosak, J. (2000). *The Birth of XML: A Personal Recollection*. World Wide Web: http://java.sun.com/xml/birth_of_xml.html.

Bosak, J. (2000). *XML, Java, and the Future of the Web*. World Wide Web: http://www.xml.com/pub/w3j/s3.bosak.html.

Buck, L., Goldfarb, C. & Prescod, P. (1999). Datatypes for DTDs (DT4DTD) 1.0. Public Specification, World Wide Web Consortium. World Wide Web: http://www.extensibility.com/dt4dtd/spec.htm

Callaway, D. (1999). *Inside Servlets: Server-Side Programming for the Java Platform*. Reading, MA: Addison-Wesley.

Fingar, P., Kumar H. & Sharma, T. (2000). *Enterprise E-Commerce: The Software Component Breakthrough for Business-to-Business Commerce*. Tampa, FL: Meghan-Kiffer Press.

Goldfarb, C. (1991). *The SGML Handbook*. Oxford: Clarendon Press.

Informix Software Inc. (2000). *Informix and XML: Smart Distributed Data*. World Wide Web: http://www.informix.com/informix/techbriefs/xml/xml.pdf.

Interactive Financial eXchange (2000). *XML Reference*. World Wide Web: http://www.ifxforum.org/ifxforum.org/Docs/Guidelines.PDF.

International Business Machines (2000). *DB2XML 1.3: Transforming relational databases into XML documents*. World Wide Web: http://www.informatik.fh-wiesbaden.de/~turau/DB2XML/index.html.

Knuth, D.E. (1984). *The TeXbook*. Reading, MA: Addison Wesley.

Kopka, H. & Daly, P.W. (1994). *A Guide to LateX, 3rd. edition*. Reading, MA: Addison-Wesley.

Lamport, L. (1994). *LaTeX - A Document Preparation System, 2nd edition for LaTeX2e*. Reading, MA: Addison-Wesley.

Maruyama, H., Tamura, K. & Uramoto, N. (1999). *XML and Java: Developing Java Applications*. Reading, MA: Addison-Wesley.

MhonArc (2000). An E-mail to HTML converter. World Wide Web: http://www.oac.uci.edu/indiv/ehood/mhonarc.html.

Oracle Corporation. (2000). World Wide Web: http://technet.oracle.com/tech/xml/info/htdocs/otnwp/about_oracle_xml_products.htm.

Sun Microsystems, Inc. (2000). *Java API for XML Parsing, Version 1.0 Final Release*. World Wide Web: http://java.sun.com/aboutJava/communityprocess/final/jsr005/jaxp-1.0-final-release.pdf.

Sun Microsystems, Inc. (2000). *JSR-000005 XML Parsing Specification*. World Wide Web: http://java.sun.com/aboutJava/communityprocess/final/jsr005/index.html.

Sybase, Inc. (2000). Java & XML in ASE 12.0. World Wide Web: http://www.sybase.com/products/databaseservers/ase/whitepapers/L01085.pdf.

Travis, B. E & Waldt, D.C. (1995). *The SGML Implementation Guide: A Blueprint for SGML Migration*. New York: Springer.

Chapter II

Search Engines, Relevancy, and the World Wide Web

Wendy Lucas
Bentley College, USA

This chapter presents a survey and discussion of the relevancy rankings assigned by search engines to pages in their indices. An examination of methodologies whose goal it is to improve the relevancy of search results follows. The chapter concludes with a look at emerging trends in search engine technologies and directions for future research.

INTRODUCTION

Recent estimates for the size of the World Wide Web range from 275 million distinct, static pages, growing by about 20 million pages per month (Bharat & Border, 1999), to 800 million publicly "indexable" pages (Lawrence & Giles, 1999), where indexable refers to those pages that are available to search engines for indexing. While estimates vary, it is undeniable that the exponential growth rate of the Web greatly complicates the task of finding relevant pages. Organizing and managing these pages therefore assumes critical importance. This role has largely been borne by search engines, which impose structure on the Web by indexing its contents and providing directed access via search interfaces.

An estimated 85% of users turn to search engines for finding information on the Web (Graphic Visualization and Usability Center, 1998). As anyone who has used a search engine knows, submitting a query to an engine often results in the listing of thousands of links to "matching pages" of dubious quality. Links to retrieved pages are listed in decreasing order of relevance, with relevancy ratings determined by proprietary algorithms. Typically, links to 10 Web pages are displayed on each page of search results. Pages whose links appear on the first page of results are the most likely to be viewed (Silverstein, Henzinger, Marais, & Moricz, 1998; Spink, Chang, & Goz, 1999). Yet, there is no guarantee that the most relevant pages will be those appearing in the "top ten" (Gordon & Pathak, 1999; Gudivada, Raghavan, Grosky, & Kasanagottu, 1997). A high-quality page that truly matches the user's information needs may therefore never be discovered if the ranking algorithm used by the search engine erroneously places its link beyond the first page or two of results with other, less relevant links appearing before it.

The focus of this chapter is on the relevancy of search results returned by the most popular search engines in response to users' queries. Descriptions of the functions performed by search engines and a review of current literature analyzing their performance are given in the next section. A preliminary study that evaluates methodologies for improving relevance, which was first presented in (Lucas, 2000), follows. This study investigates the relevance of search engine results to user-entered queries and then examines a method for reducing the incidence of irrelevant matches. Approaches that rely on the internal and external structure of Web documents are supported by recent research. Emerging trends in search engine technologies, their impact on text databases, and directions for future research are also explored.

BACKGROUND

Many of today's search engines offer two ways for users to find information on the Web. One is by submitting a query whose content is then matched to the contents of an electronically built and maintained index. The other is by making use of directories that are created by human volunteers for classifying Web sites. As the Web continues to expand exponentially, efficient means for classifying and managing the textual contents of this largest of databases will necessitate the continued use of electronic measures. These measures are therefore the focus of this chapter.

In the following section, the methods used by search engines for indexing Web pages and for determining their relevancy rankings in response to users' queries are described. The ability of search engines to successfully index and rank pages, as evidenced by recent studies of search engine performance, is then elucidated.

Indexing and Page Ranking Techniques

Search engines use software variously called "robots," "spiders," "crawlers," or "wanderers" to find new and modified pages on the Web. After collecting the contents of a page, the robot will then visit and collect the contents of all new or modified pages linked to it by recursively traversing its links. This process will be repeated until there are no more links for the robot to follow. A new starting point will then be selected and the procedure will be repeated.

Large-scale search engines seeking to maximize their coverage of the Web, such as AltaVista, Fast, and Northern Light, will visit all the pages whose links they encounter. Other search engines may prioritize the order in which pages are visited based on various criteria, such as the number of links leading to them, termed "link popularity," or the location of the page. For example, a page with an *edu* extension may be considered by some search engines as more valuable than one ending in *com.*

Indexing software is used to process a Web page's content and add it to the search engine's index. If an author does not want a page to be indexed, access by search engines can be prohibited by using the Robots Exclusion Protocol to indicate parts of a site that are off limits. A Robots META tag within a page's HTML code can also keep pages from being indexed. In addition, pages with password-based access, dynamically updated content, and specialized formats such as Acrobat or PostScript are not indexed. Those pages that do not fall into any of these categories comprise the indexable content of the Web.

A search engine may refuse to index a page or may subsequently remove it from its index if it is determined that the page's author has attempted to "spam the index." Spamming refers to any technique that attempts to deceive a search engine about the content of a Web page in order to attract viewers to that page. A common form of spamming is the repetition of a popular search term, even though that term may have little or nothing to do with page content.

All of the major search engines claim to engage in full-text indexing, in which every word from a Web page and the data associated with it is stored to the index. An exception is frequently made for "stop words," which are terms for which a search engine will not stop because they are either too common to add meaning to a search or because they have no subject-related significance. Examples include *an*, *is*, *its*, *the*, *homepage*, *Internet*, and *Web*. A search engine may also ignore content found within a frame. Other terms that may not be indexed include those appearing in comment tags and, for some engines, words in META tags. Although the function of META tags is for specifying meta data about a page, such as descriptions and keywords, they are often used for spamming, as their contents are invisible when the page is viewed via a browser.

After a user enters a query to a search interface, terms in the index are used for finding all documents that match the query, and term weightings are used in determining the rank of each matching page. While the actual indexing algorithms are propriety, it is known that the number of times each word occurs within a page, referred to as term frequency, the positions of each word, and their placement in HTML tags comprise some of the criteria used in determining weightings. Terms that appear at or near the top of the page, and particularly those that appear within title tags, are considered as being more indicative of content and will therefore be given higher weightings in the index. Many of the search engines will also give higher weightings to terms in META tags, and some will reward terms that appear in header tags. The proximity of terms to others in the page is also recorded so that if a query contains terms that are in close proximity within a page, that page's rank will be positively affected.

The queries entered by users to the search engine interface can be in a number of different formats. Term queries are ones in which one or more keywords are listed. In phrase queries, quotation marks are used to indicate that words appearing within them must also appear together within a retrieved page. Boolean and Boolean-like queries, in which the plus (+) symbol is used to indicate that a term or phrase must be included within the page and a minus (-) symbol to indicate it must not be, can also be used.

Studies have shown that most people submit short, term-based queries and few use Boolean operators. In Jansen, Spink, Bateman & Saracevic (1998), it was found that the average length of 51,473 queries in a log of submissions to the Excite search engine was 2.35 terms, and that less than 10% of these queries included any Boolean operators. A study of an AltaVista query log containing approximately one billion entries for search requests found that 72.4% of the queries had two or fewer terms, and that 79.6% did not contain any Boolean operators, including (+) and (-) signs (Silverstein et al., 1998). Analysis presented in Abdulla, Liu & Fox (1998), which looked at five log files containing 26,824 queries, also found that two terms per query was most popular, and that most queries had no Boolean operators.

After a searcher has entered a query, most of the search engines perform a disjunction comparison of query and document content, so that any page containing any of the query terms and/or phrases will be considered a match. To rank those pages, each search engine applies its own proprietary algorithm. While the specific nature of those algorithms cannot be known with certainty, they are built upon well-known information retrieval (IR) models and concepts. The Vector Space Model (Salton, 1971) is commonly used for calculating the match between the terms in a document and a query. Its basic premise is that if a query term occurs more frequently in a document than it does in the collection of documents as a whole, then the similarity ranking between that term and the document will be higher. If the query term occurs less frequently, then the ranking will be lower. While search engines do in general adhere to this principal, there is some unknown upper boundary for each search engine above which the number of occurrences of a term in a document constitutes spamming and will therefore lower the page's rank.

Probabilistic models can also be used for indexing and ranking pages. The model developed by Roberston and Sparck-Jones (1976) bases term relevance on its appearance in previously retrieved documents that were judged as being relevant to the user's query. Bayes' theorem is applied to derive the weight of a term, which can be summarized as the odds of it occurring in a relevant document versus the odds of it occurring in an irrelevant one within the collection. If the weight is greater than 0, then the document in which it appears is relevant to the query, while a weight less than 0 indicates that the document is not relevant.

Search engines may also use natural language processing (NLP) techniques for improving the likelihood of finding relevant results. A user's query can be expanded through the use of an on-line thesaurus to include synonyms for the terms found in it, so that a query on "dog" will also find documents containing the term "canine." The terms found in a document, however, are often an unreliable indicator of its true content. A statistical method called Latent Semantic Indexing (Deerwester, Dumais, Furnas, Laudauer, & Harshman, 1990) estimates the underlying latent semantic structure of a document by correlating related terms. Documents and queries are then represented by terms that may or may not actually appear within them but are closest to their meaning. Excite uses a proprietary statistical method called Intelligent Concept Extraction™ for identifying terms related to a user's query and searching for concept-related pages.

A less sophisticated NLP technique used by many search engines during query processing is word stemming, which refers to finding the stem of words in addition to the actual word entered. For example, a search on "thinking" will also find documents containing the words "think" and "thinks." GO.com, Lycos, and Northern Light automatically stem query words, while some search engines, such as HotBot, offer this option as an advanced search feature. GO.com's search capability incorporates technology called LinguistX from Inxight, a Xerox New Enterprise Company, which uses high-speed stemming to find the root for each word in a document. A search on "thinking" will therefore retrieve documents containing "thought" as well.

Independent of the relationship between query and document terms, many search engines will also consider "link popularity" when determining a page's rating. This measure of quality is based on the premise that pages with several links leading to them are more popular and hence of greater relevance, particularly if the links pointing to them originate at popular pages themselves. Excite, HotBot, GO.com, and Lycos include this measurement when determining page rankings. Another widespread practice is to factor in "page popularity," in which those pages that are visited more frequently are given higher rankings. The Direct Hit search engine analyzes the viewing behavior of its users and applies the results to the relevancy ratings of Web pages. Their technology has been integrated into the search results of many popular search engines, including HotBot, GO.com, and Lycos.

After using some combination of relevance and quality measures, each search engine creates ranked lists of links to Web pages that are displayed in response to users' queries. Some search engines, including AltaVista, Excite, GO.com, and Google, offer a relevance feedback option by providing links to similar or related pages for each of the documents listed. Relevance feedback refers to the modification of queries by adding new terms and re-weighting existing ones on the basis of user feedback. In this case, the query will be modified so that more documents like the one selected are found. While relevance feedback has been shown to yield better search results (Salton & Buckley, 1990; Harman, 1992, #83), a study of Excite's query log found that only about 5% of users' queries took advantage of the provided relevance feedback mechanism (Jansen et al., 1998).

The next section of this chapter examines the ability of search engines to find relevant results in response to users' queries using technologies that are based on the ones described here. It details the methods that are typically employed for measuring search engine performance and then looks at recent studies that use those measures for evaluating the major search engines. While such evaluations are volatile due to the evolving nature of retrieval algorithms, they do provide an indication of how well search engines are currently performing their most critical tasks, which can serve as a base-line for evaluating future advances in IR technology.

Search Engine Performance

The common goal of all search engines is to provide users with relevant responses to their queries in a timely fashion. Since search engines were first introduced in 1994, the timeliness of search results has become less of an issue, given the increases in both computer processor speeds and Internet connections. Improving the relevance of search results, on the other hand, has proven to be more elusive.

One of the first requirements for a search engine is to have a complete index of all potentially useful pages if it is going to find all relevant responses to a query. No search engine, however, comes even close to indexing all of the pages on the Web. Rather, each indexes small, varying portions, for a combined total coverage of 42% of the indexable pages (Lawrence & Giles, 1999). Another requirement for relevant results is that the index be up-to-date. Given that the indexing of new or modified pages can take several months or more (Lawrence & Giles, 1998b), those pages that are retrieved in response to a query may no longer meet the search criteria if their contents have changed but have not been updated in the index.

Metasearchers, which submit a query to multiple search engines and then display links retrieved from each of them, can compensate for the poor coverage of individual search engines. Selberg and Etzioni (1997) found that using a single search engine instead of the MetaCrawler search service could result in users missing over 77% of the references they would find to be the most relevant. Although metasearchers can provide users with a broader cross section of documents, they do not compensate for the deficiencies of the individual search engines.

A third requirement of search engines is that their ranking algorithms accurately reflect the relevance of the pages listed in response to a query. In order to make this determination, some measure of performance must be defined. Traditionally, the effectiveness of an IR system is measured using the evaluation criteria of *precision* and *recall*. *Precision* is defined as the ratio of the number of relevant documents retrieved to the total number of documents retrieved. *Recall* refers to the ratio of the number of relevant documents retrieved to the total number of relevant documents in the collection. Measuring recall is in general more problematic than measuring precision, since the former requires knowledge about the relevancy of documents in the entire collection, while the latter is limited to the relevancy of those documents that are retrieved in response to a query. Probabilistic models can be used for estimating relevance values used in recall calculations.

Ideally, one would like both precision and recall to be maximized. This is, however, an unrealistic goal. To achieve high precision, an index must focus on terms that are specific to document content, so that fewer but more relevant documents are retrieved. Indexing more general terms will result in the retrieval of a greater number of documents and hence will lead to higher recall. Due to this conflict, an IR system's effectiveness is typically measured as its precision at various recall levels (Gudivada et al., 1997).

When evaluating the relevance of Web pages, the logical choice is to measure precision at a specified recall level. The value of the recall parameter itself can never be known with certainty in this domain, due to the huge and ever-changing nature of the Web's content. Determining the precision of search results is also problematic, as the total number of relevant documents retrieved in response to a query must be known in order to accurately calculate this measure. With the possibility of millions of pages being returned, knowing the exact number that is relevant to the user's query is infeasible. To overcome this limitation, precision ratios based on the relevance of the highest-ranked pages are most often used for analyzing the relevancy of search engine results. This is commonly referred to as a precision at 10, or P@10, performance measurement when the number of pages analyzed is restricted to 10, or as precision at 20 (P@20) if 20 pages are used in making this determination.

Due to the relatively short time that search engines have existed in the form in which we know them today, the number of formal studies evaluating the precision of their results at various recall levels is limited. Most of these evaluations rely on the judgments of the evaluators for determining the relevance of a retrieved page. Chu and Rosenthal (1996) compared and evaluated the search capabilities and retrieval performances of AltaVista, Excite, and Lycos. Ten queries were submitted to the three search engines, and the first ten results returned by each one in response to each query were analyzed. Two people judged the relevancy of the pages to the query terms by assigning a score of 1 for *relevant*, 0.5 for *somewhat relevant*, and 0 for *irrelevant*. Precision was then calculated as the sum of the relevancy scores divided by the total number of pages downloaded in response to the query, which varied from 0 to the prescribed maximum of 10. AltaVista had a mean precision score of 0.78, Excite's was 0.45, and Lycos's was 0.55. The overall mean precision score was 0.59, indicating that, on average, the pages the search engines identified as being most relevant were actually only somewhat relevant to the queries entered.

Leighton and Srivastava (1999) performed a P@20 comparison on the results returned from 15 queries submitted to AltaVista, Excite, HotBot,

Infoseek (now part of GO.com), and Lycos. Pages were categorized as to whether they were active or not and if they were duplicates or not. They were also assigned degrees of usefulness that corresponded to the categories of being *irrelevant to the query*, *satisfying the query but not potentially useful*, *potentially useful to the person conducting the query*, or *useful to almost anyone who would conduct the search*. The results of this categorization were then used in calculating P@20 values. Three experiments were run in which the definition of a "good link" varied from the lowest to the highest degree of usefulness categories. The formula used in calculating relevance in these experiments gave additional weights to links that appeared earlier in the retrieved list of URLs.

The results of the experiments varied widely depending on the definition of "relevant." In the first experiment, with the loosest definition of relevance, the median precision value was 0.81. In the second experiment, with a stricter definition, the median fell to 0.39. When relevance was defined in the third experiment as those pages that are very likely to be useful, the median dropped to 0.06. In all three cases, AltaVista, Excite, and Infoseek were the top three performers.

Recently, Text REtrieval Conference (TREC) evaluation methodology has been applied to Web search engines. Preliminary research presented in Hawking, Craswell, Thistlewaite and Harman (1999) compares four popular commercial Web search engines and one research system to six TREC systems using an 18.5 million-page snapshot of part of the Web. The P@20 calculations ranged from 0.231 to 0.377 for the Web search engines, with a median value of 0.289. The median values for the TREC systems were 0.397 when only the *title* field was used in the search, 0.503 when the *title* and *description* fields were used, and 0.611 when full topics were used. Four judges rated each document as being either relevant or irrelevant on the basis of the full topic description. While the findings suggest that the search engines' ranking algorithms may not be state-of-the-art, the authors concluded that it is not possible at this stage to rule out spidering inadequacies as the source of the problem.

Gordon and Pathak (1999) compared the effectiveness of eight major search engines, namely AltaVista, Excite, HotBot, Infoseek, Lycos, Magellan, Open Text, and Yahoo!. The search capability, rather than the directory, of Yahoo! was used for the purposes of this study. Trained searchers entered queries based on the information needs of 33 faculty members at the University of Michigan Business School. The top 20 pages returned by each engine in response to a query were then judged by the faculty member for whom the query was issued as being *highly relevant*, *somewhat relevant*, *somewhat irrelevant*, or *highly irrelevant*. Recall and precision values were then computed at various cutoff values, including 1, 10, 20, and 200 pages. In the last case, a document that ranked between 21 and 200 for one search engine's results had to appear within the top 20 pages listed by another search engine in response to the same query in order to be evaluated. Otherwise, it was assumed to be irrelevant to that query.

An encoding scheme in which *highly relevant* and *somewhat relevant* pages were considered as being relevant, while *somewhat irrelevant* and *highly irrelevant* pages were deemed irrelevant, was used for most of the analysis. For the first document retrieved, the average precision measurement ranged from 12.1% for Yahoo! to 66.7% for Open Text, with the remaining six search engines falling between 20% and 40%. When the cutoff level was 10 pages, approximately half of the searches returned only one relevant document. Average precision ranged from 17.6% for Yahoo! to 40.6% for AltaVista. This range stayed approximately the same when using a cutoff value of 20 documents, with one or two being the most frequently returned number of relevant documents. Average precision for all the search engines fell to under 10% when 200 pages were considered, and four or fewer relevant documents were typically retrieved. The authors concluded that at least 20 pages should be examined to find the most relevant search results. In addition, they found little overlap between the documents retrieved by the various search engines, with approximately 93% of the documents retrieved by a single search engine across all cutoff values.

The shortcomings of using search engines to find relevant results are well known and supported by the research cited here. These include incomplete, out-of-date indices and search algorithms that appear to be far less than optimal at finding relevant results (assuming such results actually exist). The fact that one search engine may have outperformed another in a particular study is not what is of the most interest here; rather, the failure of all of the search engines to prove their worth at finding relevant documents is the most telling finding. It appears that information retrieval algorithms with proven results in traditional retrieval environments need some adjusting to reflect the uniqueness of searching in a "hyperlinked world."

IN SEARCH OF RELEVANCE

The latest advances in finding relevant Web pages in response to a user's query come from approaches that go beyond traditional information retrieval ranking algorithms by relying heavily on the structural and content-rich components of HTML documents. The premise is that the content of META and other subject-related HTML tags plus the network of hyperlinks joining Web pages can be used to improve the relevancy of search results and eliminate many of the links to irrelevant pages.

This section first describes a study that examines the relevance of pages retrieved in response to user-specified queries. Its primary purpose is to identify those cases where page content is irrelevant to query content. This is followed by a strategy that relies on the internal structure of Web documents for minimizing the likelihood of retrieving those irrelevant pages in the first place. Then, current approaches that focus on both the internal and external structure of the Web are described.

The Study

Most studies of search engine performance submit a predefined set of queries constructed by the studies' evaluators, rather than using "real-life" queries submitted by "real" end-users (Dong & Su, 1999). Then, only the most highly ranked pages returned by the engines are analyzed in measuring the precision of search results. This approach fails to examine if too many irrelevant links are returned and if relevant links appear later in the list of matches than they should.

For the purposes of this study, five test pages were posted on the Web and registered with five of the most-visited search engines at that time: AltaVista, Excite, HotBot, Infoseek, and Lycos. Estonian recipes were chosen as the topic for the test pages because of the many unique keywords that could be used to search for them. At the same time, the topic is not so popular that thousands of Web pages would include those keywords, as that would decrease the probability of anyone finding and clicking on a link to one of the test pages.

Tracking software was placed on each of these pages for collecting the queries to search engines that lead visitors to them. Theses queries differ from those found in typical studies in that they were not formed by the study's evaluators, but were submitted on an unsolicited basis by people searching the Web. Analysis of the relevance of a Web page to a user's query could therefore not be determined by comparing the searcher's true intent to the content of that page, as that intent was unknown. As is the case for the search engine to which a query is submitted, the searcher's intent was discerned solely on the basis of the query's content. The authors of the test pages judged how closely a query matched the contents of the page it retrieved. Relevance determinations were then based on those judgments. This approach mimics that of "editor's engines," in which Web documents are manually reviewed and categorized.

Another difference from other studies is that, in determining the level of agreement with search engine-assigned rankings, analysis was not limited to only those documents whose links appeared in the first page or two of a search engine's listings. Both the total number of links retrieved and where the test page fell within that list played a role in determining the level of agreement with the search engine's relevance rating for that page.

Analysis of Results

The analysis presented here examines the relevance of page content to query terms. First, the relevancy of the test pages' contents to the query terms that resulted in their retrieval, as evaluated by the creators of those pages, is presented. This is followed by an evaluation of the accuracy of the relevancy rankings assigned by the search engines to the test pages in response to those queries.

A total of 118 queries submitted to 15 search engines and metasearchers led people to the test pages, as shown in Figure 1. This number was limited due to the fact that the five leading search engines with which the pages were registered were often unable or unwilling to correctly index the five test pages (Lucas, 1999). Thirty-eight percent of the collected queries were unique (see the Appendix for the content of these queries and the number of visitors that submitted them). The format of those queries concurred with findings of other studies of query content, in that most had few terms and rarely included operators. The majority of them (92%) were term queries. Of these, 79% contained two or fewer terms. Boolean and Boolean-like operators were used in about 9% of the total queries.

Figure 1. Summary of Queries by Search Engine

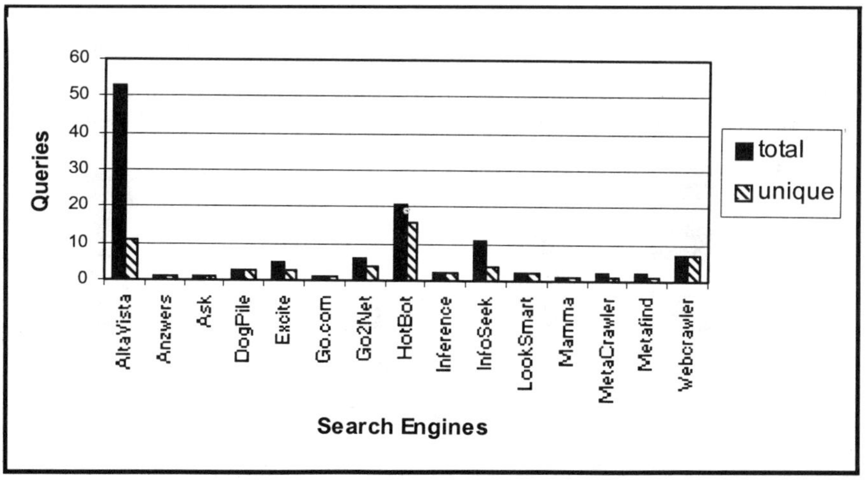

Judged Relevancy Ratings

A three-level scoring method was used for judging the relevancy of the test pages' contents to each unique query. The levels assigned were 1.0 for *relevant*, 0.5 for *somewhat relevant*, and 0 for *irrelevant*. Two independent evaluators made these judgments in order to reduce bias. Average agreement was 0.86 ± 0.07, using a 95% confidence interval. Averages of the two independently arrived-at scores were then calculated for each query. Figure 2 shows the distribution of these scores.

The average judged relevancy rating for how well the test pages' contents matched the query terms was 0.46 ± 0.13, using a 95% confidence interval. On average, the test pages were therefore somewhat relevant at best to the queries that retrieved them. Test page content was judged as being irrelevant to 35% of the unique queries. The elimination of links to those test pages would reduce the total number of matches listed in response to a query, thereby lessening the number of pages through which the user would need to wade. In addition, their elimination could make room for other, more relevant pages that would otherwise have occurred later in the listings and potentially been ignored by the query's submitter.

Test Page Relevancy Rankings

The relevancy rankings assigned by the search engines to the test pages are examined next. The "judged accuracy" of these rankings refers to the level of agreement with them. Eighty-nine percent of the unique queries had ranking data available from one or more search engine. This data was either present in the information stored with each submitted query or was obtained

Figure 2. Summary of Judged Relevancies

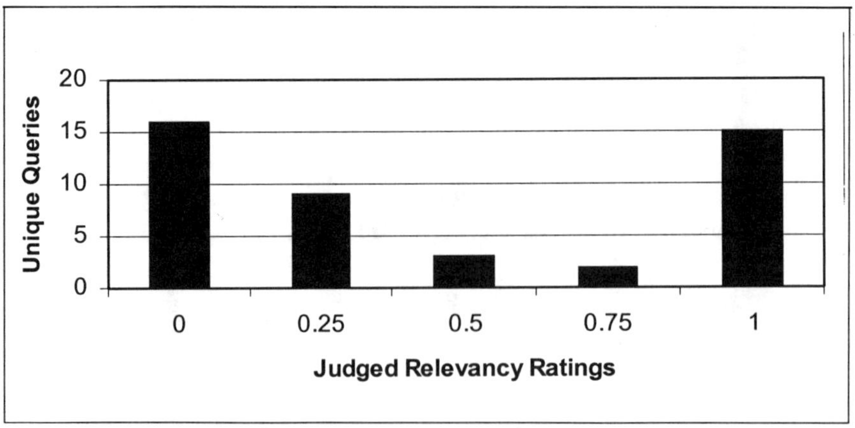

by resubmitting the original query to the search engine. In the latter case, the position of a test page link in response to a query could have changed from when that query was originally submitted. The range into which a test link fell, rather than an absolute value, was therefore used in judging the accuracy of a relevancy ranking. Percentage rating information, available from one or more search engine for 44% of the unique queries, was also considered in judging accuracy.

A three-level scoring method was used once again in making these judgments. The levels assigned were 1.0 for *agree with*, 0.5 for *somewhat agree with*, and 0 for *disagree with* the rankings assigned by the search engines. In each case, scores were arrived at independently and then averaged. The average agreement between the two sets of scores was 0.80 ± 0.11, using a 95% confidence interval.

Figure 3 shows the distribution of the judged accuracy ratings by scoring level, and Figure 4 shows the distribution by search engine. The overall average for agreement with the search engine-assigned relevancy rankings was 0.49 ± 0.13, using a 95% confidence interval, which corresponds to "somewhat agreeing" with the rankings provided by the search engines in response to the queries. Most of the disagreement with assigned rankings came from the fact that test page links appeared in the first 10% of the total number of links returned in response to all queries whose content was judged as being irrelevant to the page content. Forty percent of those links were within the top 1% of the total number of links retrieved.

Inflated ratings could be somewhat reduced by better query formation on the part of submitters. For example, a test page was listed in response to a query for **Bath Oil Making**. Both "oil" and "making" appear in a pancake recipe on that page. "Bath" never appears at all. If the terms "Bath" and "Oil" had been entered as "**Bath Oil**" then the test page would probably have

Figure 3. Judged Accuracy Distribution

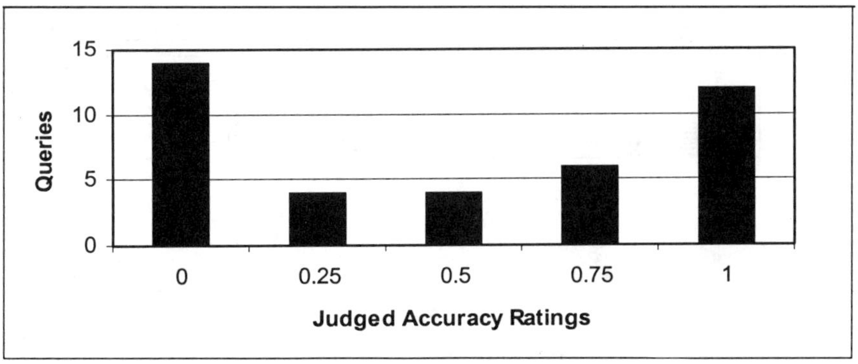

appeared later in the listing than within the range of 26-50 out of 126,788 matches. Unfortunately, it still would have appeared because of the match on the remaining query term.

Entering "**Bath Oil Making**" would have excluded the test page, but would also have excluded documents on "making bath oil," which may have been of interest to the user. The best way to exclude irrelevant pages from those retrieved by the search engine to which this query was submitted would have been to enter it as **+"Bath Oil" +Making**. This requires some degree of sophistication on the part of the query submitter, not to mention an accurate and up-to-date index, for improving the usefulness of the search results.

The relevancy of a test page in response to a query was judged as being underrated by a search engine in only one case. This was for a query on **estonian food** submitted to AltaVista. The test page did not appear until the fifth page of matches and was far more relevant than many of the links that appeared before it, such as the one leading to: **Estonian choir finds success in a post-Soviet world**.

This study corroborates previously cited findings that conducting searches with popular search engines often results in far too many links with little relevance to the user's query. Page content was found to be irrelevant to more than one-third of the queries, which strongly disagrees with the relevancy rankings assigned by the search engines to those pages. For 40% of the queries that should not have resulted in the retrieval of any of the test pages, a link to at least one of them appeared within the top 1% of retrieved links. Clearly, more should and can be done to reduce the number of links to irrelevant pages.

The data from this study is used next for examining the effectiveness of a methodology for improving the relevance of search results by reducing the number of irrelevant pages returned in response to a query.

Figure 4. Judged Accuracy by Search Engine

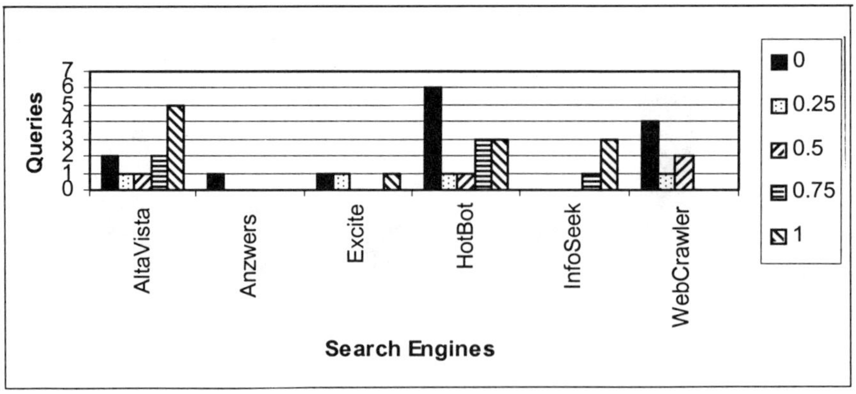

Addressing the Relevancy Problem

The internal structure of Web documents provides information about page content that can enhance traditional IR ranking algorithms. Following is an evaluation of an approach for reducing the number of irrelevant documents retrieved in response to users' queries. Matches between the test pages and the queries used to retrieve them are calculated based on the occurrence of query terms in content-rich HTML tags. The goal of this approach is to reduce to zero the match between a query and a test document for all those cases in which the study's evaluators found no correlation between their contents. This would have the effect of minimizing the number of irrelevant documents retrieved in response to a query, thereby improving the overall relevance of the search results.

Term Ranking

An evaluation metric is needed for determining the relevancy of a test page to a query based on the terms contained in each. A common approach for calculating the match between documents and queries is to represent each as a vector of the form (t_1, t_2, t_3, . . ., t_n), in which *n* is the number of unique terms (Harman, 1992). The value of t_i is 0 if term *i* is absent or 1 if term *i* is present in the document or query being represented. Taking a dot product of the two vectors yields a simple Boolean match between a query and a document. Weighted matches can be computed by increasing the weights of certain terms found within the document on the basis of frequency, position, or some other criteria.

As a starting point, frequency was used as a weighting factor in composing vectors for the test pages. Each term in a page (excluding stop words) was assigned a value of 1 if it occurred only once. If the term occurred more than once, its weighting doubled to 2. Phrases, which contain two or more terms, were given a weighted value of 2 if they occurred once. This weighting was also doubled if the phrase occurred twice. The higher value placed on phrases reflects the significance of finding a set of terms, rather than a single term, within the test page. Additional occurrences of a term or a phrase beyond a count of two did not affect its weighting in the document vector. Given the short length of the test pages, repetitions beyond that number could be considered as spamming.

Figure 5 shows the dot products calculated from vectors representing the 45 unique queries and the test pages they retrieved. For Boolean queries containing an AND condition, the dot product was 0 if both query terms did not appear in the test page. For an OR condition, if both query terms appeared in the page, the higher score of the two was used.

Figure 5. Original Dot Products

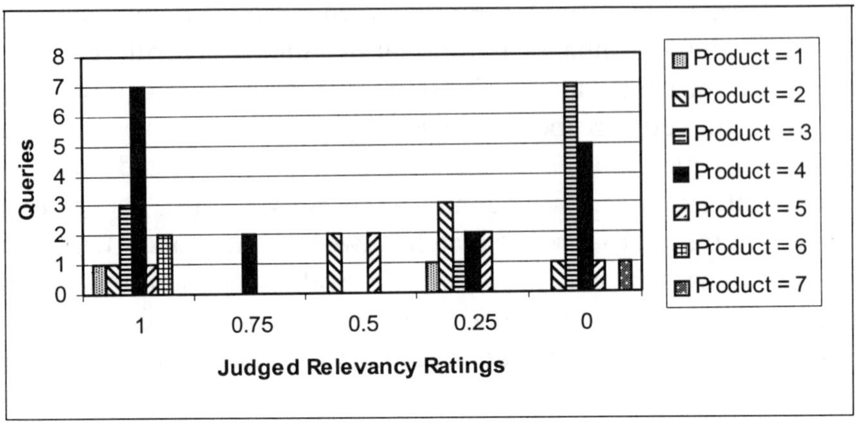

These dot products, which reflect the match between query and page content on the basis of term and phrase frequency alone, provide a base-line to which other dot products involving different vector compositions can be compared.

Content-Related HTML Tags

The major search engines all list any page containing at least one of the terms entered by the user in response to a query. As has been shown, this methodology frequently results in far too many pages being retrieved, making it all but impossible for the user to sift through the results to find the most relevant pages. One of the goals of improved search engine performance must therefore be to reduce the number of irrelevant pages retrieved.

In pursuit of this goal, the approach described here considers only those terms residing in certain HTML tags when calculating relevance. By composing document vectors based on the appearance of terms and phrases in those tags alone, it is possible to observe the effect on dot product calculations using this criterion. The desired outcome is to reduce the number of irrelevant pages retrieved, without adversely affecting the retrieval of relevant pages. To optimally achieve this result, the calculated match between test pages and queries must fall to 0 when the content of the former is irrelevant to the latter and be unchanged or improved when the content is relevant.

The document type definition (DTD) for HTML declares the element types that may appear as tags embedded within HTML documents (Raggett, Le Hors, & Jacobs, 1999). In addition to informing browsers on how to display and treat their contents, document title, heading, and META tags contain information directly related to the subject matter of a Web page. It is the terms residing in these tags that are used here as the sole determinants of page rank.

To see the effects of using only these terms, new document vectors were constructed for use in the dot product calculation. The weighting of terms found in title and META tags was increased to 2, while phrases were increased to 4. The DTD specifies six levels of headings, ranging from most to least important. The test pages contained only the top two levels of headings. Weightings of terms found in either level were increased to 1.5, while phrase weightings were increased to 3. Once again, if a term or phrase appeared more than once in the test page, its weighting was doubled. Figure 6 shows the change in dot product values from those shown in Figure 5 as a result of using this methodology.

The dot products that were most affected were those for which the test pages were either judged to be the most relevant or the least relevant in response to the queries. The match between query content and page content typically rose for the former and fell for the latter. The desired effect of improving the rank of the test page when it is relevant to a query and decreasing its rank when it is irrelevant was therefore achieved.

Figure 7 shows the average amount of change to the dot products by relevancy rating. Overall, the average change was -0.122 ± 0.841, based on a 95% confidence interval, when only terms from HTML tags were used in the matching process.

Table 1 shows the 14 queries, as entered by search engine users, to which test page content was no longer relevant when the dot product was calculated using terms from the title, heading, and META tags. Page content had judged relevancy ratings of 0 for nine of these queries, and from 0.25 to 0.50 for the remaining five. For 56% of the cases where page content was irrelevant to the

Figure 6. Dot Products Affected by Matching on Tag Terms

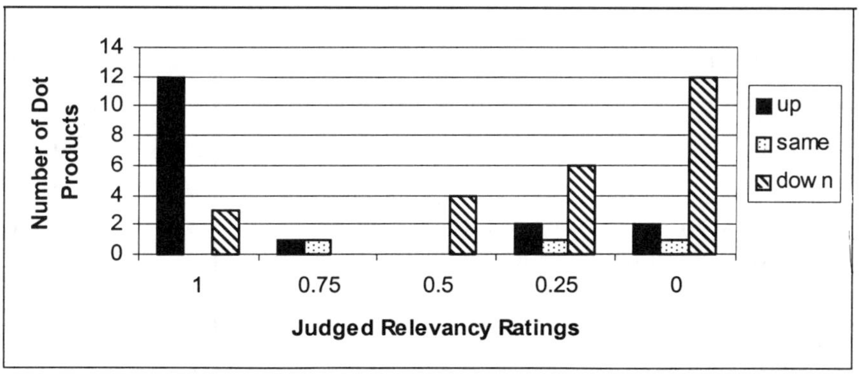

Figure 6. Average Amount of Change in Dot Products Using Tag Terms

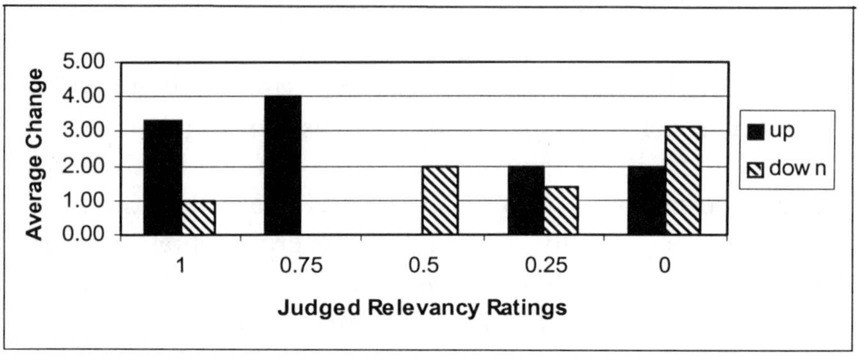

query and for 42% of the cases where it was slightly to somewhat relevant, the relevancy rating fell to 0.

Given the uneven quality and varying scope of documents on the Web, basing relevancy calculations on matches between query terms and all terms appearing in a document frequently leads to the retrieval of far too many Web

Table 1. Queries with Dot Products of 0

Query	Judged Relevancy
cleargelatin	0.50
sauerkraut+cooking	0.50
"pork"	0.25
potatoes	0.25
sauerkraut	0.25
Bath Oil Making	0.00
hard boil eggs	0.00
making butter	0.00
salt pickles	0.00
crock pot	0.00
neck bones	0.00
reefer pot marijuana chronic not trucks and not houseware and not pain and not pottery and not sex	0.00
ruff salad	0.00
small intestines	0.00

pages. The findings presented here provide preliminary evidence on the effectiveness of using the content of descriptive HTML tags to reduce the incidence of irrelevant pages. Metadata classification standards would enhance the ability of authors to use these tags for representing the content of their pages, which would also assist search engines in indexing the Web.

The Hyperlink Factor

A shortcoming to the approach of relying on the internal structure of Web pages for determining page rank is that, in order to be truly useful in the indexing and searching processes, the contents of the HTML tags must accurately reflect the subject matter. While this was the case in the study presented here, page authors may be neither truthful nor accurate in providing information on page content, given that most have a monetary incentive for achieving top positions in search results. It is therefore unlikely that metadata from user-supplied tags can ever be relied upon as the sole determinant of page content.

The integration of views about page content from sources external to the page's author is needed to reduce bias and improve the accuracy of ranking algorithms. Such information can be derived from the hypertext structure of the Web and then used for indexing and ranking pages. Graphically, the Web can be represented as nodes joined together by directed links. Recent IR efforts have focused on applying the Web's graphical structure to the task of searching for relevant documents (Kumar et al., 2000). Anchor tags within HTML documents define the links between Web pages and include the address of the referenced page as well as a label describing it. The ancestors of a page, its descendents, and the contents of its anchor tags can be used for providing information about a page's subject matter and the perceived quality of that page. The approaches described here combine the external structure of the Web with the internal structure of Web pages for improved search performance.

Structure-Based Approaches for Improving Search Performance

Adding structural components of HTML documents to a standard information retrieval function is shown to improve that function's performance in Boyan, Freitag Joachins (1996). The LASER (Learning Architecture for Search Engine Retrieval) Web-indexing prototype uses a retrieval function that is based on the Vector Space Model. Inverse document frequency, or *idf*, is used as a weighting factor for giving higher weightings to terms that appear infrequently in the collection. It can be computed as log N/*n*, where N is the number of documents in the entire collection, and n is the number of documents in which the term occurs (Sparck-Jones, 1972). The relevance of a query term to a document can then be calculated as the product of term frequency times the inverse document frequency (TFIDF), or *tf x idf* (Salton & Buckley, 1988).

A total of 18 parameters can be used by Laser's retrieval function in determining HTML document rankings, including parameters for weighting words that fall within the title, anchor, and top three heading tags. Hyperlink structure is also incorporated by adding into the calculation of a document's relevancy rating the discounted values for the relevancy ratings of all the documents descending from it. The further removed a document is from the original one, the more the value of its rating is discounted. Laser's retrieval function was found to significantly outperform functions based on simple count, in which the number of query terms that appears in a document is counted, and those based on standard TFIDF, which provides a better measure of relevance than counting but ignores the HTML structure of documents.

The content of the hyperlinks leading to a document can also be used to rank that document's relevance to query terms. Li (1998) claims that the Vector Space Model, which rewards the use of rare words, is not valid on the Web, where documents vary in quality and purpose. Using a method called Hyperlink Vector Voting (HVV), a document's content is selected on the basis of how it is described by others, rather than the author, in the links that lead to it from other Web pages. Vectors are used to represent links, rather than documents. Ranking is determined on the similarities between link and query vectors as well as the number of links leading to the document.

An experimental HVV-based search engine called Rankdex was used for conducting tests on the performance value of this approach (Li, 1998). The top 10 results from sending 10 queries to four commercial search engines plus Rankdex were compared to the results from submitting those same queries to LookSmart, an editor's engine. Thus, the judgments of external reviewers, rather than the study's evaluator, were used for determining relevance. The editors of LookSmart selected 79 Web pages as matching the query criteria. Rankdex matched about 22.7% of those pages, Excite matched about 6.3%, Infoseek matched about 5%, AltaVista matched about 1.2%, and Lycos matched none.

The Google search engine makes extensive use of link structure and link text to increase the relevancy of search results (Brin & Page, 1998). It calculates a Web page's PageRank™ by using an iterative algorithm that factors in the number of pages containing links to it and the importance, or quality, of each of those pages. The total number of links within a page that contains a link to the page being ranked is used to normalize the calculation. This normalization is based on the premise that a link coming from a page containing fewer links should weigh more than one coming from a page containing a greater number of links.

Google's algorithm models a user who starts at a random Web page and clicks on links, without going backwards, until boredom sets in and another random page is selected. Some pages are arrived at more frequently than others, indicating they are more important, which increases their rating. Another feature used in calculating rank is the association of text in an anchor tag with the page in which it appears as well as with the page to which the link points. Term proximity and the font size of terms are also used in Google's ranking calculations.

A comparison study of Google, AltaVista, and AllTheWeb (a search engine launched by Fast Search & Transfer™ in partnership with Dell Computer Corporation) was reported in Ljosland (1999). Twelve queries were sent to each engine, and the first 10 documents retrieved were evaluated using a relevance scale of 1 for *relevant*, 0.5 for *partly relevant*, and 0 for *not relevant*. When only relevant documents were counted, the P@10 values were 0.4 for AltaVista, 0.7 for Google, and 0.4 for AllTheWeb. When partly relevant documents were also included, the P@10 values were 0.5 for AltaVista, 0.9 for Google, and 0.5 for AllTheWeb. Recall values were estimated as 0.3 for AltaVista, 0.5 for Google, and 0.3 for AllTheWeb, where the sum of the relevant, retrieved documents across all three engines was used to represent the total number of relevant documents in the collection.

The CLEVER search engine makes use of the directed graph structure of the Web in its information retrieval algorithms (Chakrabarti et al., 1998). It is built upon a link-based algorithm called HITS (Kleinberg, 1999) that distinguishes between two types of pages: *authorities*, which are the best sources of information on a topic, and *hubs*, which are collections of links leading to authority pages. Initial numerical hub and authority scores are assigned to each page. The hub score is subsequently updated as the sum of the authority scores of the locations to which the page points, while the authority score becomes the sum of the hub scores of the locations that point to it.

The precision scores of CLEVER, AltaVista, and Yahoo! were compared on the basis of user-provided relevance judgments. AltaVista was chosen for this study because of its status as the best-known automatic search engine, while Yahoo! was chosen as the best-known human-compiled directory. A total of 27 broad-topic queries were submitted to each. The top 10 pages returned by AltaVista, the top five hubs and five authorities returned by CLEVER, and 10 random pages from the most relevant node or nodes of Yahoo!, in response to each of the queries, were collected, merged, and sorted alphabetically. Thirty-seven users then ranked the usefulness of each page as *bad*, *fair*, *good*, or *fantastic*. Pages within the latter two categorizations were deemed as relevant in computing precision measurements. AltaVista was never judged as the best source on any of the topics. On 50% of the topics, CLEVER was judged the best. Yahoo! was judged the best on 19% of the topics. For the remaining 31% of topics, the difference between Yahoo! and CLEVER was insignificant.

The effectiveness of the approaches that use the internal and external structure of hypertext documents for making determinations about page quality and content is attested to by the studies described here. Search engines whose indexing and ranking algorithms incorporate these structural components often outperform more popular search engines when it comes to finding relevant pages.

EMERGING TRENDS AND FUTURE WORK

The Web presents many unique challenges that were not previously encountered in working with text databases. Its tremendous scope, coupled with its lack of structure, makes it difficult for search engines to maintain up-to-date indices. Search algorithms that work well with traditional text databases do not provide the most relevant results when applied to the Web. A further complication arises from the fact that most users of the Web are novices, with little understanding of optimal query formulation techniques.

Metasearchers have helped to bridge the gap in the coverage of the major search engines, but have failed to compensate for other shortcomings. They can do so by extending their role beyond that of providing an interface to a variety of search engines. Inquirus (Lawrence & Giles, 1998a), a demonstration and research metasearch service, improves over the performance of individual search engines in a number of ways, including providing more useful document summaries, showing the context in which the query terms appear, using proximity information to improve document ranking, and identifying pages that no longer exist or no longer contain the query terms.

Standard metadata classifications are also needed and are currently being developed for providing structured information about page content. The Dublin Core (http://purl.oclc.org/dc/) is a metadata element set for describing Web resources. The use of this and other such schemas is supported by the World Wide Web Consortium (W3C), which has published a Resource

Description Framework that provides an architecture for metadata (Brickley & Guha, 1999). The use of standardized metadata should improve search engine capabilities by supplying machine-understandable information about Web resources (Lassila, 1998).

To be truly effective, however, metadata must be associated with the majority of documents residing on the Web. Marchiori (1998) describes an automated approach for achieving this association. The use of "fuzzy" metadata is coupled with the hyperlink structure of the Web for determining page relevance. Unlike Boolean logic values, which are either 0 or 1, fuzzy logic specifies values that range from 0 to 1. This enables the use of intermediate values for denoting the relevancy of metadata to a document. Metadata is back-propagated from a page that has some sort of metadata classification to those pages linked to it. The value of that attribute is multiplied by a "fading factor" that falls between 0 and 1, so that it decreases as the distance between the originating page and the page being assigned a metadata value increases. Test results from using this approach for providing pages on the Web with metadata classifications indicate that only 16% of the Web must have metadata classifications to be truly useful, as opposed to 50% when back-propagation is not used.

Traditional ranking algorithms that rely on such calculations as TFIDF for determining the match between query and document terms are no longer the most effective means of finding relevant data. Both the internal and external structure of Web documents need to be factored into search algorithms if they are to be effective at finding relevant documents from the millions of pages of dubious quality residing on the Web. Many of the leading search engines have begun to consider link and page popularity in determining a page's rank. The optimal combination of factors for improved search performance remains to be determined, but the research efforts described here show that great progress is being made in that direction.

Many advances remain to be made in the area of natural language processing. The use of advanced NLP techniques is still rare in Web search engines and typically limited to word stemming and finding synonyms to terms in a user's query. A more difficult problem arises from the fact that words have more than one meaning, which is termed "polysemy." The intent behind a query on "java" could be to learn more about coffee, or it could be to learn more about the programming language. Relevance feedback techniques can facilitate the determination of which meaning was intended. The SimpliFind™ search engine uses a semantic network built upon the WordNet® on-line lexical reference system developed at Princeton University for generating a pull-down menu of meanings for a search term. If a term is not in the database, users are prompted to enter a meaning, which is then added to the search engine's database for future use. Words associated with that meaning are then used for expanding the query. Usable interfaces that support such techniques and succeed in persuading searchers to make use of them will have a significant impact on search results.

Search interfaces must also support the query formulation and reformulation processes of novice users and provide ample grounds for future research efforts. Prior to the introduction and widespread use of Web search engines, users of information retrieval systems were dedicated searchers who were willing to view many documents and engage in repeated query reformulations (Harman, 1994). This profile no longer fits the average user of Web search engines, as evidenced by the preponderance of queries containing two or fewer terms with no Boolean operators, and the limited use of relevance feedback options. In addition to providing easier to use interfaces, visualizations of search results that provide alternative views of the retrieved pages can also enhance a user's understanding of the relationship between documents and query terms. Improvements in the query formation processes of users coupled with advanced indexing and ranking algorithms would have a major impact on the relevancy of search results.

CONCLUSIONS

As the fastest growing database in the world, the Web represents a unique set of challenges. Its unstructured content comes from a wide spectrum of sources, resulting in the broadest range of topics imaginable covered with varying degrees of accuracy. Users of search engines enter short, simple queries that often return thousands of matches. Yet, most do not look beyond the first page or two of search results, giving great incentive to page authors to have their links listed in the top 10. Many resort to spamming techniques, which hinder a search engine's ability to retrieve relevant pages in response to a query. Search engines must also keep up with the rapidly changing content of the Web in order to provide accurate, up-to-date responses to users' queries.

To date, the ability of search engines to maintain full-text indices of the entire Web has been far from optimal. Given the Web's rapid rate of growth, the future success of search engines at achieving this goal seems doubtful. Rather, it is more reasonable to expect metasearchers to provide the breadth of coverage. Search engines could then focus on accurately indexing a portion of the Web and developing ranking algorithms that effectively calculate the relevance of a query to a page.

Ranking algorithms have begun to diverge from the standard information retrieval models used in the past by incorporating the hypertext structure of the Web. Internal structural components based on the elements found within documents can provide a truer picture of page content than can be discerned from counting the number of occurrences of terms within documents. Metadata standards are needed, and are currently being developed, to provide classifications that search engines can use for more accurate indexing of page content.

It will take some time, however, before these standards are completed and even a greater amount of time before Web page authors adopt their use. In addition, their accuracy will be hard to ascertain, given authors' incentives to engage in spamming. External views of page content must therefore be added to the mix, and search engines have begun to look at the graphical structure of the Web as a primary source of these views. The number of ancestors to a page indicates its popularity and, if those ancestors are also of high quality, then that reflects well on the quality of the page. A page's descendents provide valuable data about its usefulness as a resource locator. The text found in anchor tags for describing the destination of a link can also be used for providing a less biased view of a page's content.

It still remains to be determined what combination of factors will be most effective at maximizing the precision of search results at various recall levels. And, no matter how effective the algorithms are, they will be of little use if search engine users are unable to optimally form and reformulate queries and to interpret their results. Improved query interface design and meaningful visualizations of search results will greatly help users in these efforts and present tremendous opportunities for future research.

REFERENCES

Abdulla, G., Liu, B., & Fox, E. A. (1998). *Searching the World-Wide Web: Implications from Studying Different User Behavior.* Paper presented at the WebNet98 Conference, Orlando, FL.

Bharat, K., & Border, A. (1999). *Measuring the Web.* Available Online: http://www.research.digital.com/-SRC/whatsnew/sem.html.

Boyan, J., Freitag, D. & Joachins, T. (1996). *A Machine Learning Architecture for Optimizing Web Search Engines.* Paper presented at the AAAI Workshop on Internet-Based Information Systems.

Brickley, D. & Guha, R.V. (1999). *W3C Resource Description Framework (RDF) Schema Specification, Proposed Recommendation.* Available:

http://www.w3.org/TR/PR-rdf-schema/.

Brin, S. & Page, L. (1998). *The Anatomy of a Large-Scale Hypertextual Web Search Engine.* Paper presented at the 7th International World Wide Web Conference.

Chakrabarti, S., Dom, B., Gibson, D., Kumar, S. R., Raghavan, P., Rajagopalan, S., & Tomkins, A. (1998). *Experiments in Topic Distillation.* Paper presented at the ACM SIGIR Workshop on Hypertext Information Retrieval on the Web, Melbourne, Australia.

Chu, H., & Rosenthal, M. (1996). *Search Engines for the World Wide Web: A comparative study and evaluation methodology.* Paper presented at the ASIS 1996 Annual Conference.

Deerwester, S., Dumais, S. T., Furnas, G. W., Laudauer, T. K., & Harshman, R. (1990). Indexing by Latent Semantic Analysis. *Journal of the Society of Information Science, 41*(6), 391-407.

Dong, X., & Su, L. (1999). Search engines on the World Wide Web and information retrieval from the Internet: a review and evaluation. *Online & CDROM Review, 21*(2), 67-81.

Gordon, M. & Pathak, P. (1999). Finding information on the World Wide Web: the retrieval effectiveness of search engines. *Information Processing & Management, 35*(2), 141-180.

Graphic Visualization and Usability Center (1998). *GVU's 10th WWW User Survey.* Available: http://www.cc.gatech.edu/gvu/user_surveys/survey-1998-10/.

Gudivada, V. N., Raghavan, V. V., Grosky, W. I., & Kasanagottu, R. (1997). Information Retrieval on the World Wide Web. *IEEE Internet Computing, 1*(5), 58-68.

Harman, D. (1992). Ranking Algorithms. In W. B. Frakes & R. Baeza-Yates (Eds.), *Information Retrieval: Data Structures & Algorithms,* 363-392, Upper Saddle River, NJ: Prentice Hall.

Harman, D. (1994). *Overview of the Second Text REtrieval Conference (TREC-2),* NIST SP 500-215, National Institute of Standards and Technology, Gaithersburg, MD.

Hawking, D., Craswell, N., Thistlewaite, P., & Harman, D. (1999). *Results and Challenges in Web Search Evaluation.* Paper presented at the Eighth International World Wide Web Conference, Toronto, Canada.

Jansen, B. J., Spink, A., Bateman, J., & Saracevic, T. (1998). Real Life Information Retrieval: A Study of User Queries on the Web. *ACM SIGIR Forum, 32*(1), 5-17.

Kleinberg, J. M. (1999). Authoritative sources in a hyperlinked environment. *Journal of the ACM, 46*(5), 604-632.

Kumar, R., Raghavan, P., Rajagopalan, S., Sivakumar, D., Tompkins, A., & Upfal, E. (2000). *The Web as a graph.* Paper presented at the nineteenth ACM SIGMOD-SIGACT-SIGART symposium on Principles of database systems.

Lassila, O. (1998). WEB METADATA: A Matter of Semantics. *IEEE Internet Computing, July-August*, 30-37.

Lawrence, S., & Giles, C. L. (1998a). *Inquirus, The NECI Meta Search Engine.* Paper presented at the Seventh International World Wide Web Conference, Brisbane, Australia.

Lawrence, S., & Giles, C. L. (1998b). Searching the World Wide Web. *Science Magazine, 280*(5360).

Lawrence, S., & Giles, C. L. (1999). Accessibility of Information on the Web. *Nature Magazine, 400*(6740), 107-109.

Leighton, H. V., & Srivastava, J. (1999). First 20 Precision among World Wide Web Search Services (Search Engines). *Journal of the American Society for Information Science, 50*(10), 870-881.

Li, Y. (1998). Toward a Qualitative Search Engine. *IEEE Internet Computing, 2*(4), 24-29.

Ljosland, M. (1999). *Evaluation of Web search engines and the search for better ranking algorithms.* Paper presented at the ACM SIGIR '99 Workshop on Evaluation of Web Document Retrieval, Berkeley, CA.

Lucas, W. T. (1999). *(Mis)Management of Information on the World Wide Web.* Paper presented at the Information Systems Analysis and Synthesis/Systemics, Cybernetics and Informatics Conference, Orlando, FL.

Lucas, W. T. (2000). *The Noise Factor: Irrelevant Search Results on the World Wide Web.* Paper presented at the 11th International Conference of the Information Resources Management Association, Anchorage, Alaska.

Marchiori, M. (1998). The limits of Web metadata, and beyond. *Computer Networks and ISDN Systems, 30*, 1-9.

Raggett, D., Le Hors, A., & Jacobs, I. (1999). *HTML 4.01 Specification, W3C Recommendation.* Available: http://www.w3.org/TR/REC-html40.

Robertson, S. E., & Sparck-Jones, K. (1976). Relevance Weighting of Search Terms. *Journal of the American Society for Information Science, 27*(3), 129-146.

Salton, G. (1971). *The SMART Retrieval System — Experiments in Automatic Document Processing*. Englewood Cliffs, NJ: Prentice-Hall.

Salton, G., & Buckley, C. (1988). Term-Weighting Approaches in Automatic Text Retrieval. *Information Processing & Management, 24*(5), 513-523.

Salton, G., & Buckley, C. (1990). Improving Retrieval Performance by

Relevance Feedback. *Journal of the American Society for Information Science, 41*(4), 288-297.

Selberg, E., & Etzioni, O. (1997). The Metacrawler Architecture for Response Aggregation on the Web. *The IEEE Expert, 12*(1), 8-14.

Silverstein, C., Henzinger, M., Marais, J., & Moricz, M. (1998). *Analysis of a Very Large Alta Vista Query Log* (Technical 1998-014). Palo Alto, CA: Compaq Systems Research Center.

Sparck-Jones, K. (1972). A Statistical Interpretation of Term Specificity and Its Application in Retrieval. *Journal of Documentation, 28*(1), 11-21.

Spink, A., Chang, C., & Goz, A. (1999). *Users' Interactions with the Excite Web Search Engine: A Query Reformulation and Relevance Feedback Analysis.* Paper presented at the CAIS Conference, Quebec.

APPENDIX: DATA COLLECTION

User-Entered Queries	Number of Occurances
"Estonian recipe"	1
"Estonian recipes"	8
"parsley root" recipes	1
"pork"	1
4 ingredients recipes	1
a few Estonian recipes	1
Bath Oil Making	1
celery root pancakes	1
cleargelatin	1
cream of wheat recipes	1
crock pot	1
crock pot recipes	1
estonian recipes	3
Estonian and recipes	2
Estonian cousines	1
Estonian food	2
Estonian recipe	2
Estonian recipes	57
Estonian sauerkraut recipes	2
hard boil eggs	1
How do I prepare intestines for sausages	1
International Estonian Child adoption	1
lemon butter fish	1
making butter	1
meat or blood	1
neck bones	1
pork chop recipes	2
potatoes	1
potatoes in vinegrette	1
recipes +neck +bones	2
recipes beets	1
recipes desserts estonian	1
recipes estonian	2
recipes for jam and bacon	1
recipes+making+sausages	1
reefer pot marijuana chronic not trucks and not houseware and not pain and not pottery and not sex	1
ruff salad	1
salt pickles	1
sauerkraut	1
sauerkraut recipes	1
sauerkraut soup	1
sauerkraut+cooking	1
small intestines	1
stuffed pork chop recipes	2
Vinegrette	1

Chapter III

Addressing the Metadata Gap: Ad Hoc Digital Documents in Organizations

Lisa D. Murphy
Louisiana State University, USA

INTRODUCTION

In today's World Wide Web, Napster, Active Server Page world, distinctions among text, databases, and documents are disappearing both inside and outside a firm's firewall. This chapter brings out of the shadows a key issue related to document work in organizations: metadata for ad hoc digital documents. Ad hoc digital documents are those created, stored, and used outside the purview of formal text databases or document management systems. When every end user is a potential publisher and every desktop computer a potential server, document management is not just the concern of records retention personnel and information systems professionals. And, researchers and technologists applying their sophisticated automated summarization and full-text searching tools to documents under user control must prove the worth and improve the effectiveness of their tools.

Digital documents are crucial for day-to-day organizational work, but as yet their management is personalized, erratic, unsystematic; both the research on text databases and the practice of document management can benefit from an improved understanding of this complex context and the roles of metadata in it. We will review empirical studies of document work in organizations and consider both traditional and emerging roles for metadata in ad hoc document work settings. After identifying these roles, we will analyze a metadata standard implemented in HTML (the Dublin Core) for its suitability for supporting metadata use in this context. Directions for practice and research are offered prior to the concluding remarks.

BACKGROUND

In organizations, document workers with a typical networked desktop computer can create complex, multimedia, multi-application, hyperlinked, digital documents with embedded procedures, sophisticated metadata, and automatically generated summaries. They can distribute the documents electronically through e-mail, file sharing, and Web pages, and enforce a variety of controls over the documents' use, including file attributes, annotation controls, peer-to-peer networking, and passwords. Those with Lotus Notes can intermingle documents, data, and e-mail, revise the structure and relationship of documents over time, and use the software's sophisticated replication functions to keep distributed copies of these "databases" synchronized. Often document workers can do all this without involving an information systems or document management professional. However, the presence of advanced publishing capabilities does not guarantee good document practice, make appropriate information available to others, or assure compliance with company policies, regulatory requirements, or legal needs.

Beyond the complications of these new and more powerful technologies, today's ways of working also have implications for document management. Digital documents move quickly, and generally without impediment, around organizations and across hierarchies, and often between them as well (Murphy, 1999). Traditional boundaries of information processing within organizations—task, work group, department, division (e.g., Daft and Macintosh, 1981)—are no barrier to digital documents transmitted as e-mail attachments or as copies put on shared hard drives. Adding to the complexity is the increasing use of nonhierarchical organizational structures such as task forces, virtual teams, and communities of practice (Wegner & Snyder, 2000).

The new ways of organizing work interact with the new technologies. Groupware of various stripes can be used to support group activities ranging from a onetime meeting to a globally distributed virtual team. Computer-based communication tools such as these have been identified as the "backbone of many organizations, supplanting the formal hierarchical structure to achieve coordination and manage relationships" (Daft & Lewin, 1993, p. iv). However, a group-based orientation to electronic document work is a powerful but imperfect one. Ad hoc organizing arrangements such as teams eventually come to an end, "orphaning" their information, knowledge, and documents (Paepcke, 1996b; Schultze & Boland, 1997). Also, people may belong to multiple teams simultaneously while others are occasional members, joining as stand-ins for regular members or as temporary troubleshooters. Such deviations from the exemplar of one-person-one-group can cause problems in the implementation, management, and use of these technologies.

As management becomes aware of how digital documents are proliferating in their organizations and anticipates some of the potential consequences (e.g., liability), records retention and document management professionals may be called on to bring order to this document "adhocracy." Outside their traditional domain document management practitioners have little authority to enact change; their familiar technologies fall short of serving the wide range of document types and uses; and, in general, the situation does not call for the system-based approaches at which they excel. However, one resource familiar to document management personnel may help bring order to the situation: metadata.

METADATA TO THE RESCUE?

Metadata—data describing data to enhance usefulness—are a key element of traditional and digital libraries (Marshall, 1998; Smith, 1996; Weibel, 1995), Electronic Document Management Systems (EDMS) (Bielawski & Boyle, 1997; Boyle, 1997; Sprague, 1995), and databases (Cammarata et al., 1994; Gillenson & Frost, 1993). Associated with entering documents into a repository, creating metadata has conventionally required a professional to catalog each item using a single list of entities and often a controlled vocabulary. Each metadata record is specific to a document in the particular context of its repository; each provides descriptive information about the document available for searching, retrieval, access control, disposition management, and other needs. Metadata do not have to be compiled at the level of a collection (Murphy, 1998); an individual document can be described with its own unique attributes. However, when different documents use different structures of metadata, each document then becomes a collection of one, increasing the effort associated with searching and browsing, and reducing the ability to make linkages between documents or collections (Marshall, 1998).

Metadata can be identified as being separate from (vs. integrated within) the document itself both physically and logically (Murphy, 1998). Physically separable metadata are those that can be stored independently of the document and therefore can persist after the document itself is no longer available. Logically separable metadata are informational elements that cannot be determined by direct access to the document content, such as the birth and death date of the author or the existence of subsequent versions. Many document technologies provide capabilities for physical and logical integration and separation. Common examples of integrated metadata include HTML "meta" tags and a word-processor's "properties" box; other metadata can be extracted from integrated content such as tables of contents, list of figures, captions, indexes, and glossaries. Examples of separable metadata include an automatically-generated summary file extracted from a text document such as can be created by Word 2000 (Microsoft Corporation, 1999a) and the descriptors displayed by Web search portals such as Yahoo. However, choices between physical and logical integration or separation have consequences. For example, using integrated metadata requires tools that can distinguish metadata from the document content and manipulate it for display or searching. For separable metadata, issues include the ability to associate the metadata with the document object, including reflecting the fact that the object may have changed since the metadata record was generated (e.g., works in progress). The nature of the metadata needed (e.g., logically or physically separable or integrated or both) varies by organizational demands for document work and documentation. For instance, the requirements for evidence (Bearman & Sochats, 1996) may necessitate that some metadata be logically and physically separable (e.g., an index of destroyed documents) while other metadata remain physically integrated (e.g., information on format of content) to enable access and to allow the assessment of the extent of congruence between the document and its descriptors stored separately.

The technologies of the Web have exploited text-searching capabilities to index millions of digital documents, most of which lack formal metadata (Eztioni,1996; Lynch, 1997). Both through intranets (DeJesus, 1997) and through the capabilities built into popular operating systems such as Microsoft Windows 95/98/NT/2000 (Microsoft Corporation, 1999b), these automated approaches have been implemented in corporations, universities, hospitals, and government agencies and provide end users with powerful tools more familiar to them from libraries and WWW search engines. These tools create physically separable metadata from logically integrated content (as anyone who has been linked by a search engine to a "HTTP 404 File Not Found" Web page has seen).

Origins of these technologies lie in what Kuhlthau (1991) calls the "bibliographic paradigm." This paradigm reflects decades of focus on developing tools to better support access to documents in both physical and digital collections such as traditional libraries, digital libraries, and EDMS. Technologies such as natural language queries, context-based searching, and algorithms that associate meanings by location and use patterns facilitate information seeking via the exploitation of metadata accessible from document content and file attributes (DeJesus, 1997; Etzioni, 1996; Lynch, 1997).

In a book on text databases and document management, we should ask whether implementing technologies from this bibliographic paradigm effectively addresses the needs of organizations in using and managing ad hoc documents. For example, do automated metadata and full-text, advanced searching capabilities have a significant impact on the locating, sharing, accessing, statusing, and other needs of people working with ad hoc digital documents in organizations? Because so little research has been conducted in these contexts, evidence on the topic is sparse. However, when Paepcke (1996a) insists the "image of what users should do with Digital Libraries is far too narrow," he is challenging the application to organizational use of the very paradigm that engendered these technologies.

Looking at the technology per se will not tell us about the needs of document workers in organizations. Indeed, many studies of document work have been framed in an application-centric paradigm, specifically Lotus Notes (see Karsten, 1998 for a review of 17 Notes studies). Such research tells us something about the fit between some types of work and workers and implementations of this technology, but not much about the needs of people using ready-to-hand technologies for whatever their job requires and however their situation affords.

AD HOC DIGITAL DOCUMENT WORK IN ORGANIZATIONS

Because no specific investigation of metadata needs for ad hoc document work in organizations could be located, we will look at studies that can at least throw light on the context of this work. Briefly, we review the results of studies of digital genres in organizations, the findings of a digital libraries researcher who tested his assumptions about document work at a manufacturing company, and a cross-sectional survey of digital document workers at 12 firms.

Genre-framed studies have confirmed the variety and centrality of document work in organizations (e.g., Orlikowski & Yates, 1994; Schultze & Boland, 1997; Yates, Orlikowski & Rennecker, 1997). Starting with familiar (non-digital) genres, document workers use the capabilities of collaborative technologies such as Lotus Notes and e-mail to evolve new digital forms. These genres are deployed in patterns based on local norms to create what Orlikowski and Yates (1998) call genre systems. Also, researchers found that over time, genres shift; changes they observed included combining genres to take advantage of "overlap and interlock" functionality and imposing more structure over time (moderated by task characteristics and relationships). In particular, Schultze and Boland (1997) found that the more equivocal the task, the more people relied on information with lower structure such as documents. Thus, genre research confirms the importance of locally emerging and evolving document forms that respond to context needs by retaining their flexibility and autonomy.

As a part of the Stanford Digital Library Project, Paepcke (1996a; 1996b) conducted an interview and observation study of low-structured information creation and use (both paper and technology-based information) inside a computer manufacturing firm. He found document creators are rabid plagiarists who repackage existing material with new into "document compounds." People often revise and recombine the same information for various audiences, in various formats, and for various purposes. Identifying documents and interpreting them are important for document work; some people expressly seek to learn about the context of a document they want to reuse, such as who created it and for what purpose, along with the constraints under which they operated. Based on these findings, Paepcke proposes that information discovery is the beginning of a process of document reuse and recombination whereby the membership of a document in a collection is unimportant, ownership of a document is indistinct, and information about the document's circumstances is the lynch pin. The key to appropriating documents for new purposes and new audiences seems to be not finding them so much as understanding the context of their creation and creators.

A field survey at 12 organizations presents a picture of digital document work in organizations as widespread, continual, and promiscuous (Murphy, 1999; 2000). In a typical week, people work with 30 digital documents; over three quarters of employees have access to the WWW, team/project directories, and intranets from their desk. Document workers frequently reuse documents created by others (54% three or more times per week) and share their own work electronically, usually as an attachment to an e-mail message (78% three or more times per week).

Murphy (2000) found that the frequency of use of different sources for completed documents decays with distance—the closer the document, the more likely it is to be reused; the farther away, the less likely. People reuse their own work most often (2.56, where 3 = often and 0 = never), the work of their group or team next (2.02), internal reference materials (1.64) and the work of other teams (1.55) after that, and, finally, externally published materials (1.35). Work-in-progress (their own and their team members') is also an important source for reuse (2.46 and 1.86, respectively).

Document workers were often aware of the existence of digital documents of interest (even if they had never seen them) by virtue of both the workers' and the documents' being embedded in a shared environment (Murphy, 1999; 2000). Of course, people know the documents they create themselves, but they also frequently receive documents electronically from others, are aware of documents because the document (or the work it supports) is in progress (e.g., they heard about it in a meeting, in an e-mail, in a newsletter, or in a status report), and believe that certain documents *must exist* because the needs of the business require it even though they have neither heard about them specifically nor seen them.

To summarize: In organizations, people freely work with multiply-formatted digital documents from a variety of sources, including repositories (Murphy, 1999; 2000). The quantity of documents and the frequency of both sending and receiving documents in their digital form are high. The concepts of publication and ownership have little importance in this environment, and searching is associated with locating a document that exists rather than attempting to discover what documents may be available. In general, these studies show documents in motion: "Migration of information in and out of different information spaces is constant, as information is created, imported, and moved from one individual or group to another" (Paepcke, 1996b, p. 87). Candidate documents are everywhere—my work, our work, their work—and occasionally even aggregated (i.e., company reference materials). These objects of work are not treated like members of a collection, but more like supplies cached against future need (chances are that it is the author who needs it later).

Contrary to the digital library model, document workers in organizations don't just find the document and go on their way (Paepcke, 1996a); they receive or locate documents rather than discover them (Murphy, 1999). Once the document is found, they learn its context to use it (Paepcke, 1996b), then modify its genre to suit local needs (Orlikowski & Yates, 1994). Precepts of "publication" don't apply to internal materials, and topic-based support is less important (i.e., the relevance of content is already high because organizations make or use information on a relatively narrow range of topics). Where does metadata fit in this use model?

DOCUMENT METADATA IN ORGANIZATIONS

Of course, organizations have been using metadata to manage documents for decades. As ad hoc digital documents become more embedded in the daily functioning of organizations, metadata appear to be taking on some new roles. We will first identify traditional roles for metadata and then look at emerging ones. Later, we will analyze a public metadata standard for its contribution to the needs of these roles.

Traditional Metadata Roles

The metadata of document management traditionally have played the following major roles (shown in Table 1):

- to enable document search and retrieval, particularly by locating files or documents such as medical records, insurance claims, or engineering CAD files (Bielawski & Boyle, 1997; Marshall, 1998; Sprague, 1995);
- to serve as evidence for legal or audit purposes such as financial records or contracts (Bearman & Sochats, 1996);
- to restrict access to files or assign costs to do so such as military security authorizations or usage logs for document services (Bielawski & Boyle, 1997; Cammarata et al., 1994; Gillenson & Frost, 1993);
- to document retention and destruction policies for records management to meet regulatory requirements or limit liability (e.g., Berkery, 1997);

Table 1. Roles for Document Metadata in Organizations (In No Particular Order).

Traditional Roles	Emerging Roles
1. Search and retrieval	7. Interpretation and re-use
2. Evidence	8. Describing document status
3. Limitations on use	9. Organizational memory
4. Records retention	10. To persuade or increase visibility
5. Work flow	11. Individual memory aid
6. Direct physical management	12. To allocate resources

- to control the flow of documents in structured processes such as insurance claims handling (Boyle, 1997; Sprague, 1995);
- to identify the locations at which documents are logically or physically stored and the means to access them (Marshall, 1998; Thibadeau, 1996).

Emerging Metadata Roles

The broadening of document work has increased the number and variety of functions and people interacting with metadata; this change points to emerging roles for document metadata in organizations. Ad hoc document workers in organizations also may rely on metadata for the following roles:

- to facilitate document interpretation and reuse, such as through cues about the content of a document and the effort necessary to access and use it (Murphy, 1999, 2000; Paepcke, 1996b);
- to describe costs, rights, responsibilities, and limitations of use particular to organizational environments by applying classification such as proprietary, attorney-author only, or regulation-required distribution (Murphy, 1998; Paepcke, 1996b);
- to build institutional memory perhaps through representing personal, project, and organizational history via document roles, dispositions, and relationships (Murphy, 2000; Schultze & Boland, 1997).

Document creators themselves may create metadata:

- to persuade an audience by promoting a document as suitable for a certain purpose or to raise its visibility such as by increasing the likelihood of discovery by a search engine (Murphy, 1998);
- to aid authors' own memories (Murphy, 1999; Paepcke, 1996b).

Finally, a company's administration may use metadata to manage networks and allocate resources so that document work has appropriate storage, sufficient priority in support and services, is properly secured, and so forth (Murphy, 2000).

With the exception of the last, these emerging roles for organizational metadata (Table 1) seem to highlight the social and "intertextual" aspects of digital documents in organizations. Orlikowski and Yates (1994) observed that digital genres and their adaptation to local needs is less a "means" of work than the work itself. If we recognize the value of documents in building and sustaining communities (Brown & Duguid, 1996; Wegner, 1998), the social orientation of these new organizational metadata roles should come as no surprise. As the most flexible form of recorded information in organizations, digital documents can be bent to the needs of a situation more easily than more structured types information (Schultze & Boland, 1997), thus engendering a wide range of use contexts.

A FIRST LOOK AT AD HOC METADATA

Metadata developed for a customized EDMS can tell us much about the specific application need and its environment. However, two issues arise: Of the dozens of document management systems implemented in organizations, which one should be privileged over the others, and what criteria should we use to choose among them? Because metadata in EDMS make no claim to generality, it is more appropriate to start with a metadata structure that was intended for use by authors to describe their own digital work. Such a metadata system exists. It is called the Dublin Core.

Introducing the Dublin Core

The Web makes information resources that do not have professional information provider involvement accessible to millions. However, relying on the document content alone produces noisy metadata of low quality (Etzioni, 1996; Lynch, 1997; Pollock & Hockley, 1997); in response to that confusion, a simple metadata structure called the Dublin Core (DC) has been developed (Dublin Core Metadata Initiative, 1999). DC metadata are intended to be created by authors themselves without the aid of a cataloger, to support more than text-based information resources, and to be implemented in a variety of syntaxes (Weibel, 1999). Table 2 describes the 15 elements of the DC. The standard has been implemented in collection-oriented systems such as USMARC (Dempsey, 1996; Weibel, 1999) and in author-oriented environments such as HTML (Brickley & Guha, 2000; Kunze, 1999).

Analyzing the Dublin Core for Ad Hoc Documents

As a general standard for author-provided metadata for electronic documents, particularly Web pages, the DC is a candidate to address the ad hoc organizational metadata gap. The goal of the DC developers is a robust yet simple metadata structure that can evolve greater capabilities and adapt to new technologies and use situations (Weibel, 1999). Implementations of the DC for specialized contexts are conceived of as building on the core 15 elements in one of three ways: by repeating these elements as needed (e.g., multiple "date" fields to accommodate successive updates), by customizing the application of the elements for a specific situation (e.g., creating a controlled vocabulary for an element or mapping a narrower definition onto an element), and, less often, by adding entirely new elements.

Based on literature reviewed previously, the author analyzed each DC element for its applicability to the environment of organizational ad hoc digital document work. Table 3 aligns directly usable DC elements with their

Table 2. Dublin Core Metadata Element Set Version 1.1: Reference Description. (From Dublin Core Metadata Initiative, 1999).

Element	Description	Examples
TITLE	A name given to the resource.	"The Elements of Style"; "Form 1040"
CREATOR	An entity (person, organization, or service) primarily responsible for the intellectual content of the resource.	Authors; artists; photographers; illustrators
SUBJECT	The topic of the resource, or key-words or phrases that describe the subject or content of the resource.	Selections from controlled voc-abularies such as the Library of Congress Subject Headings
DESCRIPTION	An account of the content of the resource.	Abstracts for document-like objects or content descriptions for visual resources
PUBLISHER	An entity responsible for making the object available in its current form.	Publisher; university depart-ment; corporation
CONTRIBUTOR	An entity responsible for making contributions to the content of the resource.	Editors; illustrators; transla-tors; conveners
DATE	A date associated with an event in the life cycle of the resource; typically associated with creation or availability of resource.	Published 1999-12-03
TYPE	The nature or genre of the content of the resource.	Home page; novel; poem; working paper; preprint; tech-nical report; essay; dictionary
FORMAT	The physical or digital mani-festation of the resource.	Text/HTML; ASCII; Postscript file; executable application; JPEG image; MIME type
IDENTIFIER	An unambiguous reference to the resource within a given context.	URL; ISBN; any unique resource file name or key
SOURCE	A reference to a resource from which the present resource is derived.	Paper version from which elec-tronic source was transcribed; earlier version of same document
LANGUAGE	A language of the intellectual content of the resource.	English; Japanese; Visual Basic 6.0
RELATION	A reference to a related re-source.	Chapters in a book; images in a document; items in a collection
COVERAGE	The extent or scope of the con-tent of the resource, typically including spatial location, temporal period, or jurisdiction.	North America; 18th century; before 1922
RIGHTS	Information about rights held in and over the resource.	Copyright notice; patent number; rights-management statement

potential intra-organizational equivalents, a presentation which first appeared in Murphy (1998). The mappings between some elements seem quite straightforward, including description, format, language, resource type, resource identifier, subject, source, and title. However, organizational equivalents for other elements show greater divergence, such as coverage, date, other contributors, publisher, and relation.

A gap between conventional metadata and organizational metadata lies in the concepts of "publisher" and "publication." Certainly, organizations use and produce much material that is published in the sense that the documents are available for public distribution and subject to relevant laws in that regard. However, for most organizations, the volume of internal-use documents dwarfs that from outside sources. Because in most business corporations all documents produced by the employees are the property of the firm, when workers search for documents, the organization's status as publisher has limited "news" value for assessing whether or not a found document is worth accessing or can be used (Paepcke, 1996b). Instead, we see a host of intra-organizational alternatives implied by role of publisher such as sponsor, approved by, authorizing party, and contact information.

Further, the state of "being published" does not have the same status inside as it does outside the organization: A draft publication is different from a final publication which is different from a superceded one (Murphy, 1998). Nor are "published" documents automatically more valuable than "unpublished" ones. In fact, organizational insiders (and some unscrupulous outsiders) may be most interested in works-in-progress, a status public law considers unpublished. In other cases, a document may not be usable until it reaches a certain state or authorization, regardless of the "publicness" of access to it. While not exempt from issues of copyright and intellectual property, digital documents created and used internally may be subject to a wide variety of controls over who can use them, and when, how, and for what purposes. Beyond basic modes of company proprietary and confidential, internal documents may range in use status from being restricted to attorney/executive interaction (e.g., results of an environmental audit) to being required by regulation to be posted in a public location (e.g., annual OSHA injury and illness summary).

The Dublin Core reflects a conventional author-title-publisher model of document descriptors; when genres diverge from that model, elements that reflect intra-organizational issues must substitute. Table 4 describes six metadata elements appropriate to organizational environments that do not directly map to the DC elements.[1] Without attempting to be comprehensive, and lacking empirical data of organizational metadata practice, the elements

Table 3. Organizational Equivalents and Variants to the Dublin Core Elements

Dublin Core Element	**Potential Organizational Equivalent**	**Intra-Organizational Examples**
TITLE	[same]	Report name; subject line from memo
CREATOR	Author, Compiler, Manager, Producer, Team	CQI Team; EDI Steering Committee; Supervising Engineer; Webmaster
SUBJECT	[same]	Key words; Acronym list; Project names
DESCRIPTION	[same]	Executive Summary; "Comments" from MS Word Summary Info box; Abstract
PUBLISHER	[no direct equivalent; candidates included in examples]	Department of author; Sponsor; Authorizing Manager
CONTRIBUTOR	[same plus extensions specific to organization or industry]	Additional material supplied by; Reviewed by
DATE	[same plus extensions specific to organization or industry]	Authorization date; Effective date; Release date
TYPE	Genre, Document type; Template used	Customer Service Bulletin; Engineering Change Request; Trouble report; Home page; Procedure; Action plan; Status report
FORMAT	[same]	[same]
IDENTIFIER	Document, Procedure, or Report identifier	File name; URL; Policy AB10-2
SOURCE	[same]	"Update to"; Transcription of interview, teleconference, or videoconference
LANGUAGE	[same]	[same]
RELATION	"Supersedes," Version, Phase, Stage	Addendum; Initial Draft; Part 2 of 4
COVERAGE	Duration, Extent	FY 1996; Western Division; Eastern European Markets; All <250 HP models
RIGHTS	Copyright, Distribution limitations, Legal status	Company proprietary; Internal audit result; Authorized distribution list only

in Table 4 highlight the context of the document originator and a document's intended use as reflected in the ad hoc document literature reviewed earlier. First proposed in Murphy (1998), these elements may be more important than author name and title for adequately describing documents in the contexts of interest here, because who is "author" in an organization may be determined by his or her designated role (and people move on to other positions) and similar titles may apply to many information objects (as a result of restrictions in the subject domain of the organization).

An inspection of a proprietary metadata format widely available in organizations provides some support for the new organizational metadata elements in Table 4. The "custom" tab of the document Properties window in MS Office 2000 (Microsoft Corporation, 1999a) shows the potentially relevant fields of client, department, disposition, mail stop, office, owner, purpose, received from, reference, source, and status. For many organizations, the metadata built into desktop software suites become the de facto standard with little or no attempt at customization. While proprietary standards such as these are common in information technology, their uncritical acceptance and hit-or-miss utilization may inhibit future options for document access while enforcing no real control over content or meaning (e.g., inconsistent use of "owner" and "department," use of acronyms and jargon).

Looking at Tables 3 and 4, we see the Dublin Core primarily reflects the "bibliographic" model and thus displays some areas of weakness when

Table 4. Proposed New Organizational Metadata Elements

ELEMENT	EXAMPLES
AFFILIATION	Project; program; budget; sponsorship; department name; committee name
AUTHORIZATION	Policy; procedure; regulation; strategic driver; corporate initiative; "approved by"; directive
CONTACT	Internal mail address; phone number; e-mail; delivery address
EFFECTIVITY	Date new guidelines go into force; serial number or production unit for which effective; job classification codes affected
SECURITY LEVEL	Confidentiality; access level; destruction instructions; military security rating required
STATUS	Work in progress; final; released; expired; superceded

applied within organizations. However, the potential for qualifying new elements while remaining within a public standard is promising. In particular, the adoption of DC-formatted "meta" tags in HTML (and XML) provides a viable alternative to proprietary metadata as their use spreads to intranets inside organizations (Brickley & Guha, 2000; Kunze, 1999).

Comparing Metadata Roles and Metadata Elements

It is instructive to compare the metadata elements with the organizational roles identified above. Through we lack empirically derived data for such an analysis, a "first cut" analysis was conducted by the author and is presented in Figure 1. This matrix shows metadata roles from Table 1 across the top (as column labels) and metadata elements from Tables 3 and 4 down the left side (as row labels). Because each role for metadata in effect represents a point of view for a use case or an instance of a completely new use case, this analysis is necessarily subjective; depending upon frame of reference and experience, document management practitioners, other researchers, and even the author, on another day, may disagree with the conclusion for any given cell.

Moreover, we can see that some elements are more crucial to some roles than others (e.g., rights management information is quite probably more important to the "limitations on use" role than subject) and that a given document may be subject to use scenarios involving multiple roles simultaneously (e.g., "evidence," "limitations on use," and "records retention" roles are all likely to apply to documents for financial reporting). Consequently, the analysis presented below should be seen as highly preliminary. In particular, quantifying these analysis results is discouraged; to provoke thought while avoiding overinterpretation, we discuss here only the extreme values. In the future, practitioner case histories and empirically based research will provide a more robust foundation for such analysis.

A glance at Figure 1 shows that only a few roles use most of the 21 elements, and several roles use only a few. Specifically, "interpretation and reuse" and "search and retrieval" each have two thirds or more of all the elements, and "work flow," "physical management," and "status" use only one third. We also notice that some roles use more of the DC elements, while others use relatively more of the new organizational elements. Two roles seem to make the best fit with the DC elements: "search & retrieval" and "interpretation & reuse." Three roles use all six of the new elements: "organizational memory," "allocating resources," and "interpretation & reuse."

On the element side, we can see that only one element is used by all 12 roles, and that is "status." Two others of the new organizational metadata

Figure 1. A "First Cut" At Matching Metadata Elements To Metadata Roles For Ad Hoc Digital Document Work In Organizations

	Traditional Roles							Emerging Roles				
	1 search & retrieval	2 evidence	3 limita-tions on use	4 records reten-tion	5 work flow	6 physical mgmt	7 interp. & reuse	8 status	9 organize. memory	10 persuade, visible	11 memory aid	12 allocate resources
	Dublin Core Elements											
TITLE	x	x					x				x	
CREATOR	x		x				x		x	x		
SUBJECT	x	x	x				x		x		x	
DESCRIPTION	x						x				x	
PUBLISHER	x	x	x				x		x		x	
CONTRIBUTOR	x									x		
DATE	x	x				x	x		x			x
TYPE	x						x		x			
FORMAT	x			x	x	x	x	x				x
IDENTIFIER	x	x		x	x	x	x					x
SOURCE		x					x		x		x	
LANGUAGE	x						x					x
RELATION	x	x		x	x	x	x				x	
COVERAGE	x		x	x			x		x	x	x	
RIGHTS	x		x	x			x	x		x		
	New Organizational Elements											
AFFILIATION	x	x		x	x		x	x	x	x	x	x
AUTHORIZATION	x		x	x	x		x	x	x	x	x	x
CONTACT		x	x		x	x	x		x			x
EFFECTIVITY		x	x				x	x	x		x	x
SECURITY LEVEL			x	x		x	x	x	x			x
STATUS	x	x	x	x	x	x	x	x	x	x	x	x

elements approach this with 10 role assignments each: "affiliation" and "authorization." "Language" is the element used by the fewest number of roles. This result by and large reflects the English-centric model of this author's experience; scenarios in which this may change include global operational environments and the inclusion of software document objects describable by programming languages. Without overemphasizing rankings of elements, we can see that the new organizational elements from Table 4 are used extensively for both traditional and emerging roles.

From the empirical literature reviewed above, we recognize that some metadata roles deserve more attention than others. For example, their centrality to ad hoc digital document work necessitates the exploration, explication, and validation of "interpretation & reuse," "organizational memory," and "individual memory aid" roles.

The relationship of technology to the metadata elements in Tables 3 and 4 suggests that many of the DC elements potentially may be extracted from

Table 5. Potential Sources For Automated Extraction of DC Elements

Element	**Source**	**Examples**
TITLE	content formatting	<title> tag in HTML; Heading 1 format in Word
CREATOR	software attributes	application registration information; default document properties
SUBJECT	content	automated key word extraction
DESCRIPTION	content & formatting	automated summary extraction; identification of document elements such as abstracts and summaries
PUBLISHER	software attributes	application registration information; default document properties; stored return addresses in application
CONTRIBUTOR	?	
DATE	file attributes	date saved
TYPE	file attributes	file type from extension
FORMAT	content	genre identified by document template
IDENTIFIER	file attribute	file name
SOURCE	?	
LANGUAGE	content & software	language identification using content; language choice in application
RELATION	content	hyperlinks in Web pages; version information in titles
COVERAGE	content	spatial and temporal references extracted from content
RIGHTS	content	text following

documents created with current desktop tools such as word processors, electronic presentation applications, and HTML editors. Table 5 shows potential electronic sources for 13 of the 15 DC elements.

This literature review and analysis suggest that metadata elements vary in their importance for the context of ad hoc digital document work in organizations. While topic relevance will continue to be primary (i.e., when you need labor rates, market shares won't do), there are strong indications that other descriptors are significant. In particular, because organizational information environments tend to be narrow in the range of subjects included but deep in the coverage of those subjects, cues to the context of the document may do a better job of distinguishing between similar documents than topic relevance, even when extensive topic knowledge can be brought to bear (as found by Blair & Maron, 1985, while studying retrieval from full-text databases at a law firm). Those engaged in developing advanced techniques for extracting information about documents from digital environments should see this as a challenge to exploit metadata from non-document digital sources such as online directories, discussion boards, and organizational charts.

Given the subjective, non-empirical basis of this analysis, the exercise of identifying roles and elements and their mappings has nonetheless been useful, particularly in illuminating the limitations of the "bibliographic" paradigm for ad hoc organizational document work. Approaches such as the DC are helpful, but incomplete. To be fair, the DC, like all metadata systems, is a compromise between the optimal set for multiple current and future use scenarios and the realistic set—that which can be collected at an acceptable level of quality (Weibel, 1995; 1999). Indeed, trying to be comprehensive will lead to varying degrees of frustration and failure (Marshall, 1998).

DIRECTIONS FOR PRACTICE & RESEARCH

Suspecting as we do the complexity of the ad hoc document use cases and lacking empirical data to quantify, define, or predict them, it would be inappropriate to advance more than general directions at this juncture. The author hopes that this framing of the problem proves fruitful for both practitioners and researchers, at least to the extent that it avoids gross misconceptions about ad hoc digital document work.

Directions for Practice

Experienced document management personnel should beware: Your toolkit appears inadequate for dealing with this disorderly situation. Attempts to reduce the scale of the problem to specific document types, patterns of document flow, or organizational boundaries are likely to be frustrating. While Lotus Notes has proved useful for dealing with multiple genres and for supporting document sharing, its implementation is no guarantee that it will be used that way (see Karsten, 1998); also, it lacks support for document types from other platforms (e.g., Unix CAD documents) and for those related to specialized applications on the same platform (e.g., geographic information systems maps).

In effect, document management professionals involved with ad hoc document work are in a learn-by-doing mode. Case studies of failed and successful implementations, description of a variety of use contexts, and other field reports are needed before definitive guidance can be articulated. Richly textured studies of specific use cases that identify the documents, the actions taken upon them, their life cycles and trajectories through the organization, metadata and other cues available to users, and the roles for metadata would avoid prematurely fixating on a particular solution or frame of reference. From the users' perspective, more detail on the relationships of documents to each other, users' motivations for sharing and reusing documents, and the current use (and nonuse) of metadata would be valuable. Others may be in a position to promote the creation of metadata (e.g., in HTML pages on intranets); studies of the patterns of metadata use, the relative efficacy of various methods for encouraging metadata creation, and individual differences in metadata practices (e.g., Paepcke, 1996b) would provide insight into the "who pays, who gains" dilemma.[2] Experiences implementing document management systems in environments that resemble ad hoc document work could yield some useful "lessons learned." Search logs for intranets and help desk trouble reports might highlight limitations of automated tools and provide useful direction for improvements and further research.

Directions for Research

People involved in research and development in this area have much to contribute. More must be known about these work contexts and the documents used and produced to profitably direct the development and assessment of new technologies. For example, we need to critically address for these use contexts assumptions about the goal of information technology and management in relation to ad hoc digital document work, about the methods and systems that have been applied in the past, and about the functions of new tools. Concepts such as collections, searching, and interoperability must be scrutinized for applicability and hidden traps. New directions must be sought, for example, from thinking of document reuse as Nonaka (1994) does—as an instance of the movement of knowledge across generations of organization members, with that knowledge cycling between tacit and explicit forms and back again.

Behavioral researchers are well-positioned to collect use cases and to show how these cases relate to the work of the organization, genres, communities of practice, and the technology and support infrastructure (e.g., Brown & Duguid, 1996; Wegner, 1998). We need a greater understanding of when and why people share information (e.g., Constant, Kiesler, & Sproull, 1994), the psychological and economic models of metadata creation (e.g., Thorn & Connolly, 1987), and how people evaluate the cost of accessing and using documents (e.g., Hardy, 1982)—both digital and otherwise.

Tweaking the existing generation of tools for document search and retrieval in distributed ad hoc document environments is not enough. We need big new ideas. How can context be provided to document users to help them locate, interpret, and reuse the right document for the right purpose with the least amount of effort? Some context cues may be local, others more global; some may be about the creator, and others about the expected use of the information; some may be available at the time of document creation, and other cues may emerge later. Murphy (1998) proposes the creation of an interpretation engine that provides support for learning about and evaluating the context of documents. Organizational memory systems (Stein & Zwass, 1995) offer a starting point.

We need to document and examine existing metadata. Some questions of interest include: What elements do users consider to be about context, which about content, about document management or other categories? What is the contribution of knowing a document's genre vs. the semantic label for a hyperlink? It is crucial to discover the patterns that underlie cue interpretation, especially when a single element may be meaningful for different roles.

The roles described here need to be documented and analyzed. Do roles vary by organizational factors (e.g., industry, ownership), by document factors (e.g., legal status), by use factors (e.g., who needs to have access), or by combinations of these? Cross-sectional studies of the roles identified in Table 1 need to be complemented by longitudinal studies of documents (e.g., life cycle) to identify when specific metadata elements are needed, when they come into existence, and when they change or become obsolete. The need for integrated vs. separable metadata is likely to be associated with the role; the nature of the document (e.g., its structure, genre, format) will affect the ability to extract or create the metadata using automated tools and to determine when it should be revised.

Lastly, we are in need of new and improved theories about information and its role in organization design and management. Document work as portrayed by Murphy (1999; 2000) and Paepcke (1996b) is very dynamic and often disrespectful of organizational boundaries; as rapid and effective transmitters of equivocal information, digital documents may be challenging our assumptions about the nature of jobs, work arrangements, and organizational design (Daft & Lewin, 1993; Daft & Macintosh, 1981; Wegner, 1998).

CONCLUSION

The purpose of this chapter has been to illuminate the roles of metadata associated with ad hoc digital document work in organizations. As the number of digital documents increases, cues to document contents and contexts become more important. By taking a broader conception of metadata than is typically seen with EDMS and text databases, the readers of this chapter are in a position to help document workers more effectively manage their own documents, help corporations avoid problems with inappropriate retention and disposal of digital communications, and facilitate locating, sharing, and reusing documents within (and across) organizational boundaries. Because the vast majority of documents in organizations today are created digitally and are likely to spend most if not all of their useful life in electronic forms, cues to their effective storage, use, and disposal are less likely to come from physical attributes or location (Brown & Duguid, 1996) than from electronic mechanisms such as metadata. Yet, a formalized document management system, a digital library or structured repository, and other "bibliographic" approaches are likely to fail because these ad hoc documents are more often the means of accomplishing creative, reactive, episodic, and equivocal organizational work than they are static publications, elements in collections, or the outcomes of structured work flows.

This chapter has identified some roles that metadata play and analyzed a public metadata standard with regard to these roles. While no empirical ad hoc metadata research was located, the concepts developed here are based on field studies of people in businesses, government agencies, and other institutions who work with digital documents that are outside the boundaries of EDMS. Such an approach provides a good starting point for designing investigations to fill the gaps in our understanding.

Indications are that implementing metadata would be valuable for many organizations, but success will not be automatic. Document users may lack training and incentives to create useful metadata on their own, while compliance with rigid approaches is likely to be low and the cost of enforcement high. As this analysis demonstrates, available metadata structures need additions, clarifications, and modification—but what elements, for which use case, and how will they be created? The current generation of electronic tools provide effective searching of document content but few offer any help in creating the context-related descriptors document workers need. Yet, many would agree that continuing the current laissez faire approach is untenable.

To make headway, we need to leave behind the "bibliographic" paradigm (Kuhlthau, 1991) that focuses on published documents in collections without losing what we have learned from decades of EDMS applications and fewer, but intense, years of experience with distributed digital documents on the Web and intranets. Document work in organizations is dynamic, where "migration of information in and out of different information spaces is constant, as information is created, imported, and moved from one individual or group to another" (Paepcke, 1996b, p. 87). Both practice-based experiential learning and further research are required on how ad hoc document metadata can be reliably collected with a sufficient level of accuracy for a range of workplaces and organizational needs. We need to develop new theories, build and test new tools, create linkages to resources that already exist such as online directories and other elements of organizational memory, and explore behavioral approaches to encouraging document workers to create their own metadata. Time to get busy.

REFERENCES

Bearman, D. & Sochats, K. (1996). *Metadata requirement for evidence.* [On-Line] http://www.sis.pitt.edu/~nhprc/BACartic.html.

Berkery, P. (1997). IRS issues new electronic record retention rules. *Accounting Today, 11*(6), 10.

Bielawski, L. & Boyle, J. (1997). *Electronic Document Management Systems: A User Centered Approach for Creating, Distributing, and Managing Online Publications.* Saddle River, NJ: Prentice Hall PTR.

Blair, D. & Maron, M. (1985). An evaluation of retrieval effectiveness for a full-text document retrieval system. *Communications of the ACM, 28*(3), 289-299.

Boyle, J. (1997). A blueprint for managing documents. *Byte*, May, 75+.

Brickley, D. & Guha, R.V. (Eds.) (2000). *Resource Description Framework (RDF) Schema Specification 1.0: W3C Candidate Recommendation.* World Wide Web Consortium. [On-Line] http://www.w3c.org/TR/2000/CR-rdf-schema-200000327.

Brown, J.S. & Duguid, P. (1996). The social life of documents. *First Monday, 1*(1). [On-Line] http://www.firstmonday.dk/issues/issue1/documents/index.html.

Cammarata, S., Kameny, I., Lender, J. & Repologle, C. (1994). A Metadata Management System to support data interoperability, reuse and sharing. *Journal of Database Management, 5*(2), 30-40.

Constant, D., Kiesler, S. & Sproull, L. (1994). What's mine is ours, or is it? A study of attitudes about information sharing. *Information Systems Research, 5*(4), 400-421.

Daft, L. & Macintosh, N.B. (1981). A tentative exploration into the amount and equivocality of information processing in organizational work units. *Administrative Science Quarterly, 26,* 297-224.

Daft, R. & Lewin, A. (1993). Where are the theories for the new organization forms? An editorial essay. *Organization Science, 4,* I-IV.

DeJesus, E.X. (1997). The searchable kingdom. *Byte*, June, 92NA1+.

Dempsey, L. (1996). ROADS to Desire: some UK and other European metadata and resource discovery projects. *D-Lib Magazine,* July/August. [On-Line] http://www.dlib.org/dlib/july96/07dempsey.html.

Dublin Core Metadata Initiative (1999). *Dublin Core Metadata Element Set, Version 1.1: Reference Description.* [On-Line] http://purl.org/dc/documents/rec-dces-19990702.htm.

Etzioni, O. (1996). The World Wide Web: Quagmire or Gold Mine? *Communications of the ACM, 39*(11), 65-68.

Gillenson, M. & Frost, R. (1993). The evolution of the metadata concept: Dictionaries, catalogs and repositories. *Journal of Database Management, 4*(3), 17-26.

Hardy, A.P. (1982). The selection of channels when seeking information: cost/benefit vs. least-effort. *Information Processing & Management, 18*(6), 289-293.

Karsten, H. (1998). Collaboration and collaborative information technology: What is the nature of their relationship? *International Federation for Information Processing Working Group 8.2*, Helsinki, Finland (December).

Kuhlthau, C. (1991). Inside the search process: Information seeking from the user's perspective. *Journal of American Society for Information Science, 42*(5), 361-371.

Kunze, J. (1999). Internet Engineering Task Force Network Working Group Request for Comments: *Encoding Dublin Core Metadata in HTML.* December. The Internet Society. [On-Line] http://www.ietf.org/rfc/rfc2731.txt?number=2731.

Lagoze, C. (1996). The Warwick Framework: A container architecture for diverse sets of metadata. *D-Lib Magazine,* July/August. [On-Line] http://www.dlib.org/dlib/jul96/lagoze/07lagoze.html.

Lynch, C. (1997). Searching the Internet. *Scientific American.* [On-Line] http://www.sciam.com/0397issue/0397lynch.html.

Marshall, C. (1998). Making metadata: A study of metadata creation for a mixed physical-digital collection. *Proceedings of Digital Libraries 98*, Pittsburgh, PA. Association for Computing Machinery.

Microsoft Corporation. (1999a). *Microsoft Word 2000 & Microsoft PowerPoint 2000* [software]. Redmond, WA: Microsoft Corporation.

Microsoft Corporation. (1999b). *Managing Resources with the Latest File and Print Technologies.* December 15. [On-Line] http://www.microsoft.com/windows2000/guide/server/solutions/fileandprint.asp.

Murphy, L. (1998). Metadata in organizations. *Proceedings of the Thirty-First Annual Hawaii International Conference on System Sciences (CD-ROM),* Kona, HI. Washington DC: IEEE Computing Society.

Murphy, L. (1999). Digital document interactions: what knowledge workers do everyday. *Proceedings of Americas Conference on Information Systems.* Milwaukee, WI.

Murphy, L. (2000). *Digital Documents in the Workplace: An Empirical Investigation of Document Reuse and Information Technology Infrastructure.* Unpublished doctoral dissertation, Indiana University, Bloomington, IN.

Nonaka, I. (1994). A dynamic theory of organizational knowledge creation. *Organization Science*, *5*(1), 14-37.

Orlikowski, W. & Yates, J. (1994). Genres repertoire: The structuring of communicative practices in organizations. *Administrative Science Quarterly, 39*, 541-574.

Orlikowski, W. & Yates, J. (1998). *Genre Systems: Structuring Interaction Through Communicative Norms.* Center for Coordination Science Working Paper #205, Sloan Working Paper #4030. [On-Line] http://ccs.mit.edu/appers/CCSWP205/index.html.

Paepcke, A. (1996a). Digital libraries: Searching is not enough; what we learned on site. *D-Lib Magazine*. [On-Line] http://www.dlib.org/dlib/may96/stanford/05paepcke.html.

Paepcke, A. (1996b). Information needs in technical work settings and their implications for the design of computer tools. *Computer Supported Cooperative Work: the Journal of Collaborative Computing, 5*, 63-92.

Pollock, A. & Hockley, A. (1997). What's wrong with Internet searching. *D-Lib Magazine,* March. [On-Line] http://www.dlib.org/dlib/march97/03pollock.html.

Schultze, U. & Boland, Jr., R. (1997). Hard & soft information genres: An analysis of two Notes databases. *Proceedings of Thirtieth Annual Hawaii International Conference on Systems Sciences* [CD-ROM version]. New York: IEEE Computing Society.

Smith, T.R. (1996). The meta-information environment of digital libraries. *D-Lib Magazine,* July/August. [On-Line] http://www.dlib.org/dlib/new/07smith.html.

Sprague, R. (1995). Electronic document management: Challenges and opportunities for information systems managers. *Management Information Systems Quarterly, 19*(1), 29-49.

Stein, E. & Zwass, V. (1995). Actualizing organizational memory with information systems. *Information Systems Research, 6*(1), 85-117.

Thibadeau, R. (1996). Digital labels for digital libraries. *D-Lib Magazine,* [On-Line] http://www.dlib.org/dlib/october96/cmu/10thibadeau.html.

Thorn, B. & Connolly, T. (1987). Discretionary databases: A theory and some experimental findings. *Communications Research, 14*(5), 512-528.

Wegner, E. (1998). *Communities of Practice: Learning, Meaning and Identity*. New York: Cambridge University Press.

Wegner, E. & Snyder, W. (2000). Communities of Practice: The Organizational Frontier. *Harvard Business Review*, January-February, 139-145.

Weibel, S. (1995). Metadata: The foundations of resource description. *D-Lib Magazine,* [On-Line] http://www.dlib.org/dlib/july95/07weibel.html.

Weibel, S. (1999). The state of the Dublin Core Metadata Initiative. *D-Lib Magazine*, 5(4), [On-Line] http://www.dlib.org/dlib/april99/04weibel.html.

Yates, J., Orlikowski, W. & Rennecker, J. (1997). Collaborative genres for collaboration: Genre systems in digital media. *Proceedings of Thirtieth Annual Hawaii International Conference on Systems Sciences [CD-ROM Version].* Washington DC: IEEE Computing Society Press.

ENDNOTES

1. Lagoze (1996) points out that the descriptive cataloging needs addressed by the Dublin Core are only part of the information required for an information infrastructure. Terms and conditions, administrative data, provenance, linkage or relationship data, and structural data are some other metadata types he identifies; some of these may be a closer fit to the new organizational items in Table 4.
2. The author thanks Ray Panko for his comment at HICSS in 1998 about the importance of this dilemma in organizational environments.

Chapter IV

A Learner-Independent Evaluation of the Usefulness of Statistical Phrases for Automated Text Categorization

Maria Fernanda Caropreso,*
Universidad de Buenos Aires, Argentina
Stan Matwin, University of Ottawa, Canada
Fabrizio Sebastiani,
Istituto di Elaborazione dell'Informazione, Italy

In this work we investigate the usefulness of n-grams for document indexing in text categorization (TC). We call n-gram a set g_k of n word stems, and we say that g_k occurs in a document when a sequence of words appears in d_j that, after stop word removal and stemming, consists exactly of the n stems in g_k, in some order. Previous research has investigated the use of n-grams (or some variant of them) in the context of specific learning algorithms and thus has not obtained general answers on their usefulness for TC. In this work we investigate the usefulness of n-grams in TC independently of any specific learning algorithm. We do so by applying feature selection to the pool of all k-grams ($k \leq n$), and checking how many k-grams score high enough to be selected in the top σ k-grams. We report the results of our experiments, using various feature selection measures and varying values of σ, performed on the

Reuters-21578 standard TC benchmark. We also report results of making actual use of the selected n-grams in the context of a linear classifier induced by means of the Rocchio method.

INTRODUCTION

A key issue for *information retrieval* (IR) and all other content-based text management applications is *document indexing*, i.e., the task of automatically constructing an internal representation of a text d_j that (i) is amenable to interpretation by the document management algorithms and (ii) compactly captures the meaning of d_j. The choice of a representation format for text depends on what one regards as (a) the meaningful textual units (the problem of *lexical semantics*) and (b) the meaningful natural language rules for the combination of the meanings that these units convey (the problem of *compositional semantics*). Traditionally, IR has concentrated on issue (a) and almost disregarded issue (b), assuming that a good representation for a document d_j may be obtained by simply taking into account whether and how frequently a word t_k appears in d_j and in the document collection, thus disregarding the syntactic, semantic and pragmatic contexts of such occurrences. This has given rise to the so-called *bag of words* approach to indexing, according to which a text d_j is represented as a vector of weights $d_j = <w_{1j}, \dots, w_{rj}>$, where r is the number of words that occur at least once in the document collection and $0 \leq w_{rj} \leq 1$ represents, loosely speaking, how much word t_k contributes to the semantics of document d_j. Weights $0 \leq w_{kj} \leq 1$ are computed according to the frequency of t_k in d_j and in the collection under consideration. Variants of the bag of words approach are obtained by using *word stems* instead of words (Frakes, 1992) or by disregarding frequency issues and simply using a binary assignment for w_{kj} based on either the presence or the absence of t_k in d_j (the *set of words* approach).

We will hereafter speak of a *vector of features* as a neutral expression to indicate a vector of weighted words, or stems, or whatever characteristics of a document one might decide to use for the representation. Of course, the possible choices for what counts as a feature are limited by current text processing technology, i.e., by what can be extracted in a fully automated and scalable way from the text itself. That is, although in principle it would be best to identify features with the concepts the document deals with or with the problems the document tackles, these pieces of knowledge are not within the reach of current knowledge extraction technology.

Phrase Indexing in IR and TC

In the past a number of IR researchers have expressed their dissatisfaction with the bag (or set) of words approach and have tried to use notions of what a feature is that are at the same time semantically richer and technically feasible. In particular, a number of authors have investigated *phrase indexing*, i.e., the use of *phrases*, in addition to individual words, as features. In a linguistic sense, a phrase is a textual unit usually larger than a word but smaller than a full sentence: Examples of *noun phrases* are *nuclear waste disposal*, *the dog that crossed the street,* and *Bill Clinton*, while examples of *verb phrases* are playing ice hockey and went to school. Hereafter, we will use the term *syntactic phrase* for denoting any phrase that is such according to a grammar of the language under consideration. Using syntactic phrases in indexing seems an interesting idea, in that:

- phrases come closer than individual words or their stems to expressing structured concepts;
- phrases have a smaller degree of ambiguity than their constituent words, thanks to the *mutual disambiguation effect of words*. That is, while the two words *hand* and *drill* are both ambiguous (e.g., a *hand of cards* and *shaking hands; oil drilling* and a *pronunciation drill*), *hand drill* is not, since each of its two constituent words creates a context for the unambiguous interpretation of the other;
- by using phrases as index terms, a document that contains a phrase would be ranked higher than a document that just contains its constituent words in unrelated contexts;
- current natural language processing technology (with special reference to part-of-speech tagging and parsing) allows the individuation of phrases to be performed with a good degree of robustness (Brill, 1992; Church, 1988; Zhou, 1999).

Unfortunately, a number of researches that have investigated the usefulness of indexing with syntactic phrases in IR have obtained discouraging results. The likely reason for this is that, although indexing languages based on phrases have superior semantic qualities, they have inferior statistical qualities with respect to indexing languages based on single words (Fagan, 1987; Lewis, 1992). For instance, the phrase *nuclear waste disposal* definitely denotes an interesting, articulated concept, but unless it occurs frequently enough in the document collection under consideration it is unlikely to make an impact in terms of effectiveness. This situation is worsened by the fact that the same concept may be triggered by related but linguistically different units (such as *disposing of nuclear waste, Dispose of your nuclear waste!*, etc.), each of which is usually considered, from the standpoint of frequency, a different unit unless the similar underlying concept is recognized.

Also, not every syntactic phrase denotes an interesting concept: associate professor does, but tall professor does not; and telling a phrase that does from one that does not is difficult (Kageura & Umino, 1996, call this "the termhood problem").

A number of researchers have attempted to find a way out of these problems by understanding the notion of phrase in a statistical sense, rather than in a syntactic sense. We will call *statistical phrase* any sequence of words that occur contiguously in text and do so in a statistically interesting way. Statistical phrases have a number of advantages over syntactic ones: a) they may be recognized by means of more robust and less computationally demanding algorithms; b) the effect of irrelevant syntactic variants can be factored out; and c) uninteresting phrases (e.g., tall professor) tend to be filtered out from interesting ones (e.g., associate professor). Of course, inherent in their statistical nature is the disadvantage of a non-null error rate: Some phrases are not going to be recognized as such, and some non-phrases are instead going to be incorrectly recognized as phrases.

This work deals with assessing the value of statistical phrases for document indexing in the context of *text categorization* (TC), the activity of inductively learning to classify natural language texts with topical categories from a prespecified set (Sebastiani, 1999). Previous research has investigated the impact of statistical phrases on TC in the context of specific learning algorithms and thus has not obtained general answers on their usefulness for TC *tout court*. In this work we want to analyze the problem in a learner-independent way, with the aim of obtaining an indication of the usefulness of statistical phrases for TC that are independent of the learning algorithm to be used. In order to do so, we extract word sequences from a corpus of documents and assess their value not in a "direct" way (i.e., by running classification experiments on a test collection) but in an "indirect" way, i.e., by scoring the sequences by means of a number of different *feature evaluation functions* (Yang & Pedersen, 1997).

The chapter is organized as follows. First, we briefly introduce the basic notions of text categorization. Then we define precisely our own notion of statistical phrase, that we will call *n-gram.*[1] Following this we describe our learner-independent method for the evaluation of *n*-grams and then describe the results we have obtained by applying this method on Reuters-21578, the standard benchmark of TC research. We discuss a number of further, "direct" experiments we have conducted by running the Rocchio classifier-learning algorithm on the *n*-gram-based representations and aimed at assessing whether the results from the "indirect" experiments are confirmed by field tests (we have started running a similar experiment using the Ripper system—Cohen and Singer, 1999—but its results were not ready before printing time). Some related work in phrase indexing in IR and TC is also described.

TEXT CATEGORIZATION

Text categorization (also known as *text classification*, or *topic spotting*) is the activity of automatically building, by means of machine learning (ML) techniques, *automatic text classifiers*, i.e., programs capable of labelling natural language texts with thematic categories from a predefined set $C = \{c_1, \ldots, c_m\}$.

A frequently used approach to building a text classifier for categories $C = \{c_1, \ldots, c_m\}$ is that of building m independent classifiers, each capable of deciding whether a given document d_j should or should not be classified under category c_i, for $i \in \{1, \ldots, m\}$.[2] This process requires the availability of a corpus $Co = \{d'_1, \ldots, d'_s\}$ of manually preclassified documents, i.e., documents such that for all $i \in \{1, \ldots, m\}$ and for all $j \in \{1, \ldots, s\}$ it is known whether $d_j \in c_i$ or not. A general inductive process (called the *learner*) automatically builds a classifier for category c_i by learning the characteristics of c_i from a *training set* $Tr = \{d'_1, \ldots, d'_g\} \subset Co$ of documents. Once a classifier has been built, its effectiveness (i.e., its capability to take the right categorization decisions) may be tested by applying it to the *test set* $Te = \{d'_{g+1}, \ldots, d'_s\} = Co - Tr$ and checking the degree of correspondence between the decisions of the automatic classifier and those encoded in the corpus.

Feature Selection

Many classifier induction methods are computationally hard, and their computational cost is a function of the length r of the vectors that represent the documents. It is thus of key importance to be able to work with vectors shorter than r, which is usually a number in the tens of thousands or more. For this, *feature selection* techniques are used to select, from the original set of r features, a subset of $r' << r$ features that are most useful for compactly representing the meaning of the documents; the value $\rho = r - r'/r$ is called the *reduction factor*. Usually, these techniques consist in scoring each feature by means of a *feature evaluation function* (FEF) and then selecting the r' features with the highest score. Often, feature selection is also beneficial in that it tends to reduce *overfitting*, i.e., the phenomenon by which a classifier tends to be better at classifying the data it has been trained on than at classifying other data.

Table 1. Some Feature Evaluation Functions Used in the Literature. In the $\chi^2(t_k, c_i)$ and Formula g Is the Cardinality of the Training Set

Function	Denoted by	Mathematical form
Document frequency	$DF(t_k, c_i)$	$P(t_k \mid c_i)$
Information Gain	$IG(t_k, c_i)$	$P(t_k \mid c_i) \bullet \log \frac{P(t_k, c_i)}{P(c_i) \bullet P(t_k)} + P(\bar{t}_k \mid c_i) \bullet \log \frac{P(\bar{t}_k, c_i)}{P(c_i) \bullet P(\bar{t}_k)}$
Chi-square	$\chi^2(t_k, c_i)$	$\frac{g \bullet [P(t_k, c_i) \bullet P(\bar{t}_k, \bar{c}_i) - P(t_k, \bar{c}_i) \bullet P(\bar{t}_k, c_i)]^2}{P(t_k) \bullet P(\bar{t}_k) \bullet P(c_i) \bullet P(\bar{c}_i)}$
Odds Ratio	$OR(t_k, c_i)$	$\frac{P(t_k \mid c_i) \bullet (1 - P(t_k \mid \bar{c}_i))}{(1 - P(t_k \mid c_i)) \bullet P(t_k \mid \bar{c}_i)}$

Many functions, mostly from the tradition of decision or information theory, have been used as FEFs in TC (Lam & Lee, 1999; Mladenic, 1998; Yang & Pedersen, 1997); some which are of interest to the present work are illustrated in Table 1. In the third column of this table, probabilities are interpreted on an event space of documents (e.g., $P(\bar{t}_k, c_i)$ indicates the probability that, for a random document x, feature t_k does not occur in x and x belongs to category c_i) and are estimated by counting occurrences in the training set. In the same column, every function $f(t_k, c_i)$ refers to a specific category c_i; in order to assess the value of a feature t_k in a "global," category-independent sense, either the weighted average $f_{avg}(t_k) = \Sigma^{\mu}_{i=1} f(t_k, c_i) \bullet P(c_i)$ or the maximum $f_{max}(t_k) = max^{\mu}_{i=1} f(t_k, c_i)$ of its category-specific values are usually computed.

A DEFINITION OF N-GRAMS

We start by precisely characterizing what we mean by statistical phrases. The same definition has been used in a number of IR contexts (e.g., Buckley et al., 1996; Mitra et al., 1997), but never in the case of TC.

Definition 1: A 1-gram (or *unigram*) is a word stem. An *n-gram* is an alphabetically ordered sequence g_k of n unigrams. We say that an n-gram g_k *occurs* (or manifests itself) in a document d_j when a sequence of words appears in d_j that, after stop word removal and stemming, consists of a permutation of g_k.■

For instance, *inform retriev* is a 2-gram (or *bigram*); among its possible manifestations in a text are the expressions:

a) information retrieval
b) retrieval of information
c) informative retrieval

d) the retrieving of information
e) retrieved information
f) retrieving information
g) retrieves information
h) Retrieve information!
i)* Inform the retriever!

Note that, as evident from all these examples, stop word removal, stemming, and alphabetical ordering have the effect of factoring out from the notion of *n*-gram a number of morphological, syntactic, and semantic variations. As for morphosyntactic variations, note that *noun phrases* (expressions (a) to (e)), *verb phrases* (expressions (f) and (g)), and *full sentences* (expressions (h) and (i)) can all be manifestations of the same *n*-gram. As for semantic variations, note that noun phrases with different meanings, as is the case for (a) and (e), can also give rise to the same *n*-gram. Defining *n*-grams this way is based on the hypothesis that various syntactic expressions may convey the same concept and is thus to be seen as a form of *conflation*. As for other types of conflation, the generalization we perform by means of *n*-grams has its problems too. In particular, *n*-grams as defined here suffer from

- *over-generalization:* this may be seen from the fact that example (i) does not refer to the same concept as examples (a) to (h);
- *under-generalization:* this may be seen from the fact that an expression such as *retrieving interesting information* arguably refers to the same concept as examples (a) to (h) but is not recognized as such.

Note also that, quite obviously, the mere contiguous occurrence of two words in a text does not guarantee that they refer to a complex concept. For instance, the text:

> What is recursion? It is what was illustrated in the dialogue *Little Harmonic Labyrinth*: nesting, and variations on nesting.

Contains the bigrams *illustrat recur, dialog illustrat, dialog harmon, harmon labyrinth, labyrinth nest,* and *nest var*. Arguably, none of these conveys an articulated concept, as in each case the consecutive occurrence of the two words is not indicative of a strong semantic relationship between them. It is then clear that the use of *n*-grams for indexing purposes is possible only in the presence of a method for filtering interesting *n*-grams from noninteresting ones.

Filtering is also necessary because the number of different *n*-grams that occur at least once in a collection is too high. In fact, while the number of *k*-gram occurrences increases linearly (for any *k*-gram occurrence there are two *(k+1)*-gram occurrences), the number of *different k*-grams increases much more, since the average *(k+1)*-gram occurs much less frequently than the average *k*-gram.

There are many possible filters, most of which are based on frequency of occurrence considerations. This is not surprising, since we may expect an interesting bigram such as *inform retriev* to have different occurrence patterns from an uninteresting, "occasional" bigram such as *illustrat recur*.

A CLASSIFIER-INDEPENDENT EVALUATION OF THE USEFULNESS OF STATISTICAL PHRASES IN TEXT CATEGORIZATION

Our method of establishing the usefulness of n-grams for TC purposes consists in generating all k-grams (for $k = 1, \ldots, n$) that occur in a corpus of documents, score each of them by means of a FEF of the type discussed earlier, and rank them according to the score received. The usefulness of n-grams for TC will be determined by how frequently n-grams appear at the top of this ranked list.

In order to be more precise we introduce the notion of *penetration level* of n-grams.

Definition 2: Let Tr be a training set of documents and r be the number of different unigrams that occur in it. We define the penetration level $\pi^f_\rho(n)$ of n-grams for FEF f at reduction factor ρ as the fraction of the $r' = r(1-\rho)$ top (according to f) k-grams $(k=1, \ldots, n)$ of Tr that are actually n-grams.■

The purpose of this definition is best described by an example. Suppose that there are 10,000 different unigrams in our training set Tr. If we had to apply a FEF f to each of these 10,000 unigrams with reduction factor .90, we would obtain the 1,000 unigrams that f considers the most valuable. Suppose that there are 120,000 different bigrams in Tr. In order to compute the penetration level $\pi^f_{.90}(2)$ we apply f to each of the 130,000 k-grams $(k=1,2)$ and check how many of the top 1,000 k-grams are actually bigrams. The higher $\pi^f_{.90}(2)$ is, the more worthwhile bigrams prospectively look, and the more worthwhile it looks to extract them. Or, at least, worthwhile according to our chosen FEF f and for the reduction factor ρ chosen. If we repeat the same experiment for different FEFs f_i and different reduction factors $\rho_j \leq r$, averaging the results in some way, we can get a fairly clear picture of how promising bigrams look for TC purposes, and we do so without invoking even a single learning algorithm, which means that our results are arguably going to be valid regardless of the specific learning algorithm chosen. This method is, of course, applicable for any value of n.

Pros and Cons of This Approach

Before moving to the discussion of the experimental results we have obtained, we should remark that this is not by any means the only possible approach to the evaluation of *n*-grams for TC. A possible alternative approach consists in generating only a subset of prospectively good *n*-grams (i.e., *n*-grams selected according to a particular statistical filter—Damerau, 1993—or heuristics—Enguehard and Pantera, 1995; Mladenic and Grobelnik, 1998), using them in document indexing, and checking the difference in effectiveness that a given classifier exhibits with respect to the standard "bag of words" case.

This latter method has no doubt the advantage of a better computational efficiency; for instance, a heuristics according to which all and only the *n*-grams that are composed of "valuable" unigrams and/or have certain frequency characteristics are generated allows substantial reduction of the computation time needed to generate the *n*-grams and completely avoids the computation time needed to score them. For some practical applications, this may even be the only feasible method.

The drawback of this method, though, is that the experimental results thus obtained are going to be dependent on the chosen heuristics and on the chosen classifier learning algorithm. The method we have chosen abstracts away from both aspects. While the latter aspect needs no further discussion, concerning the former we want to emphasize that

1. the method relies not on generic heuristics, but on FEFs that are both well-studied and well-founded on statistic and information theory;
2. the method relies on the application of a whole range of FEFs, so as to obtain results that are not biased towards one or the other FEF.

In a sense, the real object of this work is thus *not* using *n*-grams in a particular TC application and hence devising an efficient algorithm for extracting them. This work is more foundational in nature, as we want instead to assess whether, in principle, *n*-grams are prospectively interesting for TC applications so that it might be worth to devise such an algorithm. For this purpose, it is clear that we need to analyze *all* *n*-grams, and not just those that are generated by selective heuristics. For the same reason, we need to perform this analysis in the most general possible way, that is, without reference to specific learning algorithms and with reference to the widest possible spectrum of FEFs.

"INDIRECT" EXPERIMENTS

We have performed a number of experiments in order to test the usefulness of *n*-grams for TC according to the above-mentioned learner-independent method. The experiments reported in this chapter are limited to the case of *n*=2.

Table 2. Penetration Level For 2-Grams Computed For Different FEFs At Different Reduction Factors

# of features	Reduction Factor	DF_{avg}	IG	x^2_{avg}	x^2_{max}	OR_{avg}	Or_{max}
250	.986	.128	.192	.276	.560	.512	.564
500	.971	.176	.276	.338	.736	.686	.766
750	.957	.216	.319	.391	.797	.747	.827
1000	.943	.244	.352	.423	.833	.776	.864
1250	.928	.276	.376	.444	.859	.798	.882
1500	.914	.304	.398	.471	.877	.812	.897
1750	.900	.328	.422	.489	.883	.825	.907
2000	.885	.353	.445	.504	.883	.834	.911
2250	.871	.373	.464	.523	.891	.833	.918
2500	.857	.392	.482	.535	.899	.833	.920
2750	.842	.419	.499	.551	.902	.839	.919
3000	.828	.438	.510	.563	.897	.842	.923
3250	.814	.456	.522	.573	.898	.843	.927
3500	.799	.469	.535	.587	.902	.847	.926
3750	.785	.482	.548	.592	.906	.852	.927
4000	.771	.494	.556	.600	.903	.853	.929
4250	.756	.507	.567	.610	.906	.857	.928
4500	.742	.520	.580	.616	.909	.859	.927
4750	.728	.533	.590	.626	.910	.860	.925
5000	.713	.541	.597	.634	.911	.863	.923
6000	.656	.574	.624	.656	.910	.874	.925
7000	.599	.605	.648	.675	.908	.873	.924
8000	.541	.632	.667	.688	.911	.879	.923
9000	.484	.652	.683	.704	.910	.882	.921
10000	.427	.669	.697	.714	.913	.889	.925

Experimental Setting

For our experiments we have used the "Reuters-21578, Distribution 1.0" corpus, as it is currently the most widely used benchmark in text categorization research.[3] Reuters-21578 consists of a set of 12,902 news stories, partitioned (according to the "ModApté" split we have adopted) into a training set of 9,603 documents and a test set of 3,299 documents. The documents have an average length of 211 words (that become 117 after stop word removal) and are labelled by 118 categories; the average number of categories per document is 1.08, ranging from a minimum of 0 to a maximum of 16. The number of positive examples per category ranges from a minimum of 1 to a maximum of 3,964. According to Definition 1, Reuters-21578 contains 17,439 unigrams and 250,059 bigrams, for a total of 267,498 uni+bigrams.

We have run our experiments on the set of 115 categories with at least 1 training example, rather than on other more commonly used subsets of it. The full set of 115 categories is "harder," since it includes categories with very few positive instances for which inducing reliable classifiers is obviously a haphazard task.[4]

In all the experiments discussed in this section, stop words have been removed using the stop list provided in Lewis (1992b, pp. 117-118). Punctuation has been removed and all letters have been converted to lowercase; no number removal has been performed.

Figure 1. Penetration Level For 2-Grams Computed For Different FEFs At Different Reduction Factors

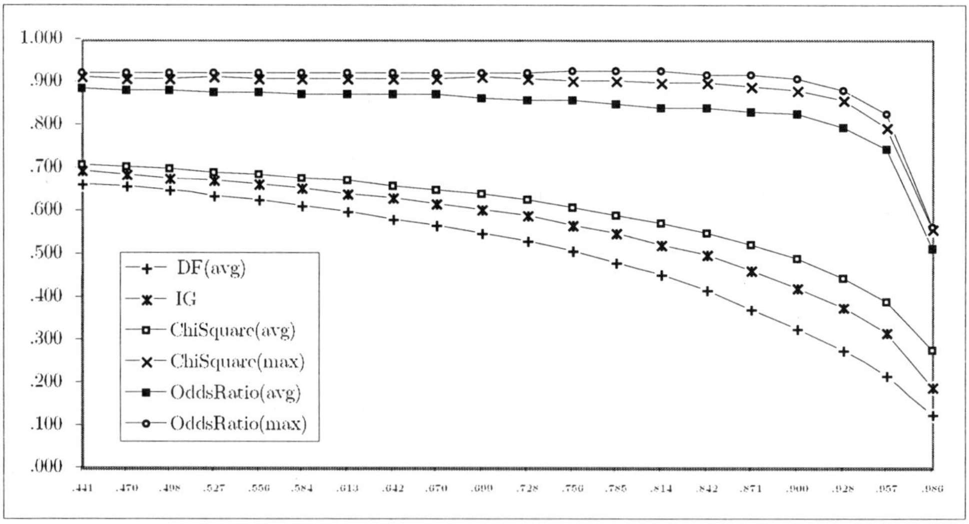

Experimental Results

Table 2 and Figure 1 report the results of computing penetration levels for bigrams by applying the four FEFs described in Table 1 with varying reduction factors. We have chosen these FEFs as they have turned out to be the best performers in the thorough comparative experiments of Mladenic (1998) and Yang and Pedersen (1997).

From these results it is evident that, for each FEF, the penetration level is a decreasing function of the reduction factor. This is not surprising because for a small reduction factor, as features are selected, less and less unigrams tend to be available for the next selection, while the number of bigrams available for the next selection tends to be substantially unaffected (given its originally huge number). For instance, in the beginning there are a total of 17,439 unigrams and 250,059 bigrams, i.e., there are 14.33 times more bigrams than unigrams. After selecting, say, the top 9,750 features by means of DF_{avg}, 3,260 unigrams and 6,490 bigrams have been chosen, which means that 14,179 unigrams and 243,569 bigrams are still available for further selection. This means that there are now 17. Eighteen times more bigrams than unigrams, a higher proportion than earlier, which means that the chances that the next selected feature will be a bigram are now higher.

Also, from Figure 1 it is evident that the six FEFs studied may be partitioned in two groups of three FEFs each ({DF_{avg}, IG, χ^2_{avg}} and , {χ^2_{max}, OR_{avg}, OR_{max}}), where the FEFs of the same group display a very similar behavior. Incidentally, this confirms one result of Yang and Pedersen (1997), who in an experiment involving two different collections had shown DF_{avg} and IG to be highly correlated and had conjectured that this pattern was general rather than corpus-dependent.

The third observation is that penetration levels are indeed high! This means that if we define bigrams as in Definition 2, many of them have statistical characteristics that, according to the FEFs we have employed, make them preferable to many of the unigrams rated high by the same FEFs.

Column 1 of Table 3 lists, for various FEFs and reduction factors, the average score obtained by a feature selected by the FEF. Each entry lists the average score of unigrams and of uni+bigrams, and the increase in average score obtained in switching from the former to the latter. In order to correctly interpret the results, note that every row of Table 3 includes two sub-rows reporting results for the unigrams and the uni+bigrams cases, respectively, *using the same number of features*. For instance, to interpret the first row of results one should note that reducing the set of 17,439 unigrams by a .70 reduction factor yields 5,232 features, which is the same number of features obtained by reducing the set of 267,498 uni+bigrams by a .9805 reduction factor. The results listed in Column 1 show that the FEFs that achieve high penetration levels (see Table 2) also achieve a high increase in the average score of a feature. This would seem to confirm that penetration levels are indeed a reasonable way to compute the contribution of *n*-grams to the quality of a feature set.

The combined results of Tables 2 and 3 seem thus to indicate that DF_{avg}, IG, χ^2_{avg} are the most "conservative" FEFs, in that they do not allow many bigrams to enter the top scoring feature set; conversely, χ^2_{max}, OR_{avg}, OR_{max} are the most "liberal."

"DIRECT" EXPERIMENTS

Evaluation Methodology

In the experiments that follow, classification effectiveness has been measured in terms of the classic IR notions of precision (Pr) and recall (Re), adapted to the case of document categorization. *Precision wrt* c_i (Pr_i) is defined as the probability that if a random document d_x is categorized under c_i (i.e., it is deemed a *positive* example of c_i), this decision is correct (i.e., it is a *true* positive for c_i). In what follows, TP, TN, FP and FN will denote the numbers of true positives, true negatives, false positives, and false negatives, respectively. *Recall wrt* c_i (Re_i) is instead defined as the probability that, if a random document d_x ought to be categorized under c_i, this decision is taken. Estimates of Pr_i and Re_i (indicated by $\hat{Pr}_i$ and $\hat{Re}_i$) may be obtained in the obvious way by counting occurrences on the test set. These category-relative values may in turn be averaged to obtain $\hat{Pr}$ and $\hat{Re}$, i.e., values global to the whole category set C, according to two alternative methods:

- *microaveraging* (indicated by the "μ" superscript): $\hat{Pr}$ and $\hat{Re}$ are obtained by globally summing over all individual decisions, i.e.:

$$\hat{Pr}^{\mu} = \frac{TP}{TP + FP} = \frac{\sum^{m}_{i=1} TP_i}{\sum^{m}_{i=1} TP_i + FP_i}$$

$$\hat{Re}^{\mu} = \frac{TP}{TP + FN} = \frac{\sum^{m}_{i=1} TP_i}{\sum^{m}_{i=1} TP_i + FN_i}$$

- *macroaveraging* (indicated by the "m" superscript): Precision and recall are first evaluated "locally" for each category and then "globally" by averaging over the results of the different categories, i.e.:

$$\hat{Pr}^M = \frac{\sum_{i=1}^{m} Pr_i}{m} = \frac{\sum_{i=1}^{m} (TP_i / TP_i)}{m}$$

$$\hat{Re}^M = \frac{\sum_{i=1}^{m} Re_i}{m} = \frac{\sum_{i=1}^{m} (TP_i / FN_i)}{m}$$

In our experiments we have evaluated both microaveraged and macroaveraged precision and recall.

As a measure of effectiveness that combines the contributions of both $\hat{Pr}$ and $\hat{Re}$, we have used the well-known F_β function, defined as

$$F_\beta = \frac{(\beta^2 + 1) \bullet \hat{Pr} \bullet \hat{Re}}{\beta^2 \bullet \hat{Pr} + \hat{Re}}$$

with $0 \leq \beta \leq +\infty$. Similarly to most other researchers we have used the parameter value $\beta=1$, which places equal emphasis on $\hat{Pr}$ and $\hat{Re}$.

Experimental Results

Table 4 compares the effectiveness of unigrams and uni+bigrams on a linear classifier induced according to the Rocchio method for the four FEFs of Table 1 and for different reduction factors. The Rocchio parameters have been set to $\beta = 16$ and $\gamma = 4$ (see, Sebastiani, 1999, Section 6.6) for a full discussion of the Rocchio method). Term weighting has been obtained by means of the standard "ltc" variant of the *tfidf* function, i.e.,

$$tfidf(t_k, d_j) = tfidf(t_k, d_j) \bullet log \frac{|Tr|}{\#_{Tr}(t_k)}$$

where $\#_{Tr}(t_k)$ denotes the number of documents in Tr in which t_k occurs at least once and

$$tf(t_k, d_j) = \begin{cases} 1 + log\#(t_k, d_j) & if\ \#(t_k, d_j) > 0 \\ 0 & otherwise \end{cases}$$

where $\#(t_k, d_j)$ denotes the number of times t_k occurs in d_j. Weights have been further normalized by cosine normalization, i.e.:

Table 3. Average Score Of A Feature (Column 1), Average Number Of Documents In Which A Feature Cccurs (Column 2) and Average Number Of Categories In Which A Feature Occurs (Column 3), Computed For Various FEFs At Different Reduction Factors. Every Entry Lists the Score For the Unigrams Case (Upper Sub-Row), For the Uni+Bigrams Case (Lower Sub-Row), and the Percentage Increase Between the Former and the Latter.

	Reduction Factor	Average Score	Average Document #	Average Category #
DF_{avg}	.70	80.393	80.393	14.751
DF_{avg}	9805	118.498 (+47.4%)	118.498 (+47.4%)	19.937 (+35.2%)
DF_{avg}	.80	116.861	116.861	19.783
DF_{avg}	.9870	164.113 (+40.4%)	164.113 (+40.4%)	24.247 (+22.6%)
DF_{avg}	.90	214.195	214.195	30.096
DF_{avg}	.9935	281.220 (+31.3%)	281.220 (+31.3%)	32.795 (+9.0%)
IG	.70	-2.907	80.037	14.653
IG	9805	-2.903 (-0.1%)	114.478 (+43.0%)	18.873 (+28.8%)
IG	.80	-2.904	115.996	19.506
IG	.9870	-2.900 (-0.2%)	157.681 (+35.9%)	22.345 (+14.6%)
IG	.90	-2.898	210.065	28.886
IG	.9935	-2.893 (-0.2%)	264.287 (+25.8%)	29.073 (+0.6%)
χ^2_{avg}	.70	12.516	78.922	13.759
χ^2_{avg}	9805	23.373 (+86.7%)	109.367 (+38.6%)	15.476 (+12.5%)
χ^2_{avg}	.80	17.521	113.975	18.161
χ^2_{avg}	.9870	31.339 (+78.9%)	150.118 (+31.7%)	18.646 (+2.7%)
χ^2_{avg}	.90	30.559	204.378	26.747
χ^2_{avg}	.9935	51.497 (+68.5%)	251.638 (+23.1%)	24.763 (-7.4%)
χ^2_{max}	.70	323.592	63.427	10.028
χ^2_{max}	9805	1805.572 (+458.0%)	14.025 (-77.9%)	3.062 (-69.5%)
χ^2_{max}	.80	441.239	73.628	10.141
χ^2_{max}	.9870	2183.591 (+394.9%)	14.884 (-79.8%)	2.999 (-70.4%)
χ^2_{max}	.90	713.364	73.645	9.212
χ^2_{max}	.9935	2936.242 (+311.6%)	16.622 (-77.4%)	2.631 (-71.4%)
OR_{avg}	.70	2.980	22.825	3.321
OR_{avg}	9805	8.257 (+177.0%)	16.919 (-25.9%)	1.961 (-40.9%)
OR_{avg}	.80	3.695	17.923	2.915
OR_{avg}	.9870	10.801 (+192.3%)	22.373 (+24.8%)	2.056 (-29.5%)
OR_{avg}	.90	5.506	24.107	2.990
OR_{avg}	.9935	17.721 (+221.9%)	34.618 (+43.6%)	2.052 (-31.4%)
OR_{max}	.70	411.681	18.826	6.498
OR_{max}	.9805	4003.307 (+872.4%)	5.339 (-71.6%)	2.799 (-56.9%)
OR_{max}	.80	575.073	15.278	5.823
OR_{max}	.9870	5217.889 (+907.3%)	5.113 (-66.5%)	2.464 (-57.7%)
OR_{max}	.90	982.787	12.660	5.062
OR_{max}	.9935	7583.538 (+671.6%)	3.812 (-69.9%)	1.963 (-61.2%)

Table 4. Comparison Between the Unigram and the Uni+Bigram Effectiveness Of A Rocchio Classifier For Different FEFs and Different Reduction Factors.

FEF	Reduction Factor	Micro Recall	Micro Precision	Micro F_1	Macro Recall	Macro Precision	Macro F_1
DF_{avg}	.60	.674	.778	.723	.521	.678	.589
DF_{avg}	.9740	.683	.788	.732	.530	.688	.599
DF_{avg}	.70	.674	.778	.723	.522	.679	.590
DF_{avg}	.9805	.683	.788	.732	.525	.679	.592
DF_{avg}	.80	.680	.785	.728	.528	.683	.595
DF_{avg}	.9870	.681	.785	.729	.512	.651	.573
DF_{avg}	.90	.686	.791	.734	.524	.670	.588
DF_{avg}	.9935	.669	.772	.717	.493	.616	.548
IG	.60	.674	.777	.722	.520	.679	.589
IG	.9740	.684	.789	.732	.532	.680	.597
IG	.70	.676	.780	.724	.526	.683	.594
IG	.9805	.684	.789	.733	.532	.682	.598
IG	.80	.680	.785	.728	.527	.684	.595
IG	.9870	.685	.790	.733	.536	.685	.601
IG	.90	.688	.793	.737	.531	.680	.597
IG	.9935	.682	.788	.731	.534	.697	.604
χ^2_{avg}	.60	.674	.778	.722	.520	.680	.590
χ^2_{avg}	.9740	.686	.791	.734	.538	.693	.606
χ^2_{avg}	.70	.676	.780	.724	.522	.680	.591
χ^2_{avg}	.9805	.686	.792	.735	.538	.695	.606
χ^2_{avg}	.80	.681	.786	.730	.534	.690	.602
χ^2_{avg}	.9870	.685	.790	.734	.520	.679	.589
χ^2_{avg}	.90	.688	.794	.737	.537	.700	.608
χ^2_{avg}	.9935	.674	.778	.722	.495	.622	.551
χ^2_{max}	.60	.676	.780	.725	.518	.676	.587
χ^2_{max}	.9740	.679	.788	.729	.537	.691	.604
χ^2_{max}	.70	.678	.783	.727	.520	.679	.589
χ^2_{max}	.9805	.658	.768	.708	.528	.688	.598
χ^2_{max}	.80	.683	.788	.732	.525	.686	.595
χ^2_{max}	.9870	.619	.748	.677	.513	.675	.583
χ^2_{max}	.90	.682	.787	.731	.530	.692	.600
χ^2_{max}	.9935	.507	.621	.558	.445	.653	.529
OR_{avg}	.60	.667	.770	.715	.518	.673	.585
OR_{avg}	.9740	.608	.711	.655	.486	.697	.573
OR_{avg}	.70	.652	.753	.699	.512	.675	.582
OR_{avg}	.9805	.583	.693	.633	.449	.661	.535
OR_{avg}	.80	.631	.731	.677	.483	.661	.558
OR_{avg}	.9870	.566	.692	.623	.437	.641	.520
OR_{avg}	.90	.607	.725	.661	.470	.650	.546
OR_{avg}	.9935	.549	.671	.604	.401	.654	.497
OR_{max}	.60	.627	.723	.671	.514	.663	.579
OR_{max}	.9740	.414	.483	.446	.422	.593	.493
OR_{max}	.70	.618	.713	.662	.524	.684	.594
OR_{max}	.9805	.387	.484	.430	.410	.597	.486
OR_{max}	.80	.565	.655	.607	.490	.665	.564
OR_{max}	.9870	.337	.470	.392	.365	.621	.460
OR_{max}	.90	.460	.538	.496	.449	.644	.529
OR_{max}	.9935	.261	.666	.375	.264	.733	.388

$$w_{kj} = \frac{tfidf(t_k, d_j)}{\sqrt{\sum_{s=1}^{r'} tfidf(t_s, d_j)^2}}$$

where r' is the set of features resulting from feature selection.

The conventions used in the formatting of Table 4 are similar to those discussed for Table 3. In particular, we recall that every entry consists of two sub-rows listing the performance of the Rocchio classifier on a unigram representation (upper sub-row) and on a uni+bigram representation (lower sub-row), where these representations use the same number of features; this ultimately means that the value of bigrams for TC purposes can be measured by how often the second sub-row reports a better result than the first and by the magnitude of these improvements.

The results of Table 4 show that bigrams do not always contribute to the categorization effectiveness of the Rocchio classifier; 20 out of 48 cases witness an improvement in effectiveness, while in the other 28 cases we actually have a loss in performance. Moreover, when bigrams bring about a performance improvement, this is seldom significant (the best improvement is 2.8%, obtained for macroaveraged F_1 with χ^2_{max} and ρ=.60). Conversely, when bigrams cause a deterioration in performance, this is often very significant (the worst deterioration is 35.1%, obtained for microaveraged F_1 with OR_{max} and ρ=.70). All this is in some sense unexpected, as the results of Tables 2 and 3 would seem to indicate that, particularly when penetration levels and increases in average scores are high, the overall "quality" of the feature set increases.

Improvements are evenly distributed in the microaveraged and macroaveraged cases. Rather, we may observe that:

1. Improvements are more often achieved for low than for high reduction factors. For instance, a reduction factor of .60/.9740 often tends to be associated to performance gains, while a reduction factor of .90/.9870 almost invariably brings about effectiveness losses;
2. The loss in effectiveness introduced by bigrams is higher for those FEFs that have achieved high penetration levels. For instance, the cases in which bigrams improve performance are obtained for *IG* (7 out of 8 cases), DF_{avg} (5 out of 8), and χ^2_{avg} (5 out of 8); these were the three FEFs that had yielded the smallest penetration levels (Table 2) and the smallest increases in average score (Table 3). Conversely, the FEFs that had produced high penetration levels and increases in average score perform badly (3 out of 8) or even disastrously, as is the case for OR_{avg} *and* OR_{max} (both achieve 0 out of 8);

3. Increases in the number of documents in which a feature occurs and in the average number of categories in which a feature occurs (Columns 2 and 3 of Table 3) seem to be associated with an increase in performance, although this is not a definitely clear pattern.

These observations (especially 1 and 2) seem to indicate that an excessive use of bigrams at the expense of unigrams may be detrimental to effectiveness, even if the total score of the top feature set is increased by letting bigrams in. This may indicate that important unigrams are pushed out of the top set by bigrams that somehow "duplicate" the information carried by existing unigrams. For instance, *inform retriev, inform* and *retriev* may all be selected for the top set, with *inform retriev* pushing out a unigram that is quite unrelated to all other remaining features. This is an inherent weakness of the "filtering" approach to feature selection, i.e., the fact that a feature is evaluated independently of all other features. In principle, a better approach would be the "wrapper" approach to feature selection (John, Kohavi & Pfleger, 1994), whereby feature sets are evaluated as a whole; however, this approach is impractical in TC, since in the presence of large sets of features to choose from, it is computationally infeasible.

Besides eliminating potentially informative unigrams, the selecting of too many bigrams has the further drawback that it increases the pairwise stochastic dependence between terms, a situation which is at odds with the principles underlying most text classifiers currently used (including Rocchio). There are methods designed to handle such situations, e.g., maximum entropy (Kantor & Lee, 1998). Maximum entropy combines feature selection with a classifier, somewhat similarly to Bayesian methods. When confronted with words that co-occur frequently (a situation that can be the effect of the above-mentioned "duplication"), maximum entropy avoids the conclusion that this co-occurrence is a significant predictor of class membership. In empirical applications, however, both Nigam, Lafferty and McCallum (1999) and Kantor and Lee (1998) have reported mixed performance of maximum entropy. While in some domains an improvement has been reported with respect to Bayesian classifiers, in some others a deterioration in classification accuracy has been noted (Nigam, Lafferty & McCallum, 1999). Kantor and Lee (1998) report similarly mixed results on an information retrieval task.

RELATED WORK

Phrase indexing is closely related to the problem of *automatic term recognition* (ATR) in *terminology*, a subfield of computational linguistics that investigates the identification and extraction from texts of linguistic units which characterize specialized domains. In their excellent review of ATR research, Kageura and Umino (1996) draw a distinction between research that emphasizes "unithood" (i.e., the fact that a given linguistic expression qualifies as a "term" from a *syntactic* point of view) and research that instead emphasizes "termhood" (i.e., the fact that a given linguistic expression qualifies as a "term" from a *semantic* point of view). The distinction we have drawn between syntactic and statistical phrases for use in IR and TC is very similar.

Related Work in Information Retrieval

Work on the use of either syntactic or statistical phrases in IR dates back to the early 1970s (see Fagan, 1989, for a review of this early work). However, it was not until Fagan's work (1987; 1989) that thorough experimental comparison between standard indexing, syntactic phrase indexing and statistical phrase indexing was performed. In his experiments Fagan found syntactic phrases to yield very small effectiveness improvements, notwithstanding the fact that a sophisticated linguistic technique had been employed for phrase extraction. More importantly, he also found that statistical phrases obtained by a simple method improved performance a lot more than the syntactic phrases.

Lewis and Croft (1990) have investigated the idea of extracting syntactic phrases and then clustering them in order to endow the resulting indexing language with better statistical properties, but this has not resulted in significant effectiveness improvements.

Mitra et al. (1997) have investigated the impact of both syntactic and statistical phrases in IR. Their research shows that the difference in effectiveness between the two is almost negligible and that there is a significant overlap between the sets of phrases identified by the two methods (41% of the union of the two sets is in their intersection). They have also shown that phrase indexing gives little benefits at low recall levels, but the benefits tend to increase at high recall levels. This is an important observation for TC applications, since in TC the recall level is usually a parameter learned on a validation set; this means that if phrases are used, in TC the recall level that maximizes overall performance is automatically chosen by the system. The statistical phrases of Mitra et al. (1997) are exactly equivalent to our bigrams (they do not consider *n*-grams for $n \geq 3$), with the only difference that an empirical statistical filter is used in place of our FEFs (i.e., only bigrams occurring in more that 25 documents are considered). The results of Mitra et al. (1997) concerning statistical phrases have essentially been confirmed by a later study by Turpin and Moffat (1999), who have also tried to use nonalphabetically ordered phrases without obtaining substantially different results.

Related Work in Text Categorization

While quite a few researchers have investigated the usefulness of phrase indexing for IR purposes, relatively few have done the same in a TC context. A number of researchers, although using syntactic (Fuhr et al., 1991; Lewis & Croft, 1990) or statistical (Apté, Damerau & Weiss, 1994; Schapire & Singer, 2000; Schapire, Singer & Singhal, 1998; Schütze, Hull & Pedersen, 1995) phrases for TC purposes, do not provide explicit comparisons between performance with and without phrases.

Syntactic Phrases

Lewis (1992a; 1992b) has been the first to study the effects of syntactic phrase indexing in a TC context. He reported that, in the context of a Naïve Bayes classifier, this yields significantly lower effectiveness than standard "set-of-words" indexing, regardless of whether the syntactic phrases are successively clustered or not (Lewis & Croft, 1990), it has to be remarked, that Lewis' phrase indexing language consisted of *phrases only*; this is different from most other works (including the present one), in which phrases are *added* to a unigram-based indexing language.

Dumais et al. (1998) report having noted no benefit at all from the use of syntactic phrases with a variety of text classifiers in the context of Reuters-21578 experimentation.

Fürnkranz et al. (1998) showed that syntactic phrases yield precision improvements at low recall levels, somehow confirming the results obtained by Mitra et al. (1997) in an IR context.

Statistical Phrases

Mladenic and Grobelnik (1998) have extracted *n*-grams of length up to 5 by means of a fast (although incomplete) algorithm that relies on document frequency as a statistical filter. On a Naïve Bayes classifier applied to a corpus of Web pages they have found that *n*-grams of length up to 4 give significant benefits with respect to the single word's case, while *n*-grams with a length of 5 do not provide additional benefit.

Fürnkranz (1998) uses an algorithm similar to that of Mladenic and Grobelnik (1998) to extract *n*-grams of length up to 5. On Reuters-21578 he has found that Ripper (Cohen & Singer, 1999) has a significant improvement in performance when *n*-grams of length up to 2 are used, but longer *n*-grams reduce classification performance; on another data set of Usenet newsgroup articles he also found *3*-grams to have some utility, and the negative contribution of longer *n*-grams was confirmed.

The difference between the experiments in Fürnkranz (1998) and Mladenic and Grobelnik (1998) and our experiment, apart from the obvious issue of learner-independence, is that Furnkranz (1998) and Mladenic and Grobelnik (1998) used no stemming and no alphabetical ordering. This is an important difference since, as discussed in a prior section, stemming and alphabetical ordering allow factoring out a significant number of morphological, syntactic and semantic differences between linguistic expressions.

Another difference between our research and all other works discussed in this section is that, in comparing the effectiveness deriving from standard indexing with that deriving from phrase indexing, we keep the number of features fixed (i.e., bigrams *substitute* some unigrams in the vector representations) while in all other works this is not done (i.e., bigrams *are added* to the unigrams in the representation). We have chosen to do this because, unlike in IR, in TC the dimensionality of the feature space is an important parameter, and because of this any comparison between different representation schemes is significant only if the numbers of features used are the same.

CONCLUSION

We have investigated the usefulness of bigrams in text categorization by first performing a learner-independent study and then assessing whether the indications of this study were confirmed by real text categorization experiments. We think this approach sheds some light on the role of bigrams in TC, a role that in previously published experiments had been clouded by learner-dependent issues. Further, we remark that this study uses a definition of *n*-grams that, although standard in IR contexts, has never been evaluated in TC experiments.

The learner-independent study showed that feature evaluation functions that are routinely used in text categorization experiments tend to score many bigrams higher than unigrams that they would themselves select in unigram-only feature selection tasks, sometimes giving rise to high bigram "penetration levels." This would seem to indicate that there is value added in selecting a fixed number of features from a pool that contains not only all unigrams but also all bigrams.

Our hypothesis that a high penetration level was conducive to improving effectiveness was not completely confirmed. In particular, our experiments showed that when the bigram penetration level is too high, effectiveness may decrease, and it is easy to conjecture that this is due to the elimination of informative unigrams on the part of bigrams that partly duplicate the information carried by existing unigrams.

All in all, we think that the issue of information duplication as a result of bigram insertion is central to understanding why significant penetration levels on the part of bigrams do not go on a par with classifier effectiveness improvements. This will be the main direction along which we plan to carry out further work.

ACKNOWLEDGMENTS

We thank Luigi Galavotti for making available his RealCAT text classification software environment (Galavotti, Sebastiani & Simi, 2000), which greatly simplified our experimental work; William Cohen for making available his Ripper system; and Gianni Ginesi and Emanuele Granucci for their collaboration in the implementation of the *n*-gram extraction software. Finally, thanks to Irene Loiseau for making the three of us meet.

REFERENCES

Apte, C., Damerau, F.J. and Weiss, S.M. (1994). Automated learning of decision rules for text categorization. *ACM Transactions on Information Systems*, 12(3), 233-251.

Brill, E. (1992). A simple rule-based part-of-speech tagger. In *Proceedings of ANLP-92, 3rd Conference on Applied Natural Language Processing*, 152-155, Trento, Italy.

Buckley, C., Singhal, A. and Mitra, M. (1996). Using query zoning and correlation within SMART: TREC-5. In E.M. Voorhees and D.K. Harman (Eds.), *Proceedings of TREC-5, 5th Text Retrieval Conference*, Gaithersburg, US.

Church, K.W. (1988). A stochastic parts program and noun phrase parser for unrestricted text. In *Proceedings of ANLP-88, 2nd Conference on Applied Natural Language Processing*, 136-143.

Cohen, W.W. and Singer, Y. (1999). Context-sensitive learning methods for text categorization. *ACM Transactions on Information Systems*, 17(2), 141-173.

Damerau, F.J. (1993). Evaluating domain-oriented multi-word terms from texts. *Information Processing and Management*, 29(4), 433-447.

Dumais, S.T., Platt, J., Heckerman, D. and Sahami, M. (1998). Inductive learning algorithms and representations for text categorization. In G. Gardarin, J.C. French, N. Pissinou, K. Makki, and L. Bouganim, (Eds.), *Proceedings of CIKM-98, 7th ACM International Conference on Information and Knowledge Management, Bethesda, MD*, 148-155, New York: ACM Press.

Enguehard, C. and Pantera, L. (1995). Automatic natural acquisition of a terminology. *Journal of Quantitative Linguistics*, 2(1), 27-32.

Fagan, J.L. (1987). Experiments in automatic phrase indexing for document retrieval: a comparison of syntactic and nonsyntactic methods. *PhD thesis*, Department of Computer Science, Cornell University, Ithaca, NY.

Fagan, J.L. (1989). The effectiveness of a nonsyntactic approach to automatic phrase indexing for document retrieval. *Journal of the American Society for Information Science*, 40(2),115-132.

Frakes, W.B. (1992). Stemming algorithms. In W.B. Frakes and R. Baeza-Yates, (Eds.), *Information Retrieval: data structures and algorithms*. Englewood Cliffs, NJ: Prentice Hall, 131-160.

Fuhr, N., Hartmann, S., Knorz, G., Lustig, G., Schwantner, M. and Tzeras, K. (1991). AIR/X—a rule-based multistage indexing system for large subject fields. In A. Lichnerowicz (Ed.), *Proceedings of RIAO-91, 3rd International Conference "Recherche d'Information Assistee par Ordinateur'' Barcelona*. Amsterdam: Elsevier Science Publishers, 606-623.

Fürnkranz, J. (1998). A study using n-gram features for text categorization. *Technical Report TR-98-30, Oesterreichisches Forschungsinstitut fur Artificial Intelligence,* Wien, Austria.

Fürnkranz, J., Mitchell, T.M. and Riloff, E. (1998). A case study in using linguistic phrases for text categorization on the WWW. In *Proceedings of the 1st AAAI Workshop on Learning for Text Categorization*, 5-12, Madison, US.

Galavotti, L., Sebastiani, F. and Simi, M. (2000). Experiments on the use of feature selection and negative evidence in automated text categorization. In J.L. Borbinha and T. Baker (Eds.), *Proceedings of ECDL-00, 4th European Conference on Research and Advanced Technology for Digital Libraries, number 1923 in Lecture Notes in Computer Science, Lisbon*. Heidelberg, Germany: Springer Verlag, 59-68.

John, G.H., Kohavi, R. and Pfleger, K. (1994). Irrelevant features and the subset selection problem. In *Proceedings of ICML-94, 11th International Conference on Machine Learning*, New Brunswick, US, 121-129.

Kageura, K. and Umino, B. (1996). Methods of automatic term recognition: A review. *Terminology*, 3(2), 259-289.

Kantor, P.B. and Lee, J.J. (1998). Testing the maximum entropy principle for information retrieval. *Journal of the American Society for Information Science*, 49(6), 557-566.

Lam, S.L. and Lee, D.L. (1999). Feature reduction for neural network based text categorization. In A.L. Chen and F.H. Lochovsky (Eds.), *Proceedings of DASFAA-99, 6th IEEE International Conference on Database Advanced Systems for Advanced Application, Hsinchu*. Los Alamitos, CA: IEEE Computer Society Press, 195-202.

Lewis, D.D. (1992). An evaluation of phrasal and clustered representations on a text categorization task. In N.J. Belkin, P. Ingwersen and A.M. Pejtersen (Eds.), *Proceedings of SIGIR-92, 15th ACM International Conference on Research and Development in Information Retrieval, Kobenhavn,Denmark.* New York:

ACM Press, 37-50.

Lewis, D.D. (1992). Representation and learning in information retrieval. *PhD thesis*, University of Massachusetts, Amherst, MA.

Lewis, D.D. and Croft, W.B. (1990). Term clustering of syntactic phrases. In *Proceedings of SIGIR-90, 13th ACM International Conference on Research and Development in Information Retrieval*, 385-404, Bruxelles, Belgium.

Mitra, M., Buckley, C., Singhal, A. and Cardie, C. (1997). An analysis of statistical and syntactic phrases. In *Proceedings of RIAO-97, 5th International Conference "Recherche d'Information Assistee par Ordinateur"*, Montreal, CA, 200-214. An extended version is forthcoming in Information Processing and Management.

Mladenic, D. (1998). Feature subset selection in text learning. In C. Nedellec and C. Rouveirol (Eds.), *Proceedings of ECML-98, 10th European Conference on Machine Learning, number 398 in Lecture Notes in Computer Science, Chemnitz, Germany*. Heidelberg, Germany: Springer Verlag, 95-100.

Mladenic, D. and Grobelnik, M. (1998). Word sequences as features in text-learning. In *Proceedings of ERK-98, the Seventh Electrotechnical and Computer Science Conference*, Ljubljana, SL, 145-148.

Nigam, K., Lafferty, J. and McCallum, A.K. (1999). Using maximum entropy for text classification. In *Proceedings of the IJCAI-99 Workshop on Information Filtering*, Stockholm, Sweden.

Schapire, R.E. and Singer, Y (2000). BoosTexter: a boosting-based system for text categorization. *Machine Learning*, 39(2/3), 135-168.

Schapire, R.E., Singer, Y. and Singhal, A. (1998). Boosting and Rocchio applied to text filtering. In W.B. Croft, A. Moffat, C.J. van Rijsbergen, R. Wilkinson and J. Zobel (Eds.), *Proceedings of SIGIR-98, 21st ACM International Conference on Research and Development in Information Retrieval, Melbourne, Australia*. New York: ACM Press, 215-223.

Schütze, H, Hull, D.A. and Pedersen, J.O. (1995). A comparison of classifiers and document representations for the routing problem. In E.A. Fox, P. Ingwersen, and R. Fidel (Eds.), *Proceedings of SIGIR-95, 18th ACM International Conference on Research and Development in Information Retrieval, 229-237, Seattle, WA*. New York: ACM Press.

Sebastiani, F. (1999). Machine learning in automated text categorization. *Technical Report IEI-B4-31-1999*, Istituto di Elaborazione dell'Informazione, Consiglio Nazionale delle Ricerche, Pisa, IT. Submitted for publication to ACM Computing Surveys.

Turpin, A.and Moffat, A. (1999). Statistical phrases for vector-space information retrieval. In *Proceedings of SIGIR-99, 22nd ACM International Conference on Research and Development in Information Retrieval*, 309-310, Berkeley, CA.

Tzeras, K. and Hartmann, S. (1993). Automatic indexing based on Bayesian inference networks. In R. Korfhage, E. Rasmussen and P. Willett (Eds.), *Proceedings of SIGIR-93, 16th ACM International Conference on Research and Development in Information Retrieval, Pittsburgh, PA*. New York: ACM

Press, 22-34.

Yang, Y. and Pedersen, J.O. (1997). A comparative study on feature selection in text categorization. In D.H. Fisher (Ed.), *Proceedings of ICML-97, 14th International Conference on Machine Learning, Nashville, TN*. San Francisco, CA: Morgan Kaufmann Publishers, 412-420.

Zhou, J. (1999). Phrasal terms in real-world IR applications. In T. Strzalkowski (Ed.), *Natural language information retrieval*, pages 215-259. Dordrecht, Netherlands: Kluwer Academic Publishers.

ENDNOTES

* The work of this author was partially carried out while visiting the Department of Computer Science of the University of Ottawa, supported by Grant FOMEC376 from the Universidad de Buenos Aires.

1. We remark that the term "*n*-gram" is used in the text processing literature in two quite different senses. In the first sense it is used, as here, to indicate a set of *n words* that occur sequentially in a text. In the second sense it is used to indicate a set of *n characters* that occur sequentially in a text, and that may be part of a word or of a sequence of two or more words occurring contiguously. The latter sense is typical of the literature on indexing noisy texts, such as those resulting from OCR or those in Asian languages, and will not be dealt with here.
2. In this paper we make the general assumption that a document d_j can in principle belong to zero, one or many of the categories in *C*; this assumption is indeed verified in the Reuters-21578 benchmark we use for our experiments. All the techniques we discuss in this paper can be straightforwardly adapted to the other case in which each document belongs to exactly one category.
3. The Reuters-21578 corpus may be freely downloaded for experimentation purposes from http://www.research.att.com/lewis/reuters21578.html.
4. See for a discussion on why this is the "right" subset of Reuters-21578 categories to use.

Chapter V

Interactive Query Expansion With Automatically Generated Category-Specific Thesauri*

Fabrizio Sebastiani
Istituto di Elaborazione dell'Informazione, Italy

The categorization of documents into subject-specific categories is a useful enhancement for large document collections addressed by information retrieval systems, as a user can first browse a category tree in search of the category that best matches her interests and then issue a query for more specific documents "from within the category." This approach combines two modalities in information seeking that are most popular in Web-based search engines, i.e., category-based site browsing (as exemplified by, e.g., Yahoo™) and keyword-based document querying (as exemplified by, e.g., AltaVista™). Appropriate query expansion tools need to be provided, though, in order to allow the user to incrementally refine her query through further retrieval passes, thus allowing the system to produce a series of subsequent document rankings that hopefully converge to the user's expected ranking. In this work we propose that automatically generated, category-specific "associative" the-

sauri be used for such purpose. We discuss a method for their generation and discuss how the thesaurus specific to a given category may usefully be endowed with "gateways" to the thesauri specific to its parent and children categories.

INTRODUCTION

We here report work in progress within the *Eurosearch* project, whose purpose is the design and implementation of a European federation of *n* search engines ε_1, ..., ε_n, each addressing a national Web space of documents expressed in the respective languages $L(\varepsilon_1)$, ..., $L(\varepsilon_n)$. Each search engine ε_i in the federation will be capable of answering queries[1] q_j worded in $L(\varepsilon_1)$ that ask for documents written in either of a set of languages $L(\varepsilon_{1j})$, ..., $L(\varepsilon_{mj})$ contained in $\{L(\varepsilon_1), ..., L(\varepsilon_n)\}$. The search engine will achieve this by translating, in collaboration with search engines ε_{1j}, ..., ε_{mj}, the query from $L(\varepsilon_1)$ to each of the languages $L(\varepsilon_{1j})$, ..., $L(\varepsilon_{mj})$, dispatching the translated queries to the appropriate engines, and presenting to the user the results returned by them. Of course, ε_i will also search within its own national Web space in case, as most of the times will indeed happen, $L(\varepsilon_i) \in \{L(\varepsilon_{1j})$ ..., $L(\varepsilon_{mj})\}$.[2]

Modalities of Information Seeking

One key aspect of the *Eurosearch* architecture is the combination of two information access modalities that have traditionally been addressed by separate tools.

The first modality is *keyword-based document querying*, exemplified by the AltaVista™ search engine (*http://www.altavista.digital.com/*), in which a user types in a list of keywords or phrases and receives back as a result a list of documents, ranked in decreasing probability (or estimated degree) of relevance to the query, in which these keywords play a (decreasingly) significant role (e.g., appear in the title, in headers, or in the body of the document). The second modality is *category-based site browsing*, exemplified by the Yahoo™ search engine (*http://www.yahoo.com/*), in which a user is allowed to browse a hierarchy of subject categories, each of which contains pointers to a *select* number of Web sites highly relevant to it; after navigating down to the category she is interested in, the user can then browse the sites referred therein.

The *Eurosearch* architecture integrates the two modalities by allowing the user to first browse a hierarchy of categories, thus docking to the category

C she was looking for, and from there issue keyword-based queries for documents:

1. *belonging to C*; documents satisfying this must have been categorized under *C* by the search engine, likely because they reside on the top relevant sites for *C*;
2. *related to C*; documents satisfying this need not have been categorized under *C* by the search engine, but they must nevertheless be topically related to *C*.

Traditional search engines based on category-based site browsing, such as Yahoo™, tend to incorporate functionality (1) but not functionality (2). We allow both (1) and (2) as alternative search modes, because while (1) yields high *precision* (i.e., a high proportion of the retrieved documents tend to be relevant to the user's need), the second yields high *recall* (i.e., a high proportion of the documents relevant to the user's need tend to be retrieved; Buckland & Gey, 1994). Different users have different requirements in terms of recall and precision, and their needs are properly catered for by allowing the user to choose between the two alternatives.[3]

The advantage of modality (2) over pure keyword-based document querying is that the query is less ambiguous, or more focused, than it would be if issued from a semantically neutral environment (such as AltaVista™ or the "root" category of Yahoo™), as terms contained in the query can appropriately be interpreted by the search engine in the semantic context of the category within which the query originated. For instance, the word *bank* contained in a query issued from within the *BusinessAndEconomy* category can be safely interpreted in its sense of "financial institution" rather than in its sense of "fortification of a river", and can thus be both interpreted correctly and translated correctly into the target languages. In *Eurosearch*, word sense disambiguation prior to translation into the other languages is of fundamental importance, especially given that in the architecture a "pivot" language (English) is used[4]: Word sense ambiguities rooted in the pivot language would not only degrade the performance, but would also originate results unintelligible to a user not proficient in the pivot language.

The profile of the category (typically, a vector of weighted terms that are deemed relevant to it) can be used as contextual information; the net effect is one of word sense disambiguation, both when the query is addressed to the local search engine (this is the case in which $L(\varepsilon_i) \in \{L(\varepsilon_{1j}) \ldots, L(\varepsilon_{mj})\}$) and when it is translated into the pivot language in order to be dispatched to other search engines. The typically large size of the category profile usually ensures high-quality disambiguation (Sanderson, 1994).

Query Refinement

No matter whether they are issued from within categories or from semantically neutral environments, queries always return less than perfect results: Some irrelevant documents are ranked high in the list, and some relevant documents are ranked low. It is thus necessary to offer the user tools for *query refinement*, by means of which she may interact with the system and feed it information that allows it to refine the query through further retrieval passes, thus yielding a series of subsequent document rankings that hopefully converge to the user's expected ranking. Modern query refinement methods may loosely be classified into *automatic query expansion* (AQE) methods and *interactive query expansion* (IQE) ones (e.g., Efthimiadis, 1996).

Many AQE methods rely on *relevance feedback* techniques (e.g., Salton & Buckley, 1990), whereby terms featuring prominently in documents marked relevant by the user are automatically added to the query (or reweighted, increasing their weight appropriately); other AQE methods rely instead on the use of *thesauri*, from which terms semantically related to the query terms (Grefenstette, 1992) or to the query as a whole (Qiu & Frei, 1993) are extracted and added to the query. These techniques have often given good results, but their effectiveness is known to depend on a lot of factors, including the method used for document ranking, the characteristics of the document collection being targeted, and the number of terms used.

IQE methods (also called *semiautomatic query expansion methods;* Qiu & Frei, 1993) are instead based on the idea that these automatically selected terms must be first submitted to the user (by a *term suggestion device;* Schatz, Johnson, Cochrane, & Chen, 1996), who may thus decide which to include and which not to include in the revised query.[5] Again, the suggested terms may come from relevance feedback or from lexical resources such as thesauri. While in the first case the results reported in the literature are mixed, showing that only experienced users tend to benefit from these techniques (Magennis & van Rijsbergen, 1997), in the latter case there have been promising results, that have prompted a flurry of work in the area (e.g., Chen et al., 1996; Schatz et al., 1996), especially within the context of the Digital Libraries Initiative.

Querying from within categories also requires that query refinement too be performed in a category-specific way. In the rest of the paper we discuss work in progress within Eurosearch aimed at allowing the user to interactively add new keywords (or substitute previously used keywords with more specific ones) by choosing them from a category-specific *associative thesaurus*, i.e., a graph in which nodes represent terms and edges represent (unspecific) relationships of semantic similarity between terms. The advantage of associative thesauri over other kinds of thesauri (such as conventional "hierarchical" ones) is that they may be generated automatically through statistical analysis of word occurrences in a given collection.

The rest of the paper is organized as follows. In the next section we discuss associative thesauri and the problem of their automatic generation. We then discuss the methods we intend to follow for allowing the users to exploit the generated thesauri for interactive query refinement.

ASSOCIATIVE THESAURI AND THEIR AUTOMATIC GENERATION

Thesauri have long been used for query expansion or reformulation (e.g., Efthimiadis, 1996). A *thesaurus* is a collection of words organized according to a topology that reflects the semantics of the terms and of their associations; typically, thesauri are *domain-specific*, i.e., the set of words they contain are those specific to a given discipline. In a conventional thesaurus (Foskett, 1980) words are organized into binary relations, the most important of which are

- $NT(t_1, t_2)$ ("Narrower Term"), meaning that t_1 is a more specific term than t_2;
- $RT(t_1, t_2)$ ("Related Term"), meaning that t_1 is semantically related, albeit in a non-hierarchical way, to t_2.

The *NT* relation thus induces a partial order on the set of terms, giving it the characteristic hierarchical structure. This structure makes it easier for users to *substitute* terms previously used in the query by means of more specific ones, which the user can identify by browsing the thesaurus, starting from the term to be substituted and working downwards along the hierarchy.

However, conventional thesauri have been found unsuitable for suggesting to the user new terms to *add* to a query (Schatz et al., 1996). The main reason is that these thesauri are built manually, by expert lexicographers, and the *manual* nature of this process makes it virtually impossible to identify and list by means of the *RT* relation a sufficiently large set of semantically related terms among which the user might want to choose new terms to add to the query.

A way out of this inadequacy is the *automatic* identification of semantic relationships between terms from a corpus of documents; this process originates an *associative thesaurus,*[6] i.e., a graph in which nodes represent terms and edges represent relationships of semantic similarity between terms.

Edges have an associated weight, denoting the strength of association between the two words; therefore, to each term is associated a list of related terms, ranked in decreasing order of association strength.

The automatic generation of associative thesauri, or variants thereof, has a long history, dating back at the very least to the seminal studies of Sparck Jones (1971) and Salton (1971). More or less, the process of generating a thesaurus is articulated in the following steps:

1. Standard (automatic) document indexing is performed, thereby generating the usual term-document incidence matrix that specifies a weight w_{ij} for each pair $<t_i, d_j>$ constituted by a term t_i and a document d_j.
2. A term-term matrix is generated, specifying a "semantic relatedness" value r_{ij} for each pair of terms $<t_i, t_j>$. The matrix may be symmetric or not, depending on the underlying notion of similarity, and is generated by taking into account factors such as the degree of co-occurrence or co-absence of the two terms in the collection.
3. Small values of r_{ij} are replaced by 0, thus leaving only highly related pairs with a nonzero coefficient; these latter, which determine the edges of the resulting associative thesaurus, may be identified:
   (a) as the top n coefficients for any given term, for a prespecified value of n;
   (b) as all the coefficients exceeding a pre-specified threshold value.

From step (2), it is clear that the resulting thesaurus embodies an *extensional*, rather than the standard *intensional*, notion of lexical semantics (e.g., Haack, 1978, p. 246): *The meaning of words is only determined by the documents they appear in.* It is also a collection-dependent notion of meaning, as the r_{ij} values strongly depend on the characteristics of the collection which is chosen as "training sample."

The Eurosearch Approach

In a space of documents categorized into one or more categories, such as the one *Eurosearch* deals with, good terms for query expansion are most likely to be specific to the particular domain the category is about. Therefore, our approach contemplates generating *category-specific associative thesauri*, one for each category in the categorization scheme. This generation will take place from a training set of documents previously categorized under the category of interest.

One key observation for this task is that we want to avoid pairs of terms that, although they might be deemed as strongly related in the training sample, are nevertheless extraneous to the domain-specific terminology of the category of interest. For instance, from a training sample of documents previously categorized under the *BusinessAndEconomy* label, the two words *banana* and *coconut* might (correctly!) emerge as strongly related, simply because they co-occur in a few documents (e.g., related to stock prices of exotic fruits) and they are co-absent in most of the others. In order to avoid this, before proceeding to term-term similarity computation, we first want to identify the terms that are specific to the category of interest. These can be identified as the terms whose *within-category inverse document frequency WCaIDF* is substantially smaller (i.e., smaller at least by a predetermined factor) than their *within-collection inverse document frequency WCoIDF*. If *Ca* and *Co* denote the category of interest and the collection (i.e., the whole corpus), respectively, *WCaIDF* and *WCoIDF* may be defined as[7]

$$WCaIDF(t_i) = log\left(\frac{1+ \|Ca\|}{1+\#_{Ca}(t_i,d_j)} \right) \tag{1}$$

$$WCoIDF(t_i) = log\left(\frac{1+ \|Co\|}{1+\#_{Co}(t_i,d_j)} \right) \tag{2}$$

where $\#_S(t_i, d_j)$ denotes the number of documents $d_j \in S$ in which term t_i occurs at least once and $||S||$ denotes the cardinality of set S. This criterion is based on the intuition that terms specific to a given category occur more frequently in documents belonging to the category than in "generic" documents belonging to the entire training set.

Once terms specific to the category of interest have been identified, semantic relatedness values between each pair of such terms may be computed. As mentioned in point (2) above, co-occurrence and co-absence considerations are often taken into account in this computation. We instead intend to rely on a technique developed in Schäuble and Knaus (1993), and subsequently experimented with in Qiu and Frei (1993) and Sheridan et al. (1997), that relies on an inversion of the roles that documents and terms traditionally have in information retrieval.

This approach may be better understood by recurring to a sort of *abstract indexing theory*, according to which a set of *items* forming a collection *I* are indexed by a set of *indexing features F*. Let *T* be the set of all *tokens t*, i.e., of all occurrences of an indexing feature f_r in an item i_s for some *r, s*. Let $\Phi: T \rightarrow F$ be the function that maps a token into the indexing feature of which it is an occurrence, and let $Y: T \rightarrow I$ be the function that maps a token into the item in which it occurs. We may thus define the *within-item frequency* of feature in item as the number of times f_r occurs in i_s:

$$\text{WIF}(f_r, i_s) = \| \{ t \in T: (\Phi(t) = f_r \wedge (Y(t) = i_s)\} \| \tag{3}$$

We may also define the *within-collection frequency* of feature f_r as the number of items in which the following occurs at least once:

$$WCF(f_r) = \| \{ i \in I: f_r t.(\Phi(t) = f_r \wedge (Y(t) = i) \} \| \qquad (4)$$

The *inverse within-collection frequency* of feature f_r is defined as:

$$IWCF(f_r) = log\left(\frac{1+\|I\|}{1+WCF(f_r)} \right) \qquad (5)$$

A possible weight for indexing feature f_r in item i_s may thus be

$$w_{rs} = WIF(f_r, i_s) \bullet IWCF(f_r) \qquad (6)$$

If the cosine measure (i.e., inner product with cosine normalization) is used for modelling item-item similarity, then we have

$$SIM(i_s,i_t) = \frac{\sum_{r=1}^{\|F\|} \omega_{rs} \bullet \omega_{rt}}{\sqrt{\sum_{r=1}^{\|F\|} \omega^2_{rs} \bullet \omega^2_{rt}}} \qquad (7)$$

In standard IR, documents play the role of items, terms play the role of indexing features, (3), (4) and (5) are the well-known *term frequency, document frequency and inverse document frequency* functions, respectively, while (6) is the widely used *tf * idf* weighting scheme (Salton & Buckley, 1988).

For the generation of the associative thesaurus, instead, *terms play the role of items and documents play the role of indexing features*; in other words, the method is simply based on the idea of "thinking dually." Term t_j is thus represented as a vector $t_j = < w_{ij}, ..., w_{nj}>$, where n is the cardinality of the document collection D and w_{1j} is the weight of document d_i for term t_j. This gives rise to a "dual" vector space model, in which terms are vectors in a space generated by the documents in the collection. In this way, the most similar terms to a given term t_j may be identified by issuing t_j as a "query" term and considering the top-ranked "retrieved" terms.

Adopting this simple idea has a number of consequences, first and foremost that the intuitions that underlie the standard application to IR of this "abstract indexing theory" may be applied, *mutatis mutandis*, to the new setting. In particular, it is interesting to note that, while the rationale of *IWCF* in the standard interpretation (i.e., *idf*) is that terms that occur in fewer documents are more valuable indexing features than the ones occurring in many documents, the rationale of *IWCF* in the dual interpretation is that documents consisting of fewer terms (i.e., shorter documents) are likewise more valuable indexing features: Shorter documents tend to deal with less topics and hence represent the terms that occur in them in a more significant way (Sheridan et al., 1997).

It is clear from this description that the process of associative thesaurus generation is computationally expensive. While the term-document incidence matrix may be considered as given (as it will already have been produced in indexing the documents for "standard" retrieval purposes), formula (3) needs to be calculated for every $<f_r, i_s>$ document-term pair, formula (4) needs to be calculated for every document f_r, etc. However, the fact that only terms specific to the category and only documents categorized under the category are used substantially cuts down the complexity of the process with respect to the standard, highly expensive problem of generating an *unspecific* (i.e., topic-neutral) associative thesaurus (Chen et al., 1996). This is true even once we consider that the process must be repeated for every single category, as this brings about only an additive increase in complexity, while the above-mentioned reduction in complexity is multiplicative. Besides, one should not forget that, as recalled in Qiu and Frei (1993), the generation of the thesaurus is done once for all.

USING CATEGORY-SPECIFIC ASSOCIATIVE THESAURI FOR QUERY REFINEMENT

Thesaurus Display and Navigation

We are currently evaluating different strategies for allowing the user to refine or expand her query by browsing the thesaurus through a graphical interface. One possibility is the adoption of a graph browser (Jones et al., 1995). Such a tool would display, upon clicking on a term in the previously issued query window, a star-shaped graph representing the portion of the thesaurus consisting of the clicked word and its semantically most related words, linked to it by edges; navigation in the graph would allow the user to select new words for addition to the query or for substitution (refinement) of the clicked word (standard techniques of graphical interfaces may be adopted both for distinguishing between these two types of events and for implementing other tasks mentioned below). Various visualization techniques may be employed here, among them, adaptations of those developed within the "ostensive model of information needs" (Campbell & Rijsbergen, 1996).

A possible alternative that we are also considering is the use of an even simpler thesaurus display technique based on hierarchical menus. In this case, clicking on a word appearing in the previous query window would result in the popping up of a menu consisting in the ranked list of the terms semantically related to the word, listed in decreasing order of strength of relatedness. This menu would be hierarchical, thus allowing the selection of a word several steps away in a single click (and, thanks to the ranking of the list, with likely minimum mouse travelling distance). One advantage of this technique over the previously discussed one, apart from the possible reduction of screen clutter, is that graph displays are clumsy for the representation of *non-symmetric* binary relationships, and the binary notion of semantic relatedness (or similarity) seems inherently to be such (Peat & Willett, 1991).

Jumping Across Inter-Thesauri Borders

While the methods described in an earlier section should ensure that most terms specific to a given category *C* have been captured within the thesaurus *T(C)* specific to *C*, it is quite possible that some of them have been missed. However, some of the missed terms may well have been captured within the thesaurus *T(C')* specific to the category *C'* that is the parent of *C* in the category tree or within the thesaurus $T(C_i)$ specific to one of the categories C_1, ... , C_k that are the children of *C* in the same tree. For instance, suppose that

BusinessAndEconomy/FinanceAndInvestments/
MutualFunds/IndividualFunds

represents a branch in the category tree. The term "fund screening tools" might have been captured within the thesaurus of category *MutualFunds* and not in that of categories *IndividualFunds* and *FinanceAndInvestments*; nevertheless, it might well be of interest to a user issuing a query from within either of these latter categories. Although this is in principle always possible (additionally to thesaurus browsing, a user may add new terms by simply typing them in), it is indeed useful to allow the user to cross inter-thesauri borders when the involved thesauri refer to categories that stand in a parent-child relation in the category tree.

While other methods might in principle be used, we plan to use terms common to both thesauri as "gateways". In fact, the methods outlined earlier do allow (and this will indeed be the case for several important terms) that a given term *t* be included in the two thesauri *T(C)* and *T(C')*, where *C* is the parent (or child) of *C'* . Now, suppose that while browsing *T(C)*, term *t* is reached; along with the ranked list of terms related to *t* in *T(C)*, also the list of terms related to *t* in *T(C')* may be displayed (differentiating it, quite obviously, from the previous list by means of some adequate visualization device). This allows the user, if she wishes so, to enter the *T(C')* thesaurus and select terms from therein, notwithstanding the fact that she had started her browsing activity within a different thesaurus *T(C)*. Jumping between more than one level of the tree is obviously made possible by iterating this strategy.

Interacting term suggestion devices

As recalled previously, Schatz et al. (1996) have recently pointed out that, while associative thesauri are indeed useful for suggesting terms to be added to the query (*query expansion*), they are not for suggesting terms to be substituted to previously used, more generic ones (*query refinement*). The reason of this is that the relation of semantic relatedness between terms that associative thesauri encode is *untagged*, i.e., is the result of collapsing into a single relation the *NT* and the *RT* relations of conventional thesauri. The notion of term specificity needed for query refinement is thus embodied not in an associative thesaurus, but in a conventional one. Schatz and colleagues have thus proposed that two term suggestion devices (a conventional thesaurus and an associative one) be made available to the user, who may then freely jump from one to the other, thus freely intermixing query refinement and expansion.

While this strategy is indeed attractive, it has the obvious drawback that a conventional thesaurus specific to a given discipline is neither always available nor can be generated automatically with the ease of an associative one.

However, we are considering exploiting this strategy by *allowing the category tree itself to play the role of the conventional thesaurus*. In fact, there are numerous points in favor of this decision. First, the category tree has, as the name implies, a hierarchical structure, similar to that induced by the *NT* relation on a conventional thesaurus. Second, the *RT* relation of the conventional thesaurus, that has no analogue in the category tree, is not exploited in this strategy. Third, the Yahoo™ category tree we will rely on exhibits sufficient structure and depth to be used for this purpose.[8]

REFERENCES

Buckland, M. & Gey, F. (1994). The relationship between recall and precision. *Journal of the American Society for Information Science*, 45(1), 12-19.

Campbell, I. & van Rijsbergen, C.J. (1996). The ostensive model of developing information needs. In *Proceedings of COLIS-96, 2nd International Conference on Conceptions of Library Science*, 251-268, Kobenhavn, DK.

Chen, H. & Ng, T.D. (1995). An algorithmic approach to concept exploration in a large knowledge network (automatic thesaurus consultation): symbolic branch-and-bound search vs. connectionist Hopfield net activation. *Journal of the American Society for Information Science*, 46(5), 348-369.

Chen, H., Schatz, B.R., Ng, T.D., Martinez, J., Kirchoff, A. & Lin, C. (1996). A parallel computing approach to creating engineering concept spaces for semantic retrieval: the Illinois Digital Library Initiative project. *IEEE Transactions on Pattern Analysis and Machine Intelligence,* 18(8), 771-782.

Efthimiadis, E.N. (1996). Query expansion. In M.E. Williams (Ed.), *Annual Review of Information Science and Technology,* 31, 121-187. American Society for Information Science.

Foskett, D.J. (1980). Thesaurus. In A. Kent, H. Lancour, and J.E. Daily (Eds.), *Encyclopedia of library and information science,* 30, 416-462. New York: Marcel Dekker.

Grefenstette, G. (1992). Use of syntactic context to produce term association lists for retrieval. In *Proceedings of SIGIR-92, 15th ACM International Conference on Research and Development in Information Retrieval*, 89-98, Kobenhavn, DK.

Haack, S. (1978). *Philosophy of logics.* Cambridge, UK: Cambridge University Press.

Jones, S., Gatford, M., Robertson, S., Hancock-Beaulieu, M., Secker, J. & Walker, S. (1995). Interactive thesaurus navigation: Intelligence rules OK? *Journal of the American Society for Information Science*, 46(1), 52-59.

Lancaster, F.W. (1981). Evaluation within the environment of an operating information service. In K. Sparck Jones (Ed.), *Information retrieval experiment,* 105-127. London: Butterworths.

Magennis, M. & van Rijsbergen, C.J. (1997). The potential and actual effectiveness of interactive query expansion. In *Proceedings of SIGIR-97, 20th ACM International Conference on Research and Development in Information Retrieval*, 324-332, Philadelphia, US.

Peat, H.J. & Willett, P. (1991). The limitations of term co-occurrence data for query expansion in document retrieval systems. Journal of the American Society for Information Science, 42(5), 378-383.

Picchi, E. & Peters, C. (1998). Exploiting lexical resources and linguistic tools in multilingual information retrieval: the EUROSEARCH approach. In *Proceedings of the First International Conference on Language Resources and Evaluation*, Granada, ES.

Qiu, Y. & Frei, H-P. (1993). Concept-based query expansion. In *Proceedings of SIGIR-93, 16th ACM International Conference on Research and Development in Information Retrieval,* 160-169, Pittsburgh, US.

Salton, G. (1971). Experiments in automatic thesaurus construction for information retrieval. In *Proceedings of the IFIP Congress,* volume TA-2, 43-49, Ljubljana, YU.

Salton, G. (1980). Automatic term class construction using relevance. A summary of work in automatic pseudoclassification. *Information Processing and Management,* 16:1-15.

Salton, G. & Buckley, C. (1988). Term-weighting approaches in automatic text retrieval. *Information Processing and Management,* 24(5) 513-523.

Salton, G. & Buckley, C. (1990). Improving retrieval performance by relevance feedback. *Journal of the American Society for Information Science,* 41, 288-297.

Sanderson, M. (1994). Word sense disambiguation and information retrieval. In *Proceedings of SIGIR-94, 17th ACM International Conference on Research and Development in Information Retrieval*, 49-57, Dublin, Ireland.

Schatz, B.R., Johnson, E.H., Cochrane, P.A. & Chen, H. (1996). Interactive term suggestion for users of digital libraries: Using subject thesauri and co-occurrence lists for information retrieval. In *Proceedings of DL-96, 1st ACM Digital Library Conference,* 126-133, Bethesda, US.

Schäuble, P. & Knaus, D. (1992). The various roles of information structures. In O. Opitz, B. Lausen and R. Klar (Eds.), *Proceedings of the 16th Annual Conference of the Gesellschaft fur Klassifikation*, 282-290. Dortmund, DE. Published by Springer Verlag, Heidelberg, DE.

Sheridan, P., Braschler, M. & Schäuble, P. (1997). Cross-language information retrieval in a multi-lingual legal domain. In C. Peters and C. Thanos (Eds.), *Proceedings of ECDL-97, 1st European Conference on Research and Advanced Technology for Digital Libraries,* 253-268, Pisa, Italy. Lecture Notes in Computer Science, number 1324, Springer Verlag, Heidelberg, DE.

Sparck Jones, K. (1971). *Automatic keyword classification for information retrieval.* London: Butterworths.

Sparck Jones, K. and Willett, P. (Eds.) (2000). Readings in information retrieval. San Mateo, CA: Morgan Kaufmann.

ENDNOTES

* This work has been carried out in the context of the project EUROSEARCH LE4-8303, funded by the Commission of the European Communities under the ESPRIT Telematics scheme.

1. In information retrieval, a distinction is often made between the user *request*, usually a list of words or phrases in natural language by which the user expresses her information need, and the *query*, the internal representation that the system gives to the request (e.g., by weighting the individual words differently). For simplicity we will avoid this distinction here and always use the term "query," allowing context to discriminate between the two meanings from time to time.
2. For simplicity, here we do not discuss the case in which a search engine ε_i also addresses documents that, although residing within its own national Web space, are expressed in a language different from $L(\varepsilon_i)$. This case is indeed tackled in *Eurosearch*, the obvious case being when this language is English.
3. A manager who wants a quick introduction to a novel topic is a typical precision-oriented user; she wants just a few highly relevant articles, and she wants them right away. On the contrary, an author who is preparing a review article on a given subject is a typical recall-oriented user; she wants to be certain that she reviews most or possibly all of the relevant material, and in order to do this she is also prepared to shuffle through some possibly irrelevant material. See Lancaster (1981) for a more thorough discussion on this.
4. This means that a query issued in Italian and asking for documents in Spanish is translated from Italian to English by the Italian engine and then dispatched to the Spanish engine, which receives it and translates it from English to Spanish. This not only allows cutting down on the number of required bilingual dictionaries from $O(n^2)$ to $O(n)$, but also solves the problem engendered by the non-availability of an online bilingual dictionary for a given pair of languages. See Picchi and Peters (1998) for details.
5. AQE and IQE do not exclude each other: A possible strategy may be to allow both possibilities, so that the user may, e.g., stay with AQE for the first retrieval passes and step in with IQE once she sees that AQE is not improving the ranking any more.
6. Associative thesauri are also called *term-term relationship matrices* (Salton, 1980), *concept spaces* (Chen & Ng, 1995; Chen et al., 1996), or *similarity thesauri* (Qiu & Frei, 1993; Schäuble & Knaus, 1993; Sheridan, Braschler, & Schäuble, 1997).

7. See, e.g., Salton and Buckley (1988) for a clear discussion of IDF and other term weighting strategies.
8. For instance, its *ComputersAndInternet* category alone contains 2,533 unique subcategories distributed over 7 levels.

Chapter VI

Database Concepts for Marked-up Textual Documents

Arijit Sengupta
Georgia State University, USA

INTRODUCTION

Was Xanadu (Nelson, 1987) a totally impossible concept? Ted Nelson's vision was a world in which documents will serve as the vehicle for every type of information and will be accessible in a worldwide distributed "super-database" of documents. Today's World Wide Web is a close reflection of Nelson's vision, but we still need to go long ways to actually reach the goal of worldwide database access to documents. Although Nelson's Xanadu failed to materialize, it did leave much to influence the current state of the art in document presentation and delivery. In spite of the progress of the WWW, we are still far from an ideal information resource with database-like structured querying and updating abilities. The primary goal of this chapter is to present an overview on theoretical as well as practical methodologies required for paving that path to Xanadu.

Lexicographically, the term "document" refers to writings on some material substance such as paper. However, with the advent of computers and automation, documents are no longer restricted to paper and other "hard copy" media. Instead, documents are prepared and stored electronically, with computers used for displaying, formatting, printing, searching and editing. To facilitate these tasks, software vendors have designed a number of powerful word processing applications that can be used to format, typeset, edit, print and publish such documents. In most cases, however, the final publishing medium is still paper, and the computer software is primarily used for adding formatting information directed towards printed output. Such systems do provide limited ability to search documents for words and phrases in the entire document sequentially. However, for large document collections, these types of searches often prove to be too slow and restricted, and better retrieval techniques become necessary.

Recently, the WWW (World Wide Web) has significantly changed the concept of document preparation and distribution. Documents are now being prepared less with specific formatting information and more with embedded structural information in the form of "tags." It is now possible for different viewers on different platforms to generate formatting information "on the fly," based on the capabilities of the platforms and the computer displays. These tags normally use the same encoding as the rest of the document, so that the document is readable without any formatting information and is easily interchangeable between platforms. The concept of these tags first arose with HTML (HyperText Markup Language) (Berners-Lee and Connolly, 1995; the language for the World Wide Web), and SGML (Standard Generalized Markup Language) (ISO 8879, 1986; a generalized language for creating documents with arbitrary structure). Currently, the eXtensible Markup Language (XML) (Bray, Paoli and Sperberg-McQueen, 1999), a markup language derived from SGML, is being considered as the next WWW markup language, and this should emphasize the concept of structured documents.

The primary goal of SGML was to create documents that are freely interchangeable between multiple systems and platforms. In addition to making documents portable, the SGML tags introduce structural information in the documents, information that can be used by applications for purposes other than formatting, e.g., as metadata for database-like searches. XML makes the power of SGML more accessible to the Web users. One objective of this research is to use effectively this metadata information in SGML and XML to allow querying of information contained in these documents in a manner that is currently possible only with database systems.

As an interesting illustration of the problem, let us consider an electronic document collection, such as the Chadwyck-Healey English poetry database.[1] If this collection were on paper, at an average of one poem per page, this document will have 160,000 pages, one page on average per poem. This number does not take into account the table of contents and the index, without which the collection will be virtually useless. At about 500 pages per volume, this will mean about 80 volumes—enough to fill up two bookshelves! On the other hand, this whole information can be easily accommodated in a single

CD-ROM, which is several orders smaller in physical size than the paper equivalent. The advances in storage medium technology have ensured easy and convenient storage of electronic documents, but storage is only half the problem. Efficient storage of large amounts of data is not of much use if the data cannot be efficiently retrieved from the storage. A popular method for extracting portions of information sources is using searches involving Boolean combination of search keywords. This problem of "information retrieval" [Salton, 1991] forms the basis for research in automated text extraction from a repository of documents. Information retrieval is virtually a subdiscipline in its own right within information science.

In its simplest form, primitive information retrieval techniques extract lines containing specified keywords from a document. It is often useful to restrict the searches to specific portions of the document, such as in the titles or poet names in the case of the poetry collection. As an illustration, in the poetry database, the word "love" returns over 270,000 matches, but restricting it within poem title immediately reduces the number of matches to around 5,000. To successfully introduce such granularity into the document, one needs to demarcate important regions of the document with additional information with tags. Tagged documents can be used not only for simple keyword searches as before but also to perform searches that are impossible without the structural information. With the help of tags, one can now answer questions similar to ones commonly asked in the context of relational databases.

Some common types of questions are:

- *Simple selections.* These are queries involving searches for text strings in various regions of the database (e.g., find all the poems that contain the word "love" in the poem title).
- *Projections.* These are queries that involve extraction of specific components of documents. (e.g., extract the poem titles and authors only of all poems in the database).
- *Quantification.* These are queries that involve quantifiers such as "all," "every," or "none" (e.g., find the period in which all poems had the word "love" in their titles).
- *Join.* These are queries in which multiple components of documents are combined based on one or more regions (e.g., find the names of poets who have at least one common poem title).
- *Negation.* These are queries in which a search condition is negated (e.g., find the poems that do not have the word "love" in the title).
- *Counting.* These are queries that involve computing the number of matched results, possibly based on certain conditions (e.g., how many

Shakespeare poems are there in the collection?).

- *Grouping and ordering*. These are queries in which the results need to be grouped and ordered based on certain conditions (e.g., list the different periods of poetry in the collection, in ascending order of the number of poems in each period).
- *Nested queries*. These are queries in which a query includes another query (or a subquery) as a search condition (e.g., find the names of poets who never used the word "love" in the title of any of their poems).

Queries similar to the above are common in relational database systems. If we could model the above poem collection using a relational database, we could answer all the queries. Because of the complex hierarchical structure of documents, relational databases cannot be used effectively to model document structures without causing an unacceptable amount of fragmentation in the data. Unfortunately, current information retrieval systems that only perform keyword searches cannot answer all the above queries as well. However, systems that support structured text can be used to automatically extract answers to the above queries.

The objective of this chapter is to provide the reader with a set of methodological tools for database processing of textual documents with embedded structure in the form of markup tags. Such processing includes the ability to pose and generate answers for queries similar to those discussed above. We achieve this objective by first showing that handling collections of documents in an electronic medium can be quite similar to database processing, and describing both formal and practical methods for accessing information from such structured data using both data and metadata. The goal of this chapter is not to present a method for searching the World Wide Web, although the current introduction of XML into the web does improve the chances of methods such as this to be used and incorporated into the web.

BACKGROUND

Database Systems

Databases emerged as a major research area when the necessity of taking a disciplined approach for storage and retrieval of information became obvious. The evolution of database systems is marked by three generations of database systems and models: (i) *first generation database systems*, including the hierarchical and network data models, (ii) *second generation database systems*, including the relational database models, and (iii) *third generation database systems*, including the object-oriented and object-relational database systems. In addition to these prominent generations of database systems, some specialized database systems have been proposed to model text, multimedia, spatial and temporal data during the recent years. Although technically they can be categorized in the third generation of database systems, the uses of these database systems in their specialized domains make them distinguishable from the various generations.

Document Processing

We hinted earlier that meaningful queries could be performed on documents if they contain some structural information in addition to the actual text content. In this section, we discuss the basic concept of "structured documents" as well as information retrieval for both structured and non-structured documents.

Structured Documents

In this chapter, when we refer to documents, we primarily mean documents in electronic form. The simplest type of electronic document is plain text, which contains only the natural language text of the document, with much restricted formatting and structural information. In addition to the text, these documents may only contain spacing and positioning constraints on the text to convey specialized meanings to the text. The main advantage of plain text documents is that they can be created on any platform without the use of any special software, and hence they are highly interchangeable. However, because of the lack of presentation and layout capabilities, plain text documents have limited use.

The advent of word processing and text formatting systems introduced tagged documents to substitute for plain text documents. Word processors, such as Microsoft Word™, primarily use tags specific to the system, using encoding that only particular word processors can decipher. Text processing systems, such as roff and T_EX, use special codes that can be entered using a computer keyboard. These utilities can process such documents containing appropriate layout codes for the purpose of viewing on screen or printing on paper. Roughly speaking, we term documents with additional embedded information as *tagged* or *structured documents*. Tagged documents can be classified in the following two major classes based on the type of tagging involved:

- *Specific tagging*. In this type of tagging, the tags primarily have font, size and other formatting information and do not necessarily define any logical regions in the document. Examples of this type of document include word-processor documents and documents in roff, T_EX and other related document preparation formats.

- *Generic tagging*. In this type of tagging, the tags do not specify any font or size information but are more general in nature. The primary purpose of these tags is to define logically distinct regions in the document such as chapters, sections, and headings. These tags can be translated into formatting information by applications, based on the capabilities of the platform and the screen. Documents tagged using XML and SGML are examples of this type of tagging.

Other than the two types of tags described above, there can be a mixed type of tagging, where both generic and specific tagging are involved. Tags can also be procedural, indicating some action to be performed where they appear. Documents in L_AT_EX format contain logical tags such as sections and chapters as well as font, size and spacing tags. A few of the HTML tags can also be seen under this mixed category. In addition, tags can also be *procedural*, used primarily for giving instructions to the processing application.

In the context of this chapter, however, we will use the term "*structured documents*" to denote generically tagged documents—XML and SGML documents in particular. Moreover, we will assume that the structure of the documents can be obtained from these tags and from information obtained from the tags. Hence, the contents of the documents do not need to be analyzed in order to determine the structure of the documents, which is typically the case for semistructured documents (e.g., Suciu, 1997).

Information Retrieval

As mentioned earlier, efficient storage of large amounts of text does not solve the problem of effectively extracting information from them. Fortunately, research on the issue of extracting information from large volumes of text has uncovered techniques for "information retrieval." We look at a few of these techniques in this section.

The most common method for searching information in a document repository is by using *Boolean searches* (Salton, 1991). In this type of search, a number of keywords combined with Boolean operators (such as "and," "or," "not") are specified, and the result consists of the documents that satisfy the given Boolean expression. The problem with this type of search is that all matching documents in the resulting document set are given the same importance. To avoid this, one can use the *weighted keyword search*, in which the search items are assigned weights based on their importance, and the retrieved documents can be ordered by the most relevant to the least relevant based on the number of matches and the weights of the matched terms.

Although the complexity of simple keyword search in a document is only linear to the size of the document, for very large documents this complexity turns out to be considerably expensive. For example, a simple grep[2] search for the word "tyger" in the Chadwyck-Healey poetry database mentioned earlier takes about 6 minutes (62.9 seconds system CPU time) running on a Sun Ultra Sparc 2 with 128MB of main memory. This seemingly abysmal performance is partially due to the fact that grep does not utilize the system resources intelligently, but scans the files one line at a time. Although operating systems are usually intelligent enough to cache one or more blocks of data even for single-line reads, most of the time is still in processing I/O from secondary storage and network.

The most common approach to avoid accessing the whole document repository for every search is to create indices based on the documents. The searching applications can use the indices first to determine the exact location of the file in which matches could potentially be found and retrieve data by directly accessing the document in that location. As an illustration, the same search as above using *Glimpse* (Manber & Wu, 1993), with only a small index file, on the same machine takes about 67 seconds (4.19 seconds system CPU time), an improvement of around a factor of 15 on CPU usage.

Note that this improvement is even more apparent if the search keyword appears less often. In the last example, the word "tyger" has about 400 occurrences in the database. If the same experiment is performed with the word "Casabianca" (which occurs only twice in the database), the sequential search takes about the same time as before, while the index search takes only about 2 seconds (0.19 seconds system CPU time). On the other hand, although a sequential search on the word "love" (which appears over 200,000 times) takes about the same time as before with the sequential search, it takes about 4 minutes (22.3 seconds system CPU time) with the index method. The reason for this is again because of the time spent in retrieving the results from the individual files, which is I/O intensive. Although this process involves building the indices, which takes about 2 hours, and uses about 7-8% of the size of the database, indices are only built once and can be used for all subsequent queries.

Creation of indices also requires special considerations based on the type of data to be indexed and types of queries to be supported. In any language, there are words that are used very frequently, but very rarely searched for (such as "and," "of," "or," "but," "the" in English). While creating indices, these words make the size of the auxiliary index structures larger, thus affecting the search time. Indexers often ignore such words, commonly referred to as "stop" words. While indexing, it is often useful not to create separate index entries for all forms of the same word (such as various verb forms, tenses and numbers) and only include the root word in the indices.

In summary, most of these techniques use the full text of the documents to build smaller auxiliary structures that can be searched faster than the actual documents. Worldwide availability of these documents is now possible using the WWW, which in turn is developing the concept of *digital libraries,* containing not only text, but also images, sound and other multimedia objects.

RELATED WORK

Pioneering work on document processing started with research on information retrieval as elaborated earlier. Research on structured document retrieval started much later, primarily with the advent of the Internet. Searches on structured documents differ from searches on unstructured documents in their obvious use of structure in addition to data. Henceforth, searches that use structure in addition to data will be called queries. Query processing has been a very important topic of research in database systems and quite unsurprisingly so in structured documents. Such research has produced a number of query languages and processing techniques. For the purpose of this chapter, we classify the query language research in structured documents into two broad categories:

a) top-down approaches, where a data model is developed and subsequently a query language and access methods are designed and
b) bottom-up approaches, where a data structure is designed that is capable of efficient processing of special queries, and a language and model are developed based on this structure.

The top-down approach includes the object-oriented methods used by Abiteboul and others (Abiteboul, Cluet & Milo, 1993; Christophides et al., 1994), complex-object techniques used by Desai et al. (1986) and Pistor and Traunmueller (1986) and the grammar-based approached used by Gonnet and Tompa (1987). The first two classes of this approach use an existing database model to capture document structure, and the capabilities of this database model for query processing. Abiteboul et al. use the object-oriented database O_2 (Bancilhon et al., 1988) for modeling documents, by proposing mapping techniques from SGML DTDs to object-oriented schema. Document queries are then written with simple extension to the query language O_2SQL, provided by O_2. The grammar-based approach uses context-free productions to model document structures and operations on strings on such grammars to perform searches.

The bottom-up approach includes two well-known data structures—Patricia tree (Gonnet and Baeza-Yates, 1991) and concordance list (Burkowski, 1992). The Patricia tree structure has the distinct ability of searching for strings in time linear to the query and can be extended to include structure in addition to data in its searches. The Pat software (Open Text, 1994) based on this data structure includes a query language capable of performing different types of search operations, including Boolean combinations of such operations. The concordance list structure has also been implemented in the public domain structured search tool called Sgrep (Jaakkola & Kilpelainen, 1995).

Although mapping structured documents into an existing database model seems to be viable and tempting, the mapping process does not capture all the properties of SGML documents. Moreover, the requirement of converting huge amounts of document data into a completely different format seems to be somewhat wasteful. In addition, documents are often distributed in read-only media like CD-ROMs, and keeping documents in their natural space in their natural format is very effective in creating document storage systems. Thirdly, converting documents to a database format such as the object-oriented database violates the concept of closure, even if the output of the OQL queries are converted back into a document format. The method presented in this chapter belongs to the top-down approach, but avoids the conversion of documents into standard database formats, thus attempting to include the best of both of these worlds.

In addition to unstructured information retrieval and structured query processing, a recent trend has been felt towards query processing on semistructured documents. The documents on the web are typically classified in the semistructured category since most of the documents on the web do not follow the HTML structure properly. More importantly, the HTML structure is typically abused for layout purposes and in many cases does not accurately reflect the structure of the documents. In these cases, the structure of the documents often needs to be determined from the data and the links between various documents. However, the research in this area has produced many important query languages such as *Lorel* (Abiteboul et al., 1997) that have equal impact on the structured document query processing research, although primarily designed for semistructured document processing.

Recently, the World Wide Web Consortium (W3C) has taken up the task of designing a standard query language for XML and put forward a set of requirements for such a language. A number of query languages for XML have been proposed—such as XMLQL (Deutsch et al., 1998) and XQL (Robie, Lapp and Schach, 1998). Both of these query languages use the XML structure to allow retrieval, traversal and reconstruction and restructuring of documents. XMLQL uses a WHERE-CONSTRUCT notation to specify conditions and restructuring of XML elements. On the other hand, XQL uses an extension to the XSL (eXtensible Style Language) pattern language to incorporate querying capabilities into XML.

DOCUMENT MODELING USING STRUCTURED DATA

The model of the document repository presented here is fairly simple. Our database is a set of valid or well-formed documents. A document is an instance of a hierarchical structure, which is defined by a DTD. A DTD can be represented with a quintuple $d=(\tau, G, A, C, P)$ where $\tau \in$ **doc** is a document type, $G \subseteq \mathbf{GI}$ is a set of generic identifiers, $A \subseteq$ **att** is a set of SGML/XML attributes and $C \subseteq$ **dom** is a set of constants. P is a set of production rules describing the structure of conforming document instances. Analogous to the relational database model, the DTD serves as the schema for the managed data, and documents conforming to the DTD serve as instances of the schema. In the case of well-formed XML documents without an available DTD, a DTD can be generated if necessary using methods such as Garofalakis et al. (2000).

Path Expressions

We use two path connector operators—"." and ".."—to describe our path expressions. In the rest of this chapter, we will often generalize the path expression operations with the symbol " ° "—which refers to either of the two path expression operators. These two operators, along with the assumption that they act on GIs, define the notion of "simple path expressions," as follows:

- *Null path.* ε, the null path, is an SPE.
- *Basic path.* Every ***GI x*** $\in$ **GI** is an SPE and is termed "basic path."
- *Listed path.* A listed path P is a fully expanded SPE of the form where $n \geq 1$, and for every i, $A_i \in$ **GI,** and A_{i+1} is in the *content group of* A_i.
- *Abbreviated path.* An abbreviated path P of the form $P_1..P_2..\cdots P_k$ is an SPE, where $k \geq 1$, and for every i, P_i is a basic or listed path. This notion is similar to the partial path specification in Van Den Bussche and Vossen (1993) and the ".." operator in Christophides et al. (1994).

For example, in a simple poetry database, if the top-level tag is POEM, then POEM.TITLE will reach all titles directly under POEM in the hierarchy (only poem titles), while POEM..TITLE will reach all TITLE tags reachable from POEM, any number of level deep (so these will include titles of poems as well as titles of included cantos and divisions).

DOCUMENT QUERY LANGUAGES

Based on the above document model and path expression constructs, we now present a set of query languages. We show that having (i) the means for accessing the hierarchical structure of the documents using path expressions and (ii) the ability to create new structures give these languages the power to perform searches on documents with embedded structure.

Formal Languages

Document Calculus (DC)

The main feature of the method presented here is its close resemblance with the well-known and well-established languages in the relational domain. Our algebra and calculus languages bear strong resemblance with the relational algebra and calculus. The terms in this language include constants (primarily text data), typed variables x_τ where the type τ refers to the structure of the possible values of x, specified by the corresponding GI. In addition, we have path terms of the form $x \circ P$, where $\circ$ is one of the two path operators as above, and P is a simple path expression. Notice that each term in this language (except the constants) refers to a set of documents. Hence, all operators involving terms in our language are set operators. We allow the standard set comparison operators, membership operators on sets and atoms, and two special operators $\cap$ and $\cap$ that test whether two sets intersect (i.e., whether they have a common member or not). We also allow standard logical R) and $\neg$ (NOT). Our predicates include document predicates (like relational predicates in relational calculus) and path predicates of the form $D \circ P$ where D is a document type and P is a path expression.

Based on the above notions of terms and predicates, we can define the DC formulas by induction:

1. *Atomic formula.* $R(x)$ is an atomic DC formula, where R is a predicate.
2. $x \circ P\theta c$ is a DC formula, where $\theta \in \{\ni, \ni\}$, $x \circ P$, is a path term representing a set of documents and $c \in$ **dom** is a constant.
3. $t_1 \theta t_2$ is a DC formula, where $\theta \in \{=, \neq, \subseteq, \subseteq, \cap, \cap\}$ and $t_1 = x_1 \circ P_1$ and $t_2 = x_2 \circ P_2$ are two path terms.
4. If φ and ϕ are formulas, so are $\phi \vee \varphi$, $\phi \wedge \varphi$ and $\neg\phi$.
5. If $\phi(x, x_1, x_2, \ldots, x_n)$ is a DC formula with $n+1$ free variables $x, x_1, x_2, \ldots, x_n$ $(n \geq 1)$ then $\exists x \phi(x, x_1, x_2, \ldots, x_n)$ and $\forall x \phi(x, x_1, x_2, \ldots, x_n)$ are also DC formulas.
6. If ϕ is a formula, so is (ϕ).

We also define a *safe* version of the DC formulas, in which every free variable is restricted by an expression to ensure that no variable can either be unbound or have an infinite set. Typically we represent variables in the safe formalism with the form x^Q, where Q is a previously computed finite set of documents.

A query in DC is of the form $\{x \mid \phi(x)\}$, where ϕ is a safe DC formula. We reduce all our formulas into formulas with a single variable by introducing a tuple construction mechanism. A new tuple can be constructed using an expression of the form $z=R\langle x, x_1, x_2, \ldots, x_n\rangle, n \geq 1$. A formula with multiple free variables can then be converted into a formula with a single variable as follows:

$$\phi_1(z) \neq (z=R\langle x, x_1, x_2, \ldots, x_k\rangle \wedge \phi(x, x_1, x_2, \ldots, x_k))$$

To illustrate the capabilities of this language, let's take a simple example of poems in a poetry database, and consider two queries on such a database as illustrations:

1. Find the pairs of names for poets who have at least one common poem title.

   Let $\varphi = \{z \mid poem(z)\}$. The query is then represented as:

$$\{v \mid v=R\langle w,z\rangle) \wedge \exists x,y(x^{\varphi}..title \cap y^{\varphi}..title \wedge x^{\varphi}.\varepsilon \cap y^{\varphi}.\varepsilon \wedge x^{\varphi}..poet(w) \wedge y^{\varphi}..poet(x))\}$$

2. Find the poems that do not have the word "love" in the title.

$$\{x \mid poem(x) \wedge \neg x^{\{z \mid poem(z)\}}..title \ni "love"\}\}$$

Document Algebra (DA)

In addition to the calculus, we have an algebraic language that captures the procedural counterpart of DC. Like relational algebra, DA consists of operators defined as functions from one or more sets of documents to another set of documents. Every DA operation is typed, i.e., every operation generates documents of a known type, which may be created as part of the operation. We identify a set of primary operations: path selection (°), cross product (x), selection (σ), union ($\cup$), intersection ($\cap$) and set difference (-). Other common operations that can be derived from the primary operators are join (Æ), projection (π), generalized product ($\prod$) and root addition (ρ). A summary of DA expressions involving these operators, their types and the schema productions added by these operators is shown in Table 1. Here the $\tau_i s$ represent the types of various expressions, $P_i s$ represent path expressions and $E_i s$ represent DA expressions. The functions and return the *first(P)* and *last(P)* generic identifier respectively in the path expression P.

The two illustrated queries on the poetry database of the previous section will look like the following in DA:

1. Find the pairs of names for poets who have at least one common poem title.

$$\pi_{P_1..poet,P_2..poet}\left(\sigma_{P_1..poet \neq P_2..poet}\left(\rho_{P_1} Poem \rhd\lhd^{R}_{P_1..title \cap P_2..title} \rho_{P_2} Poem\right)\right)$$

2. Find the poems that do not have the word "love" in the title.

$$Poem - \sigma_{poem..title \ni "love"} Poem$$

Table 1. Document Algebra operations, types and new created productions

Expression	Type	New productions	Semantics
D	D		Documents
$E \circ P$	$last(P)$		Traverse P from E
$E_1^{\tau_1} \cup_R E_2^{\tau_2}$	R	$R \to \tau_1 \mid \tau_2$	Untyped union
$E_1^{\tau} - E_2^{\tau}$	τ		Set difference
$E_1^{\tau_1} \times_R E_2^{\tau_2}$	R	$R \to \tau_1, \tau_2$	Cross product
$\sigma_\gamma E^\tau$	τ		Selection on E on the condition γ
$E_1^{\tau} \cup E_2^{\tau}$	τ		Typed union
$\pi^{R}_{P_1,P_2,\ldots,P_k} E^\tau$	R	$R \to first(P_1), first(P_2),\ldots first(P_k)$	Projection of the paths P_i from E
$\Pi^{R}_{E_1^{\tau_1}\ldots E_n^{\tau_n}}$	R	$R \to \tau_1,\ldots,\tau_n$	n cross products in sequence
$\rho_R E^\tau$	R	$R \to \tau$	Create a root R on top of E
$E_1^{\tau_1} \rhd\lhd^{R}_{P_1 \theta P_2} E_2^{\tau_2}$	R	$R \to \tau_1, \tau_2$	Join on E_1 and E_2

Practical Languages

Document SQL (DSQL)

This section describes our SQL-like language DSQL (Document SQL). Note that DSQL is different from SDQL (Standard Document Query Language, which is a part of the ISO 10179 DSSSL (Document Style Semantics and Specification Language) standard (ISO 10179, 1994). DSQL is language reminiscent of SQL (ANSI, 1986) and is derived from DC in the same way SQL is derived from relational calculus. The primary motivation behind having such a language is to provide users of database systems with a simple means for expressing queries using a natural language form. Also, since SQL is widely accepted as a standard query language for relational databases, it was a natural choice as a document database query language. Conceptually DSQL supports SGML documents as the objects for constructing queries. From the language point of view, however, there are only two major differences from the standard SQL, which are the following:

1. *Path expressions.* Path expressions are handled in the same way they are handled in the formal languages. To use path expressions, two main changes are made to SQL. The standard operator "." (used commonly in SQL to denote relation attributes) can now be cascaded to express listed paths. In addition, a ".." operator is introduced, which is used to construct an abbreviated path from a listed path.
2. *Complex selections.* Standard SQL deals with flat tables as primary objects and hence specifies the output as a number of columns that constitute the output table. In DSQL, the primary objects on which queries are built are documents. To ensure closure, output of queries is also specified using document formulation constructs.
   To accommodate this feature, the select clause allows the creation of composite document types from constituent components. This is similar to the tuple construction operation in DC, using which new types are created.

In this section, we present a subset of the complete DSQL language that we call core DSQL. This subset contains the core SELECT - FROM - WHERE construct of the language without any aggregate functions and nested queries. In addition, the core language does not include any grouping or ordering mechanism. This core language is used primarily to demonstrate the power of the proposed extensions to SQL. The grammar for the complete language can be obtained from Sengupta (1997).

A BNF representation for the core DSQL grammar is shown in Figure 1. In order to reduce the size of the grammar, we remove any implicit operator precedence in the logical operations. In addition, we only consider comparison predicates as in the formal language, but restrict the comparison operator to the operator as described earlier. To simplify the presentation, we represent the operator with the simple equality symbol = (i.e., the expression A = c checks if the constant c is in the set returned by A).

The BNF in Figure 1 captures the complete syntax of the core DSQL language. The basic idea is the same as the calculus language presented earlier; quantification operations are the only missing operations from the calculus presented earlier. The complete language presented in Sengupta (1997) includes all the advanced features of SQL. The primary motivation for a core subset of the language is to identify the most critical features of the language and provide methods for implementation of such features. In a subsequent section, we show how this language is implemented using available systems and languages.

The core DSQL is the most important starting point in the design of a practical document query language. The most important aspect of this language is that it provides a link to the theoretical foundations introduced earlier in this chapter and allows extensions to the language to be implemented on top of the core component with a known expressive power. We show here that any DSQL query can be expressed using an equivalent DC query.

Theorem. Any core DSQL query is equivalent to some DC query.

Proof. We prove this by taking a core DSQL query and showing how the same query is equivalent to a DC query. A completely general query is difficult to formulate, so we take a query representing all the features of the core DSQL:

SELECT	$R(D.P_{o0}, A_1.P_{o1}, A_2.P_{o2} ..., A_3.P_{ok})$
FROM	$D, D.P_{a1}\ A_1, D.P_{a2}\ A_2, ... ,D.P_{ak}\ A_k$
WHERE	$D.P_{j1} = D.P_{j2}$
AND	$A_1.P_{c1} = a_1$
OR	$A_2.P_{c2} = a_2$
AND	NOT $A_k.P_{ck} = a_k$

The previous query is not fully general, but it includes most of the

Figure 1. BNF for the core DSQL Language

query_exp	::=	SELECT output qry-body
output	::=	outputname(target)
target	::=	scalar-exp-list | *
scalar-exp-list	::=	scalar-exp [, scalar-exp]*
qry-body	::=	from-clause [where-clause]
from-clause	::=	FROM db-list
db-list	::=	db [, db]*
db	::=	path-exp [alias]
where-clause	::=	WHERE search-cond
search-cond	::=	[NOT] search-cond | search-cond AND search-cond | search-cond OR search-cond | bool-term
bool-term	::=	comp-pred | (search-cond)
comp-pred	::=	scalar-exp = scalar-exp
scalar-exp	::=	atom | col
col-list	::=	col [, col]*
col	::=	path-exp
path-exp	::=	path-list [.. path-list]*
path-list	::=	gi [. gi]*

prominent features of the core DSQL. In the above, P_{oi} represents output path expressions, A_i represents aliases, and a_i represents constants. This query is essentially a rewritten version of the following DC query:

$$
\begin{aligned}
& \{z \mid z = R\langle z_0, z_1, \ldots, z_k \rangle \wedge D.P_{a1}(A_1) \wedge D.P_{a2}(A_s) \wedge \ldots \wedge D.P_{ak}(A_k) \wedge \\
Q^{DC} = \; & D.P_{o0}(z_0) \wedge A_1.P_{o1}(z_1) \wedge A_2.P_{o2}(z_2) \wedge \cdots \wedge A_k.P_{ok}(z_k) \wedge \\
& D.P_{j1} = D.P_{j2} \wedge A_1.P_{c1} = a_1 \vee A_2.P_{c2} = a_2 \wedge \neg(A_k.P_{ck} = a_k)\}
\end{aligned}
$$

The equivalent expressions for any core DSQL query can be constructed in a similar manner.

Examples

Using this language, the queries presented earlier would be formulated as follows:

1. Find the pairs of names for poets who have at least one common poem title.
   SELECT poetpair(p1..poet,p2..poet)
   FROM Poem p1, Poem p2
   WHERE p1..title = p2..title
   AND p1..poet <> p2..poet
2. Find the poems that do not have the word "love" in their title.
   SELECT poem
   FROM Poem
   WHERE NOT (poem..title = "love")

DSQL DTD

The DSQL syntax described in the previous section can be translated into an SGML DTD, which can be used to write valid queries. There are a few distinct advantages of using SGML as a query language:

1. First and foremost, this query language retains the properties of both SQL and SGML. Being an application of SGML, this language is inherently portable and is independent of the underlying system and platform. On the other hand, since it is equivalent to DSQL, the DSQL DTD defines a first order, low complexity query language.
2. Since queries are in SGML, which is the same data format as the database itself, the queries can be stored and managed in the same way as the data itself. This leads to the concept of *compleat closure* (Sengupta, 1999), where the query itself, in addition to the input and output (and in many cases the schema as well), is in the closure domain. This immediately implies some interesting possibilities:
   - Queries can be stored as data and, subsequently, can be queried

themselves to extract information that will be very suitable in applications such as data mining and performance tuning.
- The capability of storing queries as data allows subsequent treatment of data as queries. This ability is commonly known as "reflection" in programming languages and gives a language a higher expressive power and the capability of performing metadata queries. Many attempts of providing reflection support in query languages have been researched (Jain, Mendhekar and Van Gucht, 1995), and the use of SGML as a query language for SGML databases provides a natural way to achieve this property.

3. Queries formulated and stored in SGML can easily be converted into any other query language (including visual query languages) without much effort.
4. Users posing queries in SGML can do so within their familiar environment of SGML editors. This capability also ensures that they do not have to learn the syntactic details of a new language, and a validating editor will ensure that all the queries are valid DSQL queries.
5. SGML queries can be seamlessly integrated within other SGML documents (possibly using the SUBDOC feature of SGML) for dynamic document content.
6. Queries embedded in a document can be replaced by the results obtained from the queries before presenting the final document. This is a natural way of dynamic document content generation for the WWW.

Examples

Consider the queries we used as examples earlier. Here we present the same queries written in SGML using the SQL DTD. The queries are completely normalized, so they display all the necessary open and close tags, and hence have somewhat expanded size. However, in real situations, these queries will be created using an SGML editor or a translator from the regular SQL, and most of the tags as shown here will be hidden from the users.

1. Find the pairs of names for poets who have at least one common poem title.

```
<select>
 <output><scalar><col><pathlist><gi>P1</pathlist>
  <pathlist><gi>poet</pathlist></col></scalar>
 <scalar><col><pathlist><gi>P2</pathlist>
  <pathlist><gi>poet</pathlist></col></scalar>
 </output>
<from><db alias="P1"><pathlist><gi>poem</pathlist>
```

```
 </db><db alias="P2"><pathlist><gi>poem</pathlist></db></from>
<where><cond><cond><predicat><compare EQUAL>
  <scalar><col><pathlist><gi>P1</pathlist>
   <pathlist><gi>title</pathlist></col></scalar>
  <scalar><col><pathlist><gi>P2</pathlist>
   <pathlist><gi>title</pathlist></col></scalar>
  </predicat></cond>
<logic AND>
  <cond NOT><cond><predicat><compare EQUAL>
   <scalar><col><pathlist><gi>P1</pathlist>
    <pathlist><gi>poet</pathlist></col></scalar>
   <scalar><col><pathlist><gi>P2</pathlist>
    <pathlist><gi>poet</pathlist></col></scalar></predicat></cond>
  </cond></cond>
</where></select>
```

2. Find the poems that do not have the word "love" in the title.

```
<select>
  <output><scalar><col><pathlist><gi>poem</pathlist>
   </col></scalar></output>
<from><db><pathlist><gi>poem</pathlist></db></from>
<where>
  <cond NOT><cond><predicat><compare EQUAL>
   <scalar><col><pathlist><gi>poem</pathlist>
    <pathlist><gi>title</pathlist></col></scalar>
  <scalar><atom>"love"</scalar></predicat></cond>
  </cond>
</where></select>
```

QBT: A Visual Query Language

This research generalizes the Query By Example language (Zloof, 1977) for application in databases containing complex structured data. QBE is suitable for relational databases since it uses tabular skeletons (analogous to tables in the relational model) as a means for constructing queries. Thus, the template for presenting queries in QBE is similar to the conceptual structure of the instances in the database. We use this idea to generalize QBE for databases where each data instance, albeit complex, has a simple visual model. We base this assumption on the fact that human beings form a mental model for the tasks that they intend to perform (Booth, 1989). For example, users performing a search in a dictionary may not know the internal structure and representation of each definition, but they usually have an idea about a visual structure of a dictionary entry, assuming they have used dictionaries in print. In our method, that we term "Query By Templates" (QBT), the basis of the interface is a visual template representing an instance of the database. Simple examples of templates include (i) a small poem for poetry databases, (ii) a table for relational databases, (iii) a representative word definition for a dictionary database, and (iv) a sample entry in a bibliography database.

QBT is primarily designed to be a simple point-and-click interface for posing queries in document databases without the necessity of knowing and understanding the internal structure of the database and without learning complex query language syntax. In spite of its apparent simplicity, QBT is a powerful language that can express the same class of queries as the core DSQL language introduced earlier. As in the core DSQL, the current design of QBT does not address nesting of queries.

In this section, we describe the rationale behind the QBT interface. Next, we introduce the concept of templates and describe the various types of templates considered in this design. We then describe the process of formulating queries using templates.

The main rationale for the idea of querying using templates comes from the fact that users tend to form a distinctive mental model for tasks they perform. Simply described, a mental model is a mental image of the expected task (both the process of performing the task as well as the result on completion of the task) that the users conceive of before they actually begin any task. For example, users planning to write a letter may have a mental image of what the letter would look like once it is completed. During the process of carrying out the task, users try to use a tool that can help them achieve their conceptual goal. Analogously, in order to search for information in a repository, users form similar visual images of what they are looking for. This visual image is what we try to capture using the concept of templates.

Let us explain this further with an example. Jane Doe was looking for a poem in a database of poems. She knew that Blake wrote the poem, and she knew that it mentioned the word "tiger" in the first line. However, using the conventional search techniques, she either could not retrieve the poem or had too many matching poems. On subsequent brainstorming, she also remembered the occurrence of the word "burning" in the first line, and with some effort, she could retrieve Blake's poem "The Tyger." Of course, the word "tiger" in this particular instance was spelled as "tyger."

One might correctly argue that Jane's problem could be solved using a search method that can perform approximate searches. However, the goal of this research is not to design approximate search techniques. What is more

Figure 2. (a) A simple template (b) the poem represented by the template

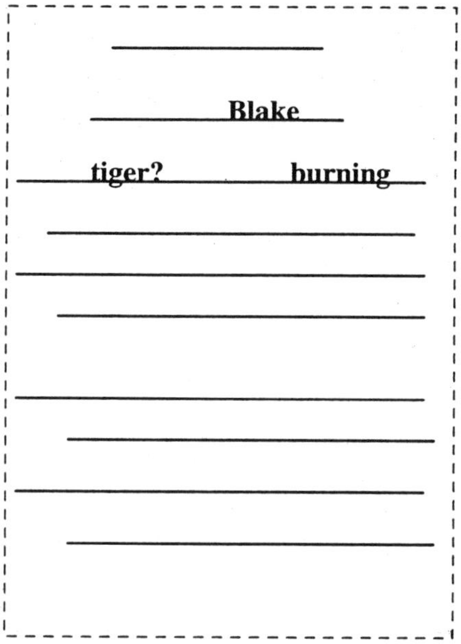

(a)

The Tyger

William Blake, 1757-1827

Tyger Tyger, burning bright,
   In the forests of the night;
What immortal hand or eye,
   Could frame thy fearful symmetry?

In what distant deeps or skies
   Burnt the fire of thine eyes!
On what wings dare he aspire?
   What the hand, dare sieze the fire?

And what shoulder, & what art,
   Could twist the sinews of thy heart?
And when they heart began to beat,
   What dread hand? & what dread feet?

(b)

important in the above instance is the fact that Jane acquired a mental image of a poem that she wanted to retrieve, and the only portions of the poem that she could remember were the poet's name and a portion of the first line. Although her initial guess was unsuccessful, a refinement of the guess eventually resulted in a match. In this case, she had a mental image of a poem (similar to Figure 2a), which resulted in a retrieved instance (in Figure 2b).

As mentioned above, the goal in this research is to capture the mental image that users develop prior to starting a search task. QBT accomplishes this by presenting the search interface using a simple representative of the database instances. Any database that has a simple visual representation of its content can be used with QBT. For databases that do not have a general visual content, we can always revert to tables (or even forms) for use as representative templates. One of the main goals for the design of QBT was to retain all the prominent properties of QBE. The intended properties of QBT that are analogous to those of QBE are (i) simplicity, (ii) equivalence, (iii) closure and (iv) completeness.

First, QBT is designed to be simple, and it does not require users' knowledge of the complex document structure. Second, it uses templates that are conceptually equivalent to the instances of the databases. Third, QBT is "closed" in its template domain by displaying the results using the same template as the query. Fourth, one can formulate most commonly occurring queries using QBT. In the rest of this section, we describe the various types of

Figure 3. A simple template for poems, with highlighted logical regions

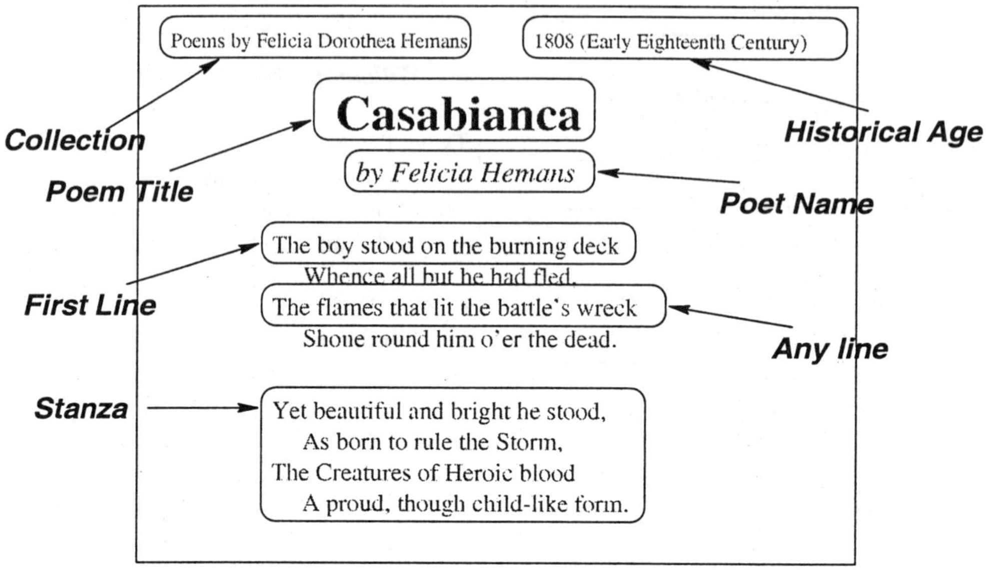

templates with illustrations, to elicit the foundation for the design of QBT.

QBT: The Basic Design

At the simplest level, a QBT interface displays a template for a representative entry of the database. The user sees an example of the type of data she would expect to find in the database, such as a poem in a poetry database. She specifies a query by entering examples of what she is searching for in the appropriate areas of the template, and the system retrieves all the database entries that match the example she provided. To illustrate the interface, we use a simple template for a poetry database, as in Figure 3. In this figure, we indicate a prominent logical region of the poem by circling it and labeling it with the corresponding region name. Physically the QBT interface consists of a small template image divided into areas corresponding to different logical regions in the database, as in Figure 3. Depending on the layout of the regions, the templates can be of different types, and these different types are described in the next sections.

Flat Templates

As described in the previous section, QBT relies on the presence of a simple visual template for the instances in the database. In most cases, this template could be planar, or flat. This means that all logical regions of the template can be displayed simultaneously in a two-dimensional image without overlapping (like in Figure 3). We call these templates "flat templates." Flat templates are usually easier to display and use, as the structural regions can be simultaneously displayed in a plane, possibly by showing multiple instances of some regions. For example, in Figure 3, the First Line and Any Line regions are subregions in Stanza. To display these subregions, the template needs to include a second stanza, which is broken into its components.

Nested Templates

Although flat templates are easy to display and navigate, they cannot model structures with deep levels of nesting. In this case, we use templates that can be nested. In nested templates, regions are allowed to overlap. In particular, certain regions can be completely inside other regions to represent subregions. To display embedded logical regions, we use one of the following methods:

Embedded regions. In this method, subregions are displayed inside the parent region. As in flat templates, all regions are displayed simultaneously in the same plane of the image. Component regions no longer need to be mutually exclusive. This method is a simple extension of flat templates, but it makes templates much more powerful while retaining the simplicity. However, this method is again limited to structures in which the nesting level is not very deep and the top-level region is physically large enough to include all the nested regions without completely obscuring itself. An example of this type of nesting in shown in Figure 4(a).

Recursive regions. This is the most general method of nesting regions. In this method, a region with subregions can be recursively expanded. During traversal, the user may "zoom in" to a parent region to display its subregions. The magnified portion of the template can be an independent template and can be subsequently magnified to get to additional levels of nesting. Although this

Figure 4. Templates with (a) Embedded regions and (b) Recursive regions

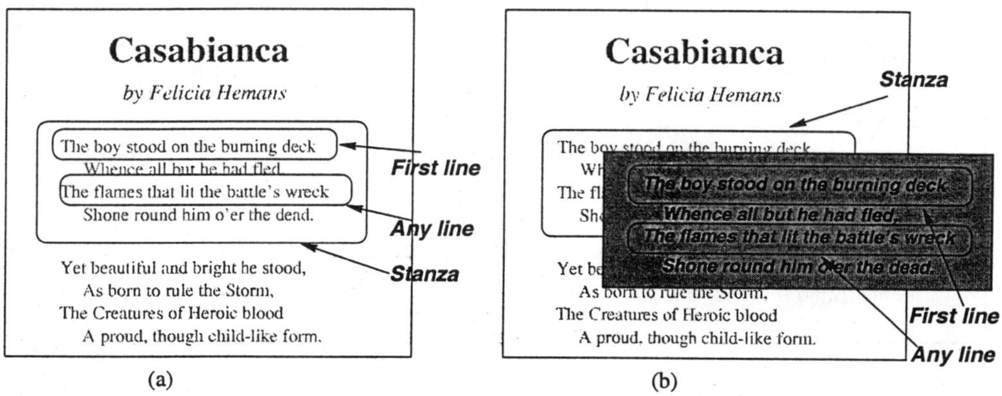

method can capture any general structure, the templates have to be cleverly designed so the nested templates do not disorient users. Figure 4(b) shows this method of displaying internal structures for the same poem example.

Structure Templates

Structures, particularly large ones, may get too complex to use nested templates. In these cases, it is often necessary to display the internal structure simultaneously with a template that displays the relative position of the current region. As mentioned earlier, most documents can be thought of as having a hierarchical structure that can be conveniently visualized as a tree. Showing a template simultaneously with a hierarchy of logical regions depicting the context simplifies the nested structure visualization. Structure templates are similar to any type of hierarchy visualization display, such as the hierarchical file structure display of Windows(tm) Explorer software. A demonstration of an actual document structure visualization can be seen in the prototype implementation of QBT.[3]

Querying With QBT

Normal keyword searches bounded by structural regions are simple in the QBT interface. As described earlier, users express their queries by indicating the search keywords in the appropriate regions of the template. In this section, we show all the different types of possible searches that can be performed with QBT.

One can treat QBE (Zloof, 1977) as a special case of QBT where the templates used are table skeletons that instantiate tables in the database. In QBE, queries are specified by entering values in proper positions of the tables. These values may be either constants (i.e., strings or numbers), variables (or

Figure 5. Query formulation with QBT: (a) simple selections and (b) logically embedded sections

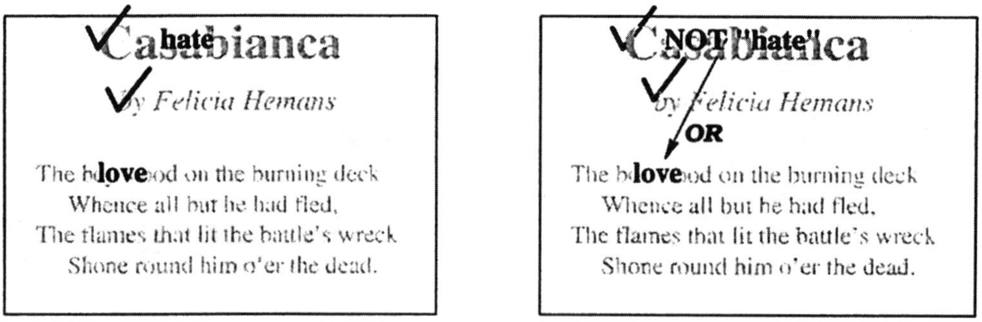

examples, usually differentiated from the constants by underlining), or expressions involving constants and variables combined with arithmetic and comparison operators. The output of the query is specified by marking the regions that need to be presented in the output. QBT uses the same basic principle, with the extension that the templates are not restricted to table skeletons but can be any visual representation of the database instances.

The primary difference between the method of expressing queries in QBT and that in QBE lies in the fact that the templates in QBE are essentially one-dimensional. Although QBE uses 2D tables for querying, the metadata (attributes of the relations) only appear along the horizontal axis as column headings of the tables. QBE uses the rows to specify multiple search conditions and logical operations between the search conditions (see examples in Zloof, 1977). In QBT, the regions (metadata) are distributed along both dimensions of the template, utilizing the whole template plane for visualizing the structure. Logical operations between regions can be expressed by physically connecting two or more regions via a logical operator. Logical operations within regions can be formed using logical expressions within the scope of that region. In the rest of this section, we discuss how different types of queries are performed using QBT.

Simple Selections

Simple selections include searching for constant strings or numbers within logical regions of the document (the whole document itself being one region). In QBT, such searches are performed by simply entering the search string in the corresponding region of the template. As a result of such a search, database instances rooted at a default region that match all the specified conditions are returned. In other words, the given search criteria are combined using a logical conjunction operation. The result of the query is by default rooted at a preselected region defined by the template. However, users can mark the regions that they want returned by placing a print-marker on them.

In the illustrations (see Figure 5), the small tick-mark is used as a print indicator. In the examples, Figure 5(a) denotes the simple query: Find the poem titles and poets of all the poems that have the word hate in the title and the word love in the first line. Note that unlike QBE, searches are substring matches instead of exact string matches. So, entering the word "love" in the region "first line" matches all poems with the first line containing the word "love" anywhere in the first line. In QBE, this is done by indicating examples before and after the search string. In case of documents, substring matches make more sense since exact searches are far less common.

Selections With Multiple Conditions

We have just seen that if multiple conditions are specified in different regions, they are combined using logical conjunctions, implying that the results returned from the query will satisfy all the specified search conditions. If this is not desired, search conditions can be combined using logical operators *AND, OR, NOT*. Negation of individual conditions is performed by placing the keyword "NOT" in front of the string. Implementations of the interface may use some visual mechanisms to place this negation keyword. Connecting various search strings using the binary operators "AND" and "OR" involves simply connecting the two strings using a pointing device and selecting the proper operation type for that connection. Figure 5(b) demonstrates how this is done by expressing the query: Find the poem titles and poets of all poems that either do not have the word 'hate' in the title or have the word 'love' in the first line. Notice the introduction of the negation and the "OR" connection.

Note that if multiple clauses are connected using logical constructs, the order in which the expressions are evaluated depends on the direction of the arrow. However, it is possible to override this order of evaluation by placing parentheses in appropriate places in a condition box, similar to QBE.

Joins and Multiple Templates

In this section, we look at a special class of query called "join." A join is an operation using which multiple fragments of a database are combined together based on some common property. Joins are indispensable in relational databases, since the relational design involves "normalizing" a schema by breaking it into flat, tabular fragments. This fragmentation necessitates combining the individual fragments together at the time of query processing using the join operation. However, in document databases, the structure is not normalized into planar fragments, but allowed to grow hierarchically, so joins are not required to combine fragments. However, joins are still useful to solve

Figure 6. Query Formulation With QBT: Joins

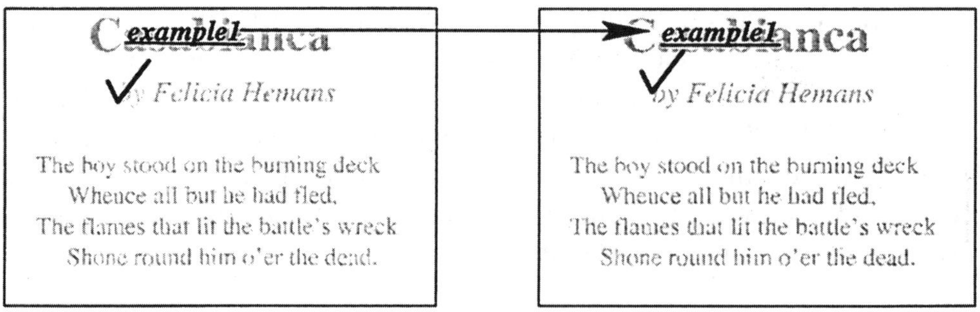

queries that require comparison of different parts of a database or different instantiations of the same database.

For example, one may try to "find the pairs of poets who have at least one poem with a common title" (as in Figure 6). In this case, we need to generate two instances of the poetry database and run the query comparing the titles of the two poems. This is achieved in QBT by using multiple templates. In the case of the above query, the same template is instantiated twice, and the join attributes are connected together. The connection can be augmented with comparison operators to specify joins other than "equi-joins" (joins that use equality on the join attributes). Once again, in the case of asymmetric comparison operations, the precedence of the operators is determined by the direction of the arrow. Although we are still using underlined examples to highlight the joins, they are redeemed unnecessarily by the use of the joining arrow.

Properties of Document Query Languages

The query languages in the above discussion exhibit many desirable properties of database query languages. Here we briefly discuss some of the significant properties and give intuitions for the proofs. The complete proofs can be obtained from Sengupta (1997).

Property 1. DA and safe DC are semantically equivalent. Any query written in DC is equivalent to some DA expression, and vice versa.

Proof sketch. We prove this in two steps:

1. *Algebra to Calculus.* We first show that if E is a DA expression, then there is an expression E^C in DC equivalent to E. We prove this by strong induction on the number of operators in the DA expression. The base case is given by the expression D with 0 operators, where the equivalent calculus query is $\{x \mid D(x)\}$. We use a strong induction hypothesis — for any DA expression E with fewer than n operators ($n \geq 1$), we can construct a safe DC formula E^C with one free variable such that $E \equiv \{x \mid E^C(x)\}$. The proof follows by taking each of the primary DA operations and showing an equivalent calculus expression, essentially by following the set theoretic definition of each of the operations. We need to make use of the tuple construction mechanism in DC for every new type created by the DA operation.
2. *Calculus to Algebra.* We now show that for every safe DC (SDC) query, there is an equivalent DA expression. To prove this, we make use of a canonical form of DC queries. We define a *distinguished query* to be a query of the following form:

$$Q_D^{\phi} = \{z \mid z = R_0\langle z_1, z_2, \ldots, z_k\rangle \wedge (z_1 = R_{x_1}\langle x_1\rangle) \wedge (z_2 = R_{x_2}\langle x_2\rangle) \wedge \cdots \wedge (z_k = R_{x_k}\langle x_k\rangle)\}$$

Here all the names R_{x0}, R_{x2}, ..., R_{xk} are distinct. The names follow the intuition that all the variables in the formula are distinguished and can be individually projected out from the query via a projection.

Given the above definition of distinguished queries, we define the following three lemmas:

Lemma 1. If $Q\emptyset D$ is the distinguished query corresponding to any SDC formula $\phi(x_1, x_2, ..., x_n)$, then there exists a DA expression $E^{\emptyset}_D$, which is equivalent to $Q^{\emptyset}_D$.

This lemma can be proved by structural induction on the queries in DC. The intuition behind this proof comes from the fact that we can always add unique roots to every sub-expression. The necessity of distinguishing arises because operations such as cross product may create branches with the same type that can not be re-extracted by following projections unless a distinguishing node is added beforehand.

Lemma 2. An algebraic expression equivalent to a distinguished query can be converted to an algebraic expression that is equivalent to the corresponding non-distinguished query $\{z \mid z=R\langle x_1, x_2, \ldots, x_k\rangle \wedge \phi(x_1, x_2, \ldots, x_k\}$.

The proof is now simple owing to the fact that all the variables x_1, x_2, ..., x_k can be distinguished from each other, even if they have same type. The algebraic expression can now be obtained by performing a projection on each of the individual variables.

Lemma 3. If $\phi(x_1, x_2, ..., x_n)$ is an SDC formula, then there exists a DA expression $E^{\emptyset}$ such that $E^{\emptyset}=\{x \mid x=R\langle x_1, x_2, \ldots, x_n\rangle \wedge \phi(x_1, x_2, \ldots, x_n\}$.

The proof of this lemma can be given in three stages. First we construct a distinguished query $Q^{\emptyset}_D$ for the formula $\phi(x_1, x_2, \ldots, x^n)$. Second, using Lemma 1, we show that there is an algebraic expression $E^{\emptyset}_D$, which is equivalent to $Q^{\emptyset}_D$. Third, using Lemma 2, we show that we can obtain $E^{\emptyset}$ from $E^{\emptyset}_D$.

The proof of the original theorem essentially follows from Lemma 3, noticing that ϕ has one single free variable, so $E^{\emptyset}\equiv\{z \mid z=R\langle x\rangle \wedge \phi(x)\}$ from Lemma 3.

Property 2. DA is safe. DA maps finite sets of documents into finite sets of documents.

Proof sketch. The proof is by structural induction on the DA expressions. The base case is given by the expression D. In the induction, we show that for each of the primary operators in DA, if the constituent expressions in the expansion of the operator are finite (given by the hypothesis), the operator produces a finite set of documents. Note that all the operations are well-defined set operations on documents, and the path expressions are on document structure in XML and do not have cycles.

Property 3. DA is in PTIME. Given a DA expression E on database D, there is an algorithm A^E that can evaluate E in O(f(|D|)) time, f being a polynomial on the size of D.

Proof sketch. To determine the database size, we include not only the number of documents in the database, but also the sizes of each of the documents. Suppose the number of documents in a database is n, and the document with the maximum number of nodes in it has m nodes in its hierarchical structure. Then the product $m \times n$ gives us an approximate size of the database in the number of actual nodes.

The proof of this property is by strong induction on the number of operators on E. The base case is for $E = D$. As induction hypothesis, we assume that for an algebraic expression E with k operators ($k > 0$), there is an algorithm A^E that can evaluate E using at most $f(m,n)$ basic operations, where f is a polynomial function. The basic operations here are (i) traversal based on node label (GI) and (ii) comparison of the leaf with a query value. Both operations are considered atomic and are assumed to take constant time. The proof now follows using strong induction on the number of operators, by considering expressions involving each of the primary DA operators. The normal set operations can be shown to be polynomial, simply following the standard set computation algorithms. The main interesting operations are $E_n=E^\circ P$ and $E_n=\sigma_\Upsilon E^\tau$, since both of them involve path expressions. For the former, we can show the PTIME result simply by performing a breadth-first search on the individual hierarchies. For the latter, we need to consider two cases based on the form of Υ. If $\Upsilon=P\theta c$ then we compute the path expression first using a polynomial number of operations as above and then perform a membership check on c. If $\Upsilon=P_1\theta P_2$, the proof proceeds the same way by computing both P_1 and P_2 and then performing an intersection on the two sets, all of which can be performed in polynomial time.

Property 4. DA is closed in documents. DA expressions always generate valid or well-formed documents if the inputs are valid or well-formed.

Proof sketch. Once again, we can prove this using structural induction on the DA expressions. The base case is given by D, which is well-formed by definition. Given a hypothesis on the validity of DA expressions, we can now show validity of the results of all DA expressions. The main intuition behind this proof lies in the type creation. For validity, the generated types get added to the DTD as a new production. For well-formed documents, the type is simply used to generate the proper open and closing tag sequences to preserve the well-formed property.

Properties 5, 6, 7. Safe DC is safe, in PTIME, and closed in documents.

the well-formed property.

Properties 5, 6, 7. Safe DC is safe, in PTIME, and closed in documents.

These properties follow using the corresponding properties on DA and the equivalence of DA and safe DC.

DOCUMENT DATABASE IMPLEMENTATION

In this section, we describe various index data structures and optimization strategies used in practice for implementing structured text-based query languages. We include traditional data structures such as the Patricia tree (Gonnet and Baeza-Yates, 1991), concordance lists (Burkowski, 1992) and how such structures can be incorporated in a generalized structured query processing system. We also discuss some of the query optimization strategies that are applicable in such implementations. In this section, we include an architectural overview of DocBase and its use of the Pat structure in query processing.

Let us briefly describe architecture as well as the actual implementation of all the components of the proof-of-concept prototype of a document database system, which we call DocBase. DocBase has a client-server architecture. The server-side applications and command-line client applications are Unix-based, but the query interface clients are Web-based and, hence, platform-independent. Here we give a brief overview of the platforms, supporting applications and languages that were used to develop this prototype. We then describe the architecture and the physical data representation used in the implementation of DocBase. We then describe the query engine architecture and how queries from the user are processed.

Languages, Platforms and Tools

C++ was the primary programming language used for the implementation of the command-line and back-end clients. The Java(tm) programming language was used for implementing the Web-based query interface client. One important consideration behind the use of object-oriented languages was that they ensure easy extensibility using inheritance and overloading. Program components specific to particular platforms were kept limited to subclasses of the platform-independent generic superclasses implemented as virtual classes in C++. This type of design assures a simple design through use of features of existing applications. In the prototype implementation, we used external applications for storage management and index building.

The prototype system was designed to run on Unix. In particular, the storage management server and SGML index management servers were Unix-based applications. Hence, all the storage and retrieval functions were limited to Unix platforms. We used a SUN Sparc-5 system as a test server for the prototype application. The query interface client developed in Java was, however, platform-independent because of the availability of Java virtual machines on most platforms. The application was developed on a Unix workstation but tested on all the platforms that support Java, and it was found to work satisfactorily.

The primary supporting applications in the prototype were storage management and index management applications. The function of the storage manager was to store the special indices and catalogs, and the function of the index management module was to create special indices on the SGML documents and to facilitate navigation of the hierarchical document structure using these indices. Query processing capabilities were built into clients of the storage management system. Figure 7 shows exactly where these applications are used in the architecture of DocBase.

An Architectural Overview of DocBase

The architecture of DocBase closely follows the tri-level design of traditional database systems (physical level, conceptual level, user level). In this architecture, there are three distinct layers: (i) a top layer involving interaction with the user, (ii) a middle layer involving query parsing, translation and optimization, and (iii) a bottom layer involving actual processing of the query using a storage manager and an index manager (see Figure 7). Figure 7 presents an overall view of the DocBase system and the lifecycle of a query during its processing. The rest of this section describes the distribution of the data and indices as well as the typical data flow process for evaluation of a query.

Data Distribution

In this section, we describe the distribution of the data in the prototype among the applications that process the data. In particular, we consider the data (in the form of SGML documents and document type definitions), the index structures and the metadata or catalog information. In the current implementation of DocBase, a structured document database is physically viewed as a collection of SGML documents, each document (or possibly a set of interlinked documents) conforming to a valid SGML document type definition (DTD). There could be multiple DTDs, but every document must conform to one of these DTDs. All of these documents are stored as standard text files in the file system. In addition to the documents, special structures for the purpose of indexing and searching are also stored. In this section, we present the details on how the data (SGML documents), indices, and catalogs are physically stored in DocBase.

Data. In the current prototype, the data is stored in the form of SGML documents in a file system. While not an ideal method for a database representation, this was necessary to allow the use of Pat for the index creation process. For this prototype, advanced storage management issues such as concurrency control and recovery of documents were not considered. In

Figure 7. Architecture of DocBase

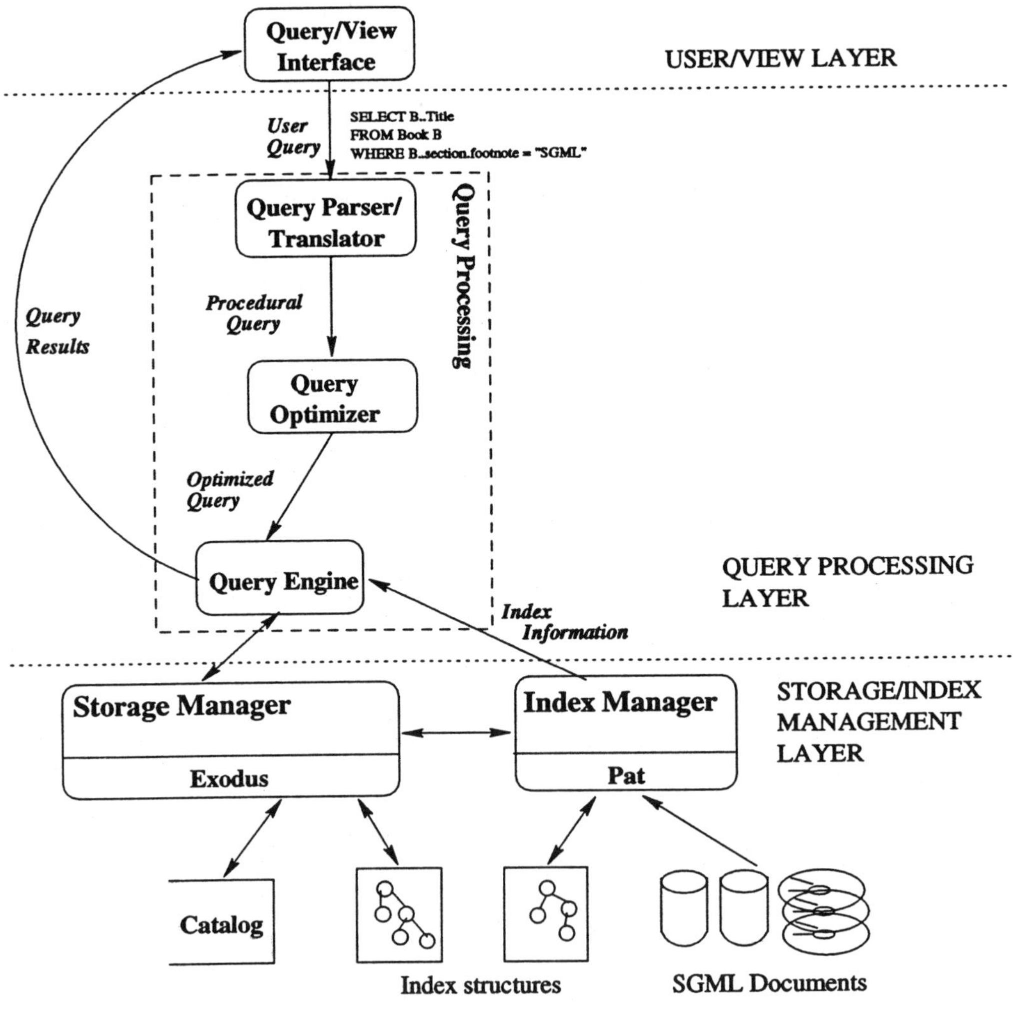

addition, in order to keep a correspondence between the documents and their physical storage, documents conforming to the same DTD were stored in the same distinct directory of the file system.

However, this distribution is not crucial for the functionality of the system. The current implementation of DocBase only has support for the core DSQL language, including simple selections and joins, and hence the input SGML data is never modified by a query. The SGML documents are only accessed by Pat and its indexing applications (see Figure 7).

Indices. Two types of indices were used for processing queries. Indices of the first type are created by the Pat indexing applications. Indices of the second type are created to speed up queries that cannot be processed using the Pat query language.[4] As shown in Figure 7, the Pat-specific index structures are accessed and modified by Pat, and the auxiliary index structures are managed by the storage manager.

1. *Pat indices*. In order to support the operations provided by the Pat query language, a Pat application needs to create some specific indices based on the input documents. The Pat indices are special binary files in a Unix file system. Pat indices of many types were created and used in this prototype: (i) word indices to speed up the search for words or phrases in the database, (ii) region indices for searching for keywords delimited by SGML elements, and (iii) fast find indices—a special auxiliary index structure supported by Pat for databases spread over multiple files in a file system. Because of the proprietary commercial nature of Pat, the internal formats of these indices were not available. However, it was known that both the word and region indices use the Patricia tree structure (Gonnet & Baeza-Yates, 1991).
2. *Join indices*. In addition to the Pat indices, auxiliary index structures were created for the processing of queries not supported by Pat (typically the queries involving joins). The auxiliary indices developed for the purpose of processing queries involving joins were created and maintained using the Exodus storage manager. These auxiliary indices can be specifically built or can be dynamically created when necessary. These join indices are created by first using a Pat query to extract the proper offsets and then indexing the result obtained from the query.

Catalog. Pat keeps track of the indices it creates in a data description file using a tagged format. This file (known as the data description file) is also stored in the file system as a regular text file. The information contained in this file is primarily for use by Pat in processing its queries. The current implementation of DocBase also creates a detailed catalog of objects in the database, including a binary representation of the document structure and a list of the different types of objects (e.g., SGML documents, DTDs, stored queries, auxiliary join indices and temporary structures). More details on these structures will be provided later in this chapter. As shown in Figure 7, the storage manager has full control over this catalog information.

The Life Cycle of a Query

This section describes the process by which a query is formulated, processed and evaluated in the current implementation of DocBase. Note that this section only describes the flow of the query as shown in Figure 7.

The user usually formulates a query by using either (i) a command-line interface to directly specify the query in DSQL or (ii) a graphical user interface such as QBT. Queries from the user are processed by a parser, which translates the query into a list of individual operations (or query fragments) in addition to determining the validity of the query.

The query components generated by the parser are optimized by a query optimizer and evaluated by the query engine. Currently the query optimizer is used primarily to determine the nature of each of the query fragments and to determine an access plan for processing each fragment. Based on the type of query fragment, the target element of the query fragment when it is evaluated, and the current state of the computed result, one of three possible decisions is made:

- *Evaluate later.* The query fragment can be easily processed by Pat, and the current state of the query allows it to be evaluated using the Pat query language. In this case, the optimizer simply generates the query in the Pat query language and stores the current result of computation as the query itself.
- *Evaluate now.* The query can be evaluated by Pat but cannot be further processed using Pat itself. In this case, the appropriate query is constructed and sent to the Pat server for evaluation. The result is left in Pat's storage space.
- *Store now.* The current state of the query and the new query fragment cannot be combined using Pat operations. This is usually the case for join queries. In this case, the results are extracted from Pat and indexed in the storage manager, while the rest of the computation continues in the storage manager or, if possible, the result is written back to Pat's storage space for use with subsequent query fragments.

The primary function of the query engine is to evaluate the query components generated by the parser using one or more of the methods described above. For the most part, the query operations are translated to corresponding index operations using the Pat query language. The results of these operations are stored as Pat queries, but the actual evaluation of the queries is delayed as much as possible. Joins are given special attention since they cannot be performed using the Pat index operations. When a join is detected, the query is processed in the following steps: (i) identifying the two components of the join operation, (ii) evaluating the components separately using Pat indices, (iii) dynamically creating storage manager indices based on the intermediate results (if such an index does not already exist), and finally, (iv) performing the join using these special index structures.

Once all the query fragments have been processed, the query engine determines the structure and format of the output and then combines the query fragments. If Pat can process all the query fragments, this final stage consists of sending the resulting Pat query to the Pat server, extracting the result, and possibly rearranging it for presentation. In the case that portions of the query cannot be evaluated using Pat, the storage manager indices are used to evaluate those portions, and the result is converted back into Pat's storage space to combine the result with the rest of the query. The final result is extracted from Pat as a set of SGML document fragments. The current prototype of DocBase does not implement nested queries. However, it allows results of queries to be stored internally as a set of "virtual documents," similar to database views in relational databases. These "virtual documents" are not proper SGML documents; they are simply a set of offsets in the document from which the fragments were extracted. These virtual documents can be used later in a query to achieve the effect of nesting.

Figure 8. Screen Images From the Prototype QBT Implementation (a) Template Screen and (b) Structure Screen.

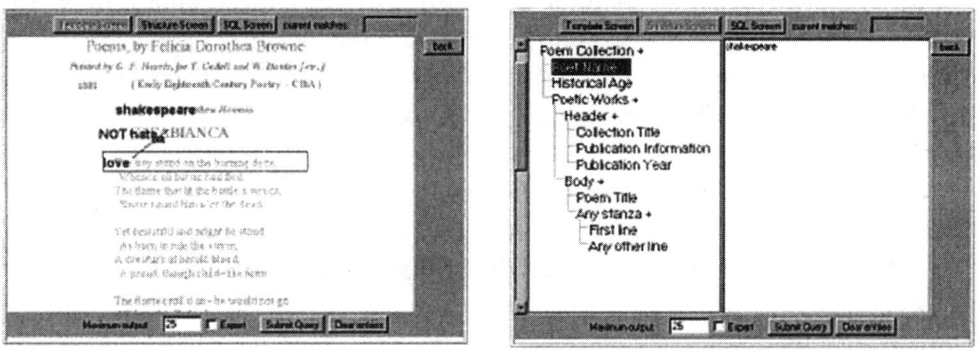

User Interface Implementation

We built a prototype[5] of the QBT interface using the Java(tm) programming language. We chose Java over other similar user-interface development languages because of its object-oriented nature and its widespread availability and use on the Web. One of our objectives in building the prototype was to be able to conduct usability experiments in the users' familiar environment. Hence the ability to run the system through the widely available WWW using Java-enabled browsers was a bonus. The prototype implements most of the querying constructs described here, including the embedded template (without recursive magnification) and the structure template. We have not yet incorporated the condition box in this prototype, but it will be added in a future release. We also included an experimental version of an SQL language translator from the QBT query. Figure 8(a) and Figure 8(b) show two parts of the screen—the template screen showing the nested template and the structure screen showing the structure template. There is a third component of the interface that displays the SQL query equivalent to the template query. This SQL query gets automatically updated as the user modifies her query using the template.

As an experiment, we used the Chadwyck-Healey English poetry database, using the poetry templates similar to those described above. In the prototype system, queries generated using the interface are sent to a query engine through HTTP (HyperText Transfer Protocol), which is run from a web server as a CGI (Common Gateway Interface) executable. The engine generates its output in HTML, which is displayed by the clients. We wrote this engine in C/C++, using the API (Application Programming Interface) provided by the Pat (Open Text, 1994) software.

QBT User Study

We performed an extensive usability analysis of the prototype interface. The main goal of this analysis was to detect differences between this interface and a standard forms-based interface with similar search capabilities. In particular, we were interested in differences with respect to *(1) accuracy, (2) efficiency and (3) satisfaction.* This section describes the method used during the experimental evaluation of the prototype Java-based (QBT) interface described above.

To compare the QBT interface with a normal form-based interface, we created a prototype form interface for searching the database with similar querying capabilities. This form uses the basic form building blocks provided by HTML in a style commonly used in web search engines. The output formats for both of these interfaces are the same and are generated by the same query engine.

Experimental Design

The experiment consisted of two primary parts. In the first part, we gave the subjects ten questions—among which we prepared nine and left the tenth question open to the subject's imagination. All subjects were given the same set of questions. The questions varied in complexity and were designed so that all except one returned some matches. The subjects were divided into two categories based on their familiarity and expertise with the subject. Each subject used one of the two interface types and answered the questions using the assigned search interface by writing down the number of matches returned by the search. The subjects were asked to ascertain that the question was interpreted properly by the searching program. At the conclusion of the experiment, the performance of each subject was evaluated based on his or her efficiency, accuracy and satisfaction. The independent and dependent variables for the experiment are outlined below.

The independent variables (determining factors) for this analysis were the following:

A. *Interface type.* (1) the QBT-based interface and (2) the form-based interface.

B. *Subject type.* (1) expert and (2) novice.

The dependent variables (evaluation factors) for the analysis were the following:

Efficiency: The amount of time in seconds the subjects take to answer each question.

Accuracy: The degree of accuracy of the queries (i.e., to what extent the queries matched the textual query given to the users).

Satisfaction: How satisfied the users were after using the interface (measured by self-reports in written debriefing).

A usability analysis procedure with a pilot test was conducted as part of this research. The first experiment was designed as a pilot test for the actual usability process. In this experiment, four subjects, one in each category (novice-form, novice-QBT, expert-form, expert-QBT), participated in this study. The main purpose of this study was to determine the appropriateness of the analysis technique and ways the experimental design could have been improved. Twenty subjects participated in the final usability analysis. We structured the study using a "between-users" strategy (Rubin, 1994), where two distinct groups of users use the two platforms. In our experiment, ten subjects were given the Java-based interface while the other ten users were given the form-based interface.

Each subject was placed in one of two distinct groups of five experts and five novices. We chose the subjects from students who volunteered to participate in the research. The only restriction imposed on the subjects was that they all be Indiana University affiliates because of the copyright restrictions on the database which we used in the experiment. We divided the subjects into two groups based on their experience with computers and databases. The subjects classified as "novices" had minimal computer expertise—generally limited to only e-mail and occasional World Wide Web access. The subjects classified as "experts" were people accustomed to using databases and the web as well as designing and programming graphical user interfaces. We made no distinctions between male and female subjects or young and old subjects, since sex and age were not considered as independent variables in this analysis. Eleven female and nine male subjects, all within the age group of 20-35, participated in this study.

We collected two types of written data: (1) the subjects' responses to the survey questions and (2) the subjects' responses to the number of matches for each search problem for the actual questions. The subjects were given ten tasks (queries) to be performed (task 1 through task 9). They were timed automatically by the server and the query engine that was actually executing the queries. The server also kept a detailed log on the actions performed by the users during the experiments, including the actual query that was executed.

This rest of this section describes in detail the results that we obtained from the usability analysis. We divide the results into three different sections, one each for the dependent variables—accuracy, efficiency and satisfaction. For each of the measures, we performed a multivariate ANOVA test with a .05 significance level. In the following, we describe the most important finding for each of the dependent variable.

Accuracy. We measured accuracy by evaluating the answers to each question on a 0-5 scale. Perfect answers were given 5 points and completely wrong answers (of course, there were none in the experiment) were given 0 points. Partially incorrect answers were given a value in the range of 1 to 4, inclusive, based on the type of mistake. The tasks 1, 2, 4 and 10 had 0 standard deviation since all users had correct answers for these tasks. For the rest of the tasks, the cumulative effect of expertise or interface was nonsignificant at the

$P<0.5$. $F(1,16)=0.02$, $p=0.886$ for interface effects, $F(1,16)=0.00$, $p=1.000$ for expertise effects, and $F(1,16)=1.05$, $p=0.322$ for their interaction: None of which show significance at $P<0.5$ level.

Efficiency. For the efficiency measure, we used the time (in seconds) between two successive submissions of queries. The absolute times at which (1) the system was first accessed and (2) the queries were submitted were logged by the query processing system. We calculated the difference between these times to get the time taken for each task by the subjects. Here, the effect of the interaction of expertise and interface was nonsignificant at the $P<0.5$ level ($F(1,15)=1.48$, $p=0.243$). However, expertise had significant effect on efficiency ($F(1,15)=25.20$, $p=0.000$). This clearly suggests that the experts were significantly more efficient than the novices using both the interfaces, so the different interfaces did not affect experts' performances. The effect of interface on efficiency, however, was marginally nonsignificant at the $P<0.5$ level ($F(1,15)=4.20$, $p=0.058$). Although this indicates that the interface does not necessarily make users significantly more efficient, this also suggests that the easier interface does not make them any slower either.

Satisfaction. For the satisfaction measure, the users were asked to grade the interface that they used in a scale of five qualitative values: (a) Much better, (b) Little better, (c) About the same, (d) Worse, (e) Absolutely worse. These five classes were assigned the ranks 5,4,3,2 and 1 respectively. This data was taken after all the actual tasks were performed and was not calculated on a task-by-task basis. From the data collected, we observe significant effect on satisfaction of the interface at $P<0.05$ level ($F(1,16) = 7.53$, $p=0.014$). However, the expertise and the interaction of expertise and interface do not show any significant results.

To summarize the above findings, we found that the QBT interface did not significantly improve the accuracy of the user queries or the efficiency of the users, but the users were significantly more satisfied with the results from the queries. Moreover, the expert users were found to be significantly more efficient with both interfaces, so the easier interface did not hurt the performance of the experts.

SUMMARY

We have proposed a language that is of low complexity, both formally and informally. Our language uses the natural hierarchical view of documents as the model and performs all operations within the domain of this model. The operations are very similar to those in the relational languages. In fact, the SQL language DSQL that is derived from DC looks and feels almost like SQL except for the path expression construct and type creation (which is also available in some form in SQL). The languages are shown to be in PTIME and have the same types of properties as their relational counterparts. We have an initial implementation of a subset of this language which has given us a fairly strong belief that such a language can be used for real structured document query processing, which will be essential as XML gains its place on the web.

FUTURE TRENDS

Recent efforts from the W3C (World Wide Web Consortium) have been applied towards finding methods to enable different types of database operations with XML. Recent research has been geared toward finding a query language for XML as well. Two languages have made significant impact on the query language audience—XQL (Robie, Lapp & Schach, 1998) and XML-QL (Deutsch et al., 1998). The query languages presented here are not specifically designed for XML, but for a generalized structured document point of view. However, they do addresses many of the issues raised by W3C. The purpose of this presentation was simply to describe a set of methodologies for document database implementation, regardless of the actual syntactic considerations. The most important notion here is that of database-like processing of documents. XML definitely holds the string to a document-centric view of future information systems. XML is general enough to represent many different types of structures, yet simple enough that it could be used by the multitude. This is clearly a sign towards the future of document repositories—maybe even a path back to Xanadu.

REFERENCES

Abiteboul, S., Cluet, S. & Milo, T. (1993). Querying and Updating the File. In *Proceedings, 19th International Conference on Very Large Databases*, 73-84.

Abiteboul, S., Quass, D., McHugh, J., Widom, J. & Wiener, J. (1997). The Lorel Query Language for Semistructured Data. *International Journal on Digital Libraries*, 1(1), 68-88.

ANSI (1986). ANSI X3. 135-1986. Database Language SQL, ANSI, 1986.

Bancilhon, F., Barbedette, G., Benzaken, V., Delobel, C., Gamerman, S., Lecluse, C., Pfeffer, P., Richard, P. & Velez, F. (1988). The Design and Implementation of O2, an Object-Oriented Database System. In K.R. Dittrich, (Ed.),. *Advances in Object-Oriented Database Systems.* LNCS 334, September.

Berners-Lee, T. & Connolly, D. (1995). HTML Markup Language - 2.0. MIT/ W3C. HTML Working Group. RFC: 1866, November.

Booth, P. (1989). *An Introduction to Human Computer Interaction.* Laurence ErlBaum Associates Publishers.

Bray, T., Paoli, J. & Sperberg-McQueen, C.M. (1999). *Extensible Markup Language 1.0.* W3C working draft, April.

Burkowski, F. (1992.). An Algebra for Hierarchically Organized Text-dominated Databases. *Information Processing and Management*, 28(3) 333-348.

Christophides, V., Abiteboul, S., Cluet, S. & Scholl, M. (1994). From Structured Documents to Novel Query Facilities. *SIGMOD RECORD,* 23(2), 313-324.

Desai, B.C., Goyal, P. & Sadri, F. (1986). A data model for use with formatted and textual data. *Journal of American Society of Information Science.*

Deutsch, A., Fernandez, M., Florescu, D., Levy, A. & Suciu, D. (1998). XML-QL: A Query Language for XML. *W3C Technical report,* available at http://www.w3.org/TR/1998/NOTE-xml-ql-19980819/.

Garofalakis, M., Gionis, A., Rastogi, R., Seshadri, S. & Shim, K. (2000). XTRACT: A System for Extracting Document Type Descriptors From XML Documents. In *Proceedings: ACM SIGMOD'2000*, Dallas.

Gonnet, G. and Baeza-Yates, R. (1991). Lexicographical Indices for Text: Inverted Files Vs Pat Trees. *Technical Report no. TR-OED-91-01*, University of Waterloo.

ISO 8879 (1986). ISO/IEC DIS 8879. Information Processing - Text and Office Systems - Standard Generalized Markup Language (SGML). Geneva.

ISO 10179 (1994). ISO/IEC DIS 10179. Document Style Semantics Specification Language (DSSSL) International Organization for Standardization and International Electrotechnical Commission. Geneva.

Jaakkola, J. & Kilpelainen, P. (1995). The Sgrep user manual. *Technical manual on-line* at http://www.cs.helsinki.fi/u/jjaakkol/sgrep.html. University of Helsinki.

Jain, M., Mendhekar, A. & Van Gucht, D. (1995). A Uniform Data Model for Relational Data and Meta-Data Query Processing. In *Proceedings of the*

Seventh International Conference on Management of Data (COMAD). 146-165.

Manber, U. and Wu, S. (1993). Glimpse: A Tool to Search Through Entire File Systems. *Technical Report no. TR-93-34*, University of Arizona.

Nelson, T. (1987). *Literary Machines.* Version 87.1, Published by Author.

Open Text (1994). Open Text Corporation. The Open Text 5.0 Users' Manual. *Technical manual,* Waterloo, Ontario, Canada.

Pistor, P. & Traunmueller, R. (1986). A database language for sets, lists and tables. *Information Systems*, 11(4), 323-336.

Robie, J., Lapp, J. & Schach, D. (1998). XML Query Language (XQL). *W3C Technical report,* available at http://www.w3.org/TandS/QL/QL98/pp/xql.html.

Rubin, J. (1994). *Handbook of Usability Testing: How to plan, design and conduct effective tests.* John Wiley & Sons, Inc.

Salton, G. (1991). Developments in Automatic Text Retrieval. *Science,* 253, 974-980.

Sengupta, A. (1997). DocBase—A Database Environment for Structured Documents. *Ph.D. Thesis.*

Sengupta, A. & Dillon, A. (1997). Query By Templates: A Generalized Approach for Visual Query Formulation for Text-dominated Databases. *Proceedings of the IEEE Symposium on Advanced Digital Libraries (ADL'97).*

Sengupta, A. (1999). The compleat closure: toward a unified view of structured document database objects. *Proceedings of the Fifth International Conference on Information System Analysis and Synthesis (ISAS '99).* Orlando, Florida.

Suciu, D. (Ed.) (1997). *Proceedings on the Workshop on Semistructured Data. Workshop associated with the SIGMOD/PODS annual conference,* Tucson, Arizona.

Van Den Bussche, J. & Vossen, G. (1993). An Extension of Path Expressions to Simplify Navigation in Object-Oriented Queries. In *Proceedings of the third international conference on Deductive and Object-Oriented Databases (DOOD),* 267-282.

Zloof, M. (1977). Query By Example: A Database Language. *IBM Systems Journal,* 16(4), 1977.

ENDNOTES

1. The Chadwyck-Healey(tm) full-text database is a collection of over

160,000 poems in digital format written by about 1,250 poets from 600 to 1900, available from Chadwyck-Healey, Inc., Alexandria, VA.

2. grep, roff, TEX, LATEX are common Unix® utilities for text processing.
3. A running demonstration of QBT, along with sample screen shots and queries, can be seen at the DocBase Web site http://www.cs.indiana.edu/~asengupt/docbase.
4. The Pat query language is part of the Open Text 5.0 Software, © Open Text Corporation, 1994.
5. The current version of the prototype implementation is available online at http://www.cs.indiana.edu/~asengupt/docbase. Note that only the interface is accessible from outside Indiana University. The results of the queries cannot be viewed from a remote location because of copyright restrictions on the data used for searching.

Chapter VII

Cooperative Document Management in Multidisciplinary Healthcare

Mareike Schoop
Aachen University of Technology, Germany

INTRODUCTION

Healthcare is a multidisciplinary setting where professionals from several disciplines need to work together to maintain or improve the health of patients. In recent years, cooperation in healthcare has become more and more important for two reasons.

The first reason is that the division of labour within healthcare has become more pronounced as patient care has become more complex with the introduction of new techniques and machines such as keyhole surgery or computer tomography. Today, nurses carry out actions that used to lie in the responsibility of doctors. For example, some nurses are allowed to give injections and nurses in hospitals can decide when it is necessary to administer drugs prescribed by doctors as "prn" (standing for "per re nata," "as required"). Some tasks previously carried out by fully qualified nurses have been taken over by auxiliary nurses or administrative staff, e.g., washing and dressing of patients, feeding patients, serving meals, requesting medical notes from patients' GPs or hospitals, etc. (Newman, 1990).

The second reason for the increased importance of cooperation in healthcare is that a more holistic approach to patient care is now taken. Patient care is no longer solely medical care but involves input from healthcare professionals coming from several disciplines (Morgan, 1993). As Newman (1990) states, the nursing profession has changed from providing subordinate duties to doctors to being responsible for patient care with autonomous nursing goals. Today, it is not permitted to discharge a patient from a hospital simply on the grounds that his or her medical treatment has finished. Nursing or social needs also have to be met before a patient can be allowed home.

As is to be expected, the areas of healthcare that see the greatest changes towards truly shared patient care are the ones where professionals from different disciplines have a large impact on the shared task of improving a patient's state of health. For example, geriatrics is a highly cooperative area. The different needs of elderly people can only be met by efficient cooperation of professionals from several disciplines (Schoop, 1998; Schoop & Wastell, 1999).

However, the reality is sometimes different: Professionals do not always understand each other and cooperation does not always work. Healthcare professionals have particular interests concerning the patients that are determined by their professional role. For example, a doctor is interested in a patient's medical complaints whereas a nurse needs to find out the care needs; a physiotherapist is interested in a patient's needs concerning daily living in order to ensure a maximal safe level of independence. According to their different interests and tasks, the professionals will notice different things when looking at the same patient which they will write down in the appropriate documents.

The move towards more cooperation is also reflected in the management of documents. The conventional practice is that each discipline manages its own documents. For example, doctors keep the medical notes which reflect the medical treatment plan; the nurses' medium of documentation is the care plan; physiotherapists and occupational therapists have again separate documents to manage. It is easy to imagine that the practice of keeping separate documents relating to the same patient can complicate or indeed inhibit communication and cooperation:

> The recording of care was held separately by each profession, the result being a collection of random notes: doctors' notes, nurses' notes, physiotherapists' notes, and occupational therapists' notes—hardly an example of an integrated, team approach to care. (...) How, in these circumstances, can there possibly be a holistic approach to patient care? (Morgan, 1993, p. 38)

For example, if a nurse needs to find out results from a medical test, (s)he would have to look in the medical notes in which (s)he might not be able to find these results since (s)he is neither familiar with the record's structure nor with the particular professional terminology used by the medical staff.

To overcome these problems, there have been attempts to develop cooperative patient record systems that would contain all clinical information about a patient and provide appropriate interfaces to the relevant data for different professional groups. For example, the PEN&PAD geriatrics project aimed at developing a cooperative system that could be used by doctors, nurses, physiotherapists, and occupational therapists (Hardiker et al., 1995; Heathfield et al., 1992, 1994). However, in the end only a nursing record system and a medical record system were designed. These systems represented the different views on patient data and the different requirements of data representation. The goal of supporting cooperation was not realised as these two systems were separate systems without the possibility of exchanging information between nurses and doctors.

Another approach to overcome the problems of keeping separate documents is the development of shared systems for documentation (Layton, 1993; Morgan, 1993; Schoop, 1998; Schoop & Wastell, 1998), which will be referred to as cooperative document management systems (CDMSs). These systems are information systems in which the documents are cooperatively managed. All information that is important for more than one discipline is recorded in the shared documents, e.g., shared objectives, multidisciplinary treatment goals, diagnoses, results from assessments. Obviously, this form of cooperative document management does not replace conventional records all together as there remain parts of the clinical record that are only relevant to one professional discipline. Cooperative document management does not mean an overload of irrelevant information but rather the support of cooperative plans of care (Schoop, 1998). It is increasingly recognised that cooperative document management systems can help to avoid cooperation breakdowns since they aim to provide a central reference point for all disciplines to focus on a cooperative plan of care (Morgan, 1993). The whole process from admission to discharge would, therefore, be visible at one glance at a level that is detailed enough to coordinate the different activities and to work towards effective discharge planning with clear responsibilities. This new initiative thus emphasises the importance of cooperative document management for effective multiprofessional cooperation and written interdisciplinary communication that are both vital to provide effective care of patients.

However, there have not been any structured approaches to cooperative document management, as shared record systems have mostly been developed by healthcare professionals on an intuitive basis to help them with their practical routines. Cooperation breakdowns cannot be prevented and communication via such cooperative systems has been shown to be problematic (Schoop & Wastell, 1999). Therefore, we argue that a fundamental overhaul of cooperative document management is required. It is not enough to provide document management systems with different interfaces according to the requirements of doctors and nurses. The fundamental problems that exist need to be solved first before any implementation can take place effectively.

In the present chapter, a novel approach to cooperative document management in multidisciplinary healthcare will be introduced that is empirically grounded while at the same time influenced by social theories and formal logics. It will be shown that most breakdowns in communication and cooperation can be avoided and, thus, effective content-based management of patient-related information is made possible. The present chapter provides the theoretical foundations for future CDMSs. Thus, we will not discuss actual implementations, but rather we will talk about the elements that need to be considered for the design of efficient CDMSs that are useful for and useable by all professionals involved.

Document management in healthcare has specific characteristics which differ significantly from those in "classical" application areas such as offices or businesses (as will become clear in this chapter). Cooperative document management is in itself an interesting area both for researchers and practitioners as it requires not only an efficient management of documents but also efficient cooperation of different professionals. In healthcare, cooperative document management concerns, on the document side, the different types of patient notes and records and, on the side of professionals involved, the multidisciplinary work of healthcare professionals from several different disciplines. Cooperative document management in healthcare is a new issue that is expected to have a great influence on work patterns and the handling of documents. The approach that will be illustrated in this chapter for the area of multidisciplinary healthcare can be applied to other areas. Thus, while healthcare is used to illustrate the approach, we can abstract from this area and will present an approach relevant to *cooperative* document management practices in general.

The outline of the chapter is as follows. In order to provide a solid empirical platform for the present work, ethnographic investigations were conducted in a multidisciplinary healthcare environment. The particular ethnographic methods that were employed will be discussed. Furthermore, the main results of the studies that are relevant for the introduction of computer-based document management systems will be summarised.

The theoretical background of the work also will be introduced. The most significant finding of the ethnographic work was that the main problems centred around communication. Fundamental communication problems between doctors and nurses existed which were an obstacle to smooth and effective cooperation. These problems were especially severe in the case of written communication which has knock-on effects on document management systems. This prompted the author to look at theories of communication as a theoretical basis for a new and more theoretically rigorous approach to the design of cooperative document management systems.

The novel approach to cooperative document management then will be introduced. The empirical data and the relevant theoretical elements are combined into a powerful framework for the design of effective cooperative document management systems. The approach will be empirically evaluated in the following section. An outlook to future trends and a final discussion will conclude the chapter.

EMPIRICAL STUDIES IN MULTIDISCIPLINARY HEALTHCARE

To collect the necessary data to provide a solid empirical platform for the work, ethnographic investigations have been carried out in a multidisciplinary healthcare setting. It was decided that the best way to find out about work practices, cooperation and documentation patterns, and potential problems would be to conduct ethnographic studies. It was felt that only by observing the work and interactions of cooperating professionals could the perspectives and the existing problems be assessed and analysed. Ethnographic studies aim to be free of the researcher's own prejudices and presuppositions to provide accounts from the participants' points of view:

> Rather than foist the categories, terminology and procedures of some academic theoretical stance, one takes the stance of the actors in that setting themselves. (Bowers, 1996, p.126)

Ethnographic investigations are relatively unobtrusive and cause little disruption to the setting observed (Burgess, 1984). The aim of our ethnographic studies was to find out in general about document management and more specifically about

- work practices,
- information flow and possible obstructions,
- documentation practices,
- cooperation structure including areas of conflict and areas where cooperation works well,

- the data and the related level of abstraction and detail that each professional group needs in order to achieve their tasks,
- what terminology is used in each professional group,
- typical communication problems,
- areas where IT could support the interaction between different healthcare professionals and the work of multidisciplinary teams.

Ethnography has been used, albeit sporadically, in relation to the design of computer systems in a variety of work settings such as offices (Rouncefield et al., 1994; Suchman, 1983), air traffic control centres (Bentley et al., 1992a, 1992b; Hughes et al., 1992, 1993), ambulance control centres (Martin et al., 1997), telephone banking centres (Martin et al., 1998), travel centres (Bullock & Goble, 1998), and the fashion industry (Pycock & Bowers, 1996). Ethnography has been mainly used as a tool for requirements analysis. As such the ethnographic findings have sometimes challenged fundamental design assumptions. For example, in a study of air traffic control (Bentley et al., 1992a, 1992b; Hughes et al., 1992, 1993) the basic assumption that routine tasks should be delegated to machines was questioned due to the ethnographic findings. It was observed that some routine tasks (such as putting flight strips in appropriate folders) include important checking procedures; this suggested that they should not be directly automated (Bentley et al., 1992a).

There has also been criticism of ethnographic approaches: Plowman et al. (1995) ask what ethnographic work studies are for as most tend not to translate their findings into concrete design recommendations.

The ethnographic methods used for the present work will be discussed and the main issues arising from the qualitative research will be summarised.

Applied Ethnographic Methods

The first step in any ethnographic study is to answer the four 'w's, i.e., where, who, what, when. The research site, the participants, the events, and the particular time need to be selected. As it is never possible to study everything in a setting, sampling methods need to be applied.

The research site was an acute geriatric ward with 26 beds which is part of a g eriatric hospital in a large English city. Geriatrics was selected because the shared care of the elderly is a highly cooperative area where many different disciplines such as doctors, nurses, physiotherapists, occupational therapists, and social workers work together to provide a shared plan of care. The ethnographic investigations concentrated on the groups of nurses and doctors as these are the main contributors to the care process. The selection of events for the research followed directly from the overall aim of the project and the selection of informants. The daily work of nurses and doctors and the ward rounds and case conferences as manifestations of multidisciplinary communication and cooperation on the ward were observed.

Participant observation is the ethnographic method that was primarily used in the present work. Participant observation involves observing people in a natural setting over a prolonged period of time and talking and listening to them. The roles that an observer can take can be distinguished into active or passive, open or covert roles (Schatzmann & Strauss, 1973). The main role of the author was "participant-as-observer," where a researcher sometimes participates but mainly observes and openly declares the role as observer. However, the author's role varied during the fieldwork: For example, in case conferences and when observing and analysing the document management practices, an observer role was mainly adopted. Here, notes were taken and no input was provided unless being invited to comment.

Once familiar with the work practices, less time was spent observing and informally talking to the participants and more time was spent carrying out interviews. Conducting interviews implies a good knowledge of the structure and dynamics of work in the setting observed. Observing is then used to confirm ideas rather than testing new ones (Schatzmann & Strauss, 1973). Semi-structured and unstructured interviews were performed with nurses and doctors about many aspects of cooperative documentation. Furthermore, interviews were carried out in the following way: A nurse was asked to summarise all relevant information about a patient for another nurse and then for a doctor; likewise a doctor was asked for a summary that (s)he would give to a colleague and one that (s)he would pass on to a nurse. These interviews showed the different information requirements as well as the assumptions of what is necessary for the other professional group.

As the focus of the ethnographic studies was on document management practices for cooperative work, document analysis played an important role. Three forms of documents were analysed: the care plan, the medical notes, and the multidisciplinary treatment goals (MDT) folder. The care plan is the nurses' main medium of documentation, whereas the doctors record in the medical notes. All information concerning more than one discipline is recorded in the shared documentation system, i.e., the MDT folder. It is confidential and may only be read by authorised healthcare professionals (as opposed to the care plan, which is stored at the end of the patient's bed and which can be read by patients and relatives).

The documents in this shared system contain the multidisciplinary goals, the responsible persons, dates, and comments relevant to the achievement of the multidisciplinary treatment goals (see Figure 1).

Observations were carried out in the ward rounds and in the case

Figure 1: An entry in the shared documentation system

Date	Multidisciplinary Goal	Action/Referral By	Review Date	Achieved Date	Comments
11/5	review disacharge plan	medics, nurses	16/5	13/5	unable to discharge due to an acute angina
17.6.	To speak with family about nursing home	social worker	24.6.	21.6.	family anxious to have her home, daughter will look after her

conferences regarding which information was documented in the shared system. Furthermore, the dynamics behind the data entries were reconstructed in the following way. Firstly, the author and the recipient of the entry were established. This was not as easy as it might seem because author and recipient are not always obvious. For example, in the second entry of Figure 1, the request was made by a nurse for the social worker to speak to the patient's family. In this case, the recipient rather than the author is recorded (as opposed to the normal practice as in the first entry). Secondly, it was found out what type of action was referred to. Thirdly, possible problems were highlighted. The last step drew on the observations of existing communication problems in that environment. For an extensive discussion of the ethnographic work conducted in the hospital, the interested reader is referred to Schoop (1998).

Results of the Ethnographic Studies

This section will summarise the results of the ethnographic studies. The discussion starts by giving an overview of the normal document management practices on the ward. Example documents of a female patient called Linda Smith[1] will illustrate the discussion. The analysis of the ethnographic work helped identify key design issues, i.e., those things that need to be considered for cooperative systems and document management in particular. The overview in this section exemplifies the key issues that will be discussed later in the chapter.

Both doctors and nurses are responsible for documentation which is a legal requirement. Doctors document in the medical notes, whereas the nurses' medium of documentation is the care plan. The staff on the ward have developed a shared documentation system which is called MDT folder or MDT system. All information concerning more than one discipline is documented in the MDT folder, for which all professionals are responsible.

On admission nurses fill in an admission form for the patient which is then stored in the MDT folder. Figures 2 and 3 show the sheet for Linda Smith.

Based on both the doctors' and the nurses' assessments, short- and long-term multidisciplinary goals and the process of shared care are then recorded in the shared system (see Figures 4 and 5[2]). The MDT folder is aimed at

Figure 2: Example of first page of admission form in MDT folder

CONFIDENTIAL HOSPITAL NHS TRUST
WARD *123*
HOSP. No. *1234* Admitted *23.1.95* CONSULTANT *WBS*

SURNAME: *Linda*
FORENAME: *Smith*
LIKES TO BE KNOWN AS:
ADDRESS: *Manchester M13*
PREVIOUS OCCUPATION:

WHO WAS INFORMED? *Husband and daughter*
TIME: *1.30 pm*
DATE: *23.1.95*

PERSON TO CONTACT IN AN EMERGENCY: *Daughter*
NAME: *Mary Miller*
ADDRESS: *Stockport SK6*
TELEPHONE NO. *4567890*

TYPE OF ACCOMMODATION:
(Tick as Appropriate)
HOUSE: √
FLAT (GROUND):
FLAT (OTHER):
BUNGALOW:
WARDE (RES.):
WARDEN (MOBILE):
E.P.H.:
NURSING HOME:
RESIDENTIAL HOME:
DELETE AS APPROPRIATE:
BED: UP/DOWN
TOILET UP/DOWN
WHO DOES PATIENT LIVE WITH? *Husband*

AGE: *66 years*
D.O.B. *8.8.28*

MARITAL STATUS:
(Tick as Appropriate)
SINGLE
MARRIED √
DIVORCED
SEPARATED
WIDDOWED

RELIGION: *C/E*

MEDICAL DIAGNOSIS

NEXT OF KIN:
RELATIONSHIP: *Husband*
ADDRESS: *Sunnyfield*
Manchester M13
TELEPHONE NO: HOME:- *9876543*
WORK:-

G.P.NAME: *Dr Hamilton*
ADDRESS *Romiley*

DOES THE PATIENT HAVE ANY DIFFICULTY WITH: REASON
STAIRS: YES/NO *uses stairs to*
BEDROOM: YES/NO *go to bed only*
TOILET/
COMMODE: YES/NO *has commode*
BATHROOM: YES/NO *downstairs*
HEATING: YES/NO

showing the whole process from admission to discharge at a glance for all professionals involved in the shared care. When the patient is ready to be discharged, a discharge sheet is filled in by the named nurse. Its purpose is to act as a checklist for the nurses who are responsible for preparing patient discharges. On it, the nurse records the discharge arrangements such as transport home, outpatient appointments, referral to district nurses, medication, etc.

Figure 3: Example of second page of admission form in MDT folder

CARERS: WHO:	 WHO:
SHOPS: *Husband* FREQUENCY: CLEANS: *Husband* COLLECTS PENSION: " COOKS: "	LAUNDRY: *Husband* GETS MEDICINES: DOES PATIENT CARE FOR ANYONE ELSE? WHO? *No*
HOME HELP: *No* HOW OFTEN: WHAT FOR?	MEALS ON WHELLS: YES/NO
DISTRICT NURSES: *No* HOW OFTEN: WHY? OTHER AGENCIES INVOLVED:	COMMUNITY NURSE FOR THE ELDERLY: NAME: CPN: YES/NO SOCIAL WORKER: YES/NO NAME: ADDRESS: TELEPHONE NO:
URGENT DOMESTIC PROBLEMS	

Figure 4: Example of first page of MDT sheet in MDT folder

HOSPITAL

Name: *Linda Smith* **Hospital Number:** *1234* **Consultant:** *WBS*
Expected Length of Stay: **Revised Discharge Date:**
Planned Discharge Date:

Short Term / Long Term Multidisciplinary Team Goals

Date	Multidisciplinary Goals	Discipline/Name	Review Date	Achieved Date	Comments
23.1.95	*To investigate cause of diarrhoea blood stained*	*Medics / Nurses*	*26.1.95*		*Stool specimen sent on 24.1.95 commenced on Loperamide*
26.1.95	*To commence 3 day faecal fat collection. Doctor will liaise with labs first and then let us know how to go about it. for ? malabsorption*	*nurses/doctor*			*weigh her* ✓ *commence on feed chart F.F.C commenced on 31.1.95 * To finish on Friday 3pm**
31.1.95	*Daughter wishes to speak to WBS*	*nurses/doctor*	*2.2.95*	*2.2.95*	*Appointment made for 12.30 pm on Thurs 2.2.95 daughter aware*
1.2.95	*To ↑ patient's mobility*	*Amy/physio*	~~*1.2.95*~~ *2.2.95*	*2.2.95*	*Patient is safe to walk with Zimmer frame*
2.2.95	*For discharge on Friday after 3pm*	*MDT*	*3.2.*	*3.2.*	*OPD with Dr. Gibbs who will review results of faecal fat collection Rels aware*
15.2.95	*RE-ADMITTED ON 15/2/95 To identify cause of re-admission (seems to be several problems)*	*MDT*	*19.2.95*		*Faecal Fat collection showed that she was passing fat not absorbing*
16.2.95	*To find out when she is due her neocytamin injection*	*Holly/Jill*	~~*17.2.95*~~ *19.2.95*	*18.2.95*	*Edith aware + will let us know*
16.2.95	*To assess social situation*	*MDT*	*22.2.95*		*Referred to Liz S/W*
16.2.95	*Poor Appetite Weight Loss*	*Dietician*	*17.2.95*		*Referred to Dietician*

Figure 5: Example of second page of MDT sheet in MDT folder

HOSPITAL

Name: *Linda Smith* **Hospital Number:** *1234* **Consultant:** *WBS*
Expected Length of Stay: **Revised Discharge Date:**
Planned Discharge Date:

Care 'Pathway'

Date	Investigations and Referrals	Action	Referral	Name	Review Date	Achieved Date	Comments
2.2.95	*To refer to gastroenterologist for opinion (Dr. Gibbs)*		✓	*doctors*			
16.2.95	*To chase up Dr. Gibb's referral*						*Hopefully to be transferred under his care and then for her to return to us*
18.2.95	*To refer to chiropody*	*Jill* →	→	→	*24.2.95*		*Form done + sent*

Key Issues

This section will summarise the key issues emerging from the fieldwork that need to be considered for introducing technology support for multidisciplinary cooperation (Schoop, 1998). Many of the issues relate to the use of documentation. Later in the chapter, the issues as a whole will be revisited and it will be discussed which of them have been accommodated in the present work and which of them have not been addressed.

1. Cooperative document management is important but breakdowns can occur.

It was found that one of the most important problems in multidisciplinary interaction is the breakdown of communication. The MDT folder is a cooperative document management system aiming to support information exchange, coordination of care, and effective cooperation. When professionals entered face-to-face dialogues they were usually able to solve their communication problems which occurred frequently. In situations where communication took place via a documentation system the problems could not be solved directly through a discussion with the communication partner. Thus, in these "non-copresence" situations communication problems could become serious obstacles for smooth and effective cooperation and could lead to breakdowns.

All members of the ward were full of praise for the newly developed MDT system. They thought that the idea was very good and indeed it was necessary to have such shared documents. However, they were not happy with the existing system.

The two extracts from the MDT sheets in Figures 4 and 5 show some typical problems: not all columns are filled in, e.g., the achieved date is sometimes missing although the action has clearly been carried out. The back page of the MDT list (the "Care Pathway") contains the columns "Action" and "Referral," which were meant to be ticked to show whether the intervention is an action or a referral. However, in this example, some professionals left both columns blank or put names in them. Furthermore, the column title "Name" is not used in a standard way either. Some professionals record the author of the entry; others record the recipient. Short-term and long-term multidisciplinary goals were supposed to be recorded on the front page of the MDT, but some of the entries for Mrs. Smith's list are clearly referrals or actions belonging to the "Care Pathway."

2. **Documentation plays a different role for doctors and nurses.** Documentation is much more a coordination tool for nurses than for doctors. The named nurse documents the daily care in the care plan, which then serves as the basis for the nurse that takes over: "So when I complete the care plan, if I'm not on on a particular day, a nurse can go to that care plan and say, right, I know all about this lady," said a senior staff nurse in an interview. Many nurses are responsible for the patient, i.e., the named nurse, the second responsible nurse, the night nurse, the team leader, and possibly other nurses; whereas, there is only one senior house officer (SHO), one (senior) registrar, and one consultant responsible for the medical care of the patients. Doctors record their medical judgement, but for them documentation serves much more as a memory aid. The nurses evaluate their care every day to assess whether the goals they set have been achieved. This is considered to be a requirement as evaluation of care must take place once every 24 hours. Doctors review their plan of treatment as well, but less frequently than the nurses. If the consultant provides input for the diagnosis or treatment of a certain patient, this prompts the ward doctor to review his or her decisions. Thus, doctors are less likely to review when they are solely responsible for the medical care. As many nurses share the care for a particular patient, the recording of evaluation is also a coordination tool.

3. **Nurses and doctors have different attitudes towards document management.** It was observed that doctors were reluctant to fill in the forms in the MDT folder although the consultant encouraged them to do so. It was mostly the nurses who recorded in it. During the ward rounds the nurses wrote down some of the doctors' statements or requests in the MDT sheets and recorded the doctors as the authors.

4. **Different linguistic styles are used by doctors and nurses.** There are major differences in both terminology and language use of doctors and nurses. Doctors use precise and short sentences whereas nurses use longer sentences and tend to explain their statements. Documentation reflects the spoken language and, therefore, different styles are used by doctors and nurses for documentation.

5. **Doctors and nurses have different professional concerns.** Obviously, doctors and nurses talk about different issues concerning the same patient. Doctors and nurses work autonomously (within the limits

of a shared plan of care). Their different aims, responsibilities, and practical concerns are reflected in their (verbal and written) utterances. For example, nurses will talk about the social background of a patient only when they speak to nurses. In an interview, a charge nurse said: "Doctors are only interested in social things if they are relevant for medical things. I tell them only if I think it is important for them." Another nurse agreed: "Medics tend to focus on medical things; nurses focus on medical, nursing, and social things."

Some misunderstandings and disagreements are due to the different pragmatic concerns. Thus, not only semantic (how does the professional interpret what (s)he sees?) but also pragmatic issues are related to the different perspectives and thus have to be considered for supporting cooperation between different healthcare professionals in general and cooperative document management in particular.

6. **Doctors and nurses have different professional terminologies.**
Doctors' and nurses' terminology is different, which can lead to problems of understanding each other. For example, a nurse might use the term "pyrexial" whereas a doctor might say "febrile." In interviews with doctors and nurses it could be seen that both professionals use a different terminology when talking to a member of the other group. Experienced nurses and doctors have learned some of the relevant terms of each other's terminology but problems still occur. They are most frequent when student nurses and SHOs talk to each other. Some examples for the different terms and phrases are:

loose stools (nurse) – diarrhoea (doctor)
hypocalcaemic (doctor) – calcium goes wrong (nurse)

7. **There are different modes of communication.**
Most of the communication between doctors and nurses takes place in the ward rounds. Here, all doctors covering the ward, the named nurse and one other nurse responsible for the patient talk about each patient. The other medium for interaction is a case conference, where all information is exchanged that also concerns other professionals involved. If something is important it should be mentioned to others; it can be done verbally but it must also be written down (because it might be meant for someone not on duty, as a reminder, etc.). This is the plan which is not always followed as can be seen in the example entries in F igures 4 and 5. The referral to physiotherapy is not recorded but it has obviously taken place as the physiotherapist records her comments in the list.

Summary

This section was about the ethnographic investigations that were carried out on a geriatric ward. These investigations focused on document management practices and common cooperation problems. It was discussed which particular ethnographic methods were used and why they were applied. An overview of the general work patterns on the geriatric ward was given, and some issues were presented that need to be considered for the design of computer systems supporting teamwork in this area.

Given the author's general interest in document management and in designing technological support for it, the MDT folder was of particular concern. Its potential for enhancing shared care by means of computer systems was clearly seen. Therefore, it was decided to develop a new approach to cooperative document management.

The key finding of the fieldwork was that cooperative document management is important but that breakdowns in cooperation can occur due to underlying fundamental communication problems. As cooperative document management in healthcare deals with "non-copresence" situations, effective communication is vital for smooth cooperation. Therefore, it is argued, the design of systems supporting cooperative document management must address communication problems that can lead to breakdowns in cooperation. Merely presenting data in different ways (e.g., in different interfaces for doctors and nurses in cooperative document management systems) according to the different viewpoints will not overcome these problems and thus not be a sufficient answer to the findings of the fieldwork. Rather, it is argued that fundamental problems that exist with respect to shared documentation in multidisciplinary healthcare need to be solved first before technical realisations can be applied.

The focus of the present work is on written communication. However, it was found to be very difficult to find out about communication problems in documentation systems. Therefore, face-to-face dialogues were also considered and analysed as they can show existing problems that will occur in some form in a written medium as well. The findings of the ethnographic studies (especially the main finding that communication problems exist and can be critical for documentation tasks) prompted the author to look at current theories of communication to determine which theories could be useful in this context. Thus, rather than developing grounded theory (cf. Glaser & Strauss, 1967) the aim was to generate a theory based on the ethnographic findings and on existing communication theories. In the next section, the two theories of communication used for this work will be introduced and the larger context in which the present work is based will be discussed.

THEORETICAL BACKGROUND

Given the ethnographic findings, the decision was made to focus the work on the use of IT to enable more effective communication through improving the design of cooperative document management systems.

The ethnographic studies showed that fundamental communication problems exist between members of multidisciplinary healthcare teams, especially between doctors and nurses. These communication problems threaten effective cooperation and thus need to be considered for cooperative document management. Therefore, it was decided to look at established theories of communication to find out whether they can provide help for the analysis and classification of the problems observed.

Two obvious candidates of communication theories were Searle's Theory of Speech Acts and Habermas' Theory of Communicative Action. Both have been influential in the area of information systems. Both theories were found to be intuitively understandable and useful for the experienced problems in communication. Therefore, it was decided to use both theories for developing a framework for an analysis of interprofessional communication problems in healthcare. The theories are located within the so-called Language-Action Perspective which forms the theoretical foundation of this work. First the two theories of communication will be introduced.

The Theory of Speech Acts

John Searle published the Theory of Speech Acts in 1969 (Searle, 1969). His aim was to show that "speaking a language is performing speech acts (...) in accordance with certain rules for the use of linguistic elements" (Searle, 1969, p.16) and to formulate these rules (Searle & Vanderveken, 1985). Searle argues that the minimal unit of an utterance is not a word or a sentence but a speech act. There are different types of speech acts: e.g., a propositional act, which is the act of uttering words whereas an illocutionary act is a complete speech act, i.e., uttering words, predicating and referring in a particular mode, such as stating, requesting, promising, etc.

Thus, the performance of an illocutionary act involves the performance of the underlying propositional act. The same propositional act can be performed in different illocutionary acts but a propositional act cannot be performed alone. For example, in the three following illocutionary acts the propositional act is that nurse Andrea takes the patient's blood pressure. This fact can be expressed as a statement, an order, or a wish; i.e., the same fact may be part of different illocutionary acts:

"Nurse Andrea takes the patient's blood pressure." (*statement*)
"Nurse Andrea, take the patient's blood pressure!" (*order*)
"I wish nurse Andrea would take the patient's blood pressure." (*wish*)

Likewise, a certain type of illocutionary act can be related to different propositional acts; e.g., "Have you already assessed the patient's activities of daily living?" and "Did the patient have a complex fracture of the femorial shaft three years ago?" are both questions but they have different contents.

Therefore, there are two distinct components of an illocutionary act: a propositional content and an illocutionary force. The propositional content describes what an utterance is about whereas the illocutionary force describes the way it is uttered. Taken together, both components provide the meaning of the utterance and both have to be known to understand the speech act. In this chapter, only complete speech acts, i.e., illocutionary acts, are considered. The term "speech act" is, therefore, used here as a synonym for the term "illocutionary act."

Each illocutionary act has got a "point" which characterises that particular type of speech act. For example, an assertion is about informing other people, a request is about getting the recipient to perform an action, etc. This purpose of the act is called the illocutionary point. Searle classifies utterances according to the illocutionary point and proposes the following five classes of speech acts:

- **Assertives** represent facts of the world of utterance or common experiences, e.g., reports or statements.
- **Directives** represent the speaker's[3] attempt to get the hearer to perform the action indicated in the propositional content, e.g., requests.
- **Commissives** represent the speaker's intention to perform the action indicated in the propositional content, e.g., promises.
- **Expressives** say something about the speaker's feelings or psychological attitudes regarding the state of affairs represented by the propositional content, e.g., apologies.
- **Declaratives** change the world through the utterance of the speech act. The speaker brings about the state of affairs represented by the propositional content solely by uttering the speech act, e.g., sentencing a prisoner or performing a marriage.

Searle argues that the illocutionary force imposes certain conditions on the propositional content of an utterance, i.e., what an utterance can be about. These conditions are called propositional content conditions. For example, a diagnosis is about medical issues; a report can only be about present or past events.

Preparatory conditions express a speaker's presuppositions when uttering a certain speech act. They have to be fulfilled for a non-defective performance of the speech act. For example, a speaker using any directive force presupposes that the hearer is capable of carrying out the requested action. Preparatory conditions can also be related to the propositional content. Most utterances presuppose the truth of certain propositions. For example, if a doctor asks a nurse to refer a patient to physiotherapy, the doctor presupposes that the patient needs this input; a nurse promising to feed a patient presupposes that the patient cannot eat herself or himself.

Each illocutionary act implies a commitment for either speaker or hearer (Schoop, 1998). The most important forms of commitment occur in commissive and directive speech acts because these types of acts deal directly with the coordination of actions and utterances between communication partners. Directives commit the hearer to carry out the action represented in the propositional content whereas commissives create a commitment for the speaker to carry out the action.

The Theory of Communicative Action

Jürgen Habermas published his Theory of Communicative Action in 1981 (Habermas, 1981). He takes Searle's theory as a starting point for his own theory reflecting his concerns with pragmatic aspects of language. Like Searle he argues that a speech act is the elementary unit of linguistic communication and that each speech act consists of an illocutionary force and a propositional content. The illocutionary force establishes the mode of communication between speaker and hearer and thus the pragmatic situation of the contents of the utterance. The propositional content establishes the relation between the utterance and the outside world.

Habermas distinguishes three types of actions:

- **instrumental actions,** which are material actions that follow technical rules; they have an effect on events and states of the world;
- **strategic actions,** which follow rational rules and try to influence a rational opponent in order to achieve personal success;
- **communicative actions,** where the motivation is a rationally grounded consensus between the communication partners.

In the following, we will refer to communicative action.

A central argument in Habermas' theory is that "we understand a speech act when we know what makes it acceptable" (Habermas, 1984, p.297). So what makes a speech act acceptable? It must satisfy conditions that enable a hearer to say "yes" to the speech act. These conditions are not specific to certain speaker-hearer pairs but are general for all possible actors uttering and hearing similar speech acts. Through the utterance of a speech act a speaker makes an offer to the hearer to accept the speech act and enter into a rationally grounded relationship. The basis for such relationships are rational agreements that can be negotiated, criticised, changed, etc. No force or threats are used; everything is out in the open. Habermas concentrates on those conditions that motivate the hearer to accept the speech act offer, presupposing that the utterance is grammatically correct and that conditions for this particular type of speech act are fulfilled. Thus, Habermas implicitly presupposes that the preparatory and propositional content conditions (using Searle's terminology) are satisfied and introduces further conditions of his own. A speech act can only be successful if the hearer says "yes" to certain validity claims raised by the speaker which are determined by the illocutionary force of the utterance.

From the viewpoint of a hearer, there are three levels of reacting to a speech act:

- The hearer understands the utterance, i.e., (s)he grasps the meaning of what is being said.
- The hearer says yes or no to claims raised through the utterance of the speech act, i.e., (s)he accepts or rejects the speech act offer.
- Following an agreement, the hearer accepts obligations and commitments arising from the speech act that are determined by social conventions for this utterance.

Habermas argues that a speaker making an utterance makes four implicit **validity claims:**

- that the utterance is **comprehensible** so that the hearer can understand the speaker;
- that the utterance is **true**, i.e., it represents a fact or a common experience, so that the hearer can share the speaker's knowledge;
- that the utterance is **truthful**, i.e., the speaker's intentions are expressed in a sincere way, so that the hearer can trust the speaker;
- that the utterance is **appropriate** in relation to a given normative context, to values, or standards so that the hearer can agree with the speaker in these values.

The four validity claims can be seen as four areas where communication can break down and requires reparative action:

- If the utterance is incomprehensible then the speaker must rephrase, explain, or translate it.
- If the truth of an utterance is challenged then the speaker must justify the utterance, e.g., by explaining it, supplying more information, pointing to common experiences, etc.

- If the hearer challenges the speaker's truthfulness then the speaker's intentions are called into question. Communication can only continue if the speaker succeeds in restoring the trust, e.g., through acting consistently, assuring the hearer of the speaker's sincerity, etc.
- If the appropriateness of an utterance is challenged then the hearer questions the speaker's right to perform the speech act, e.g., if a speaker's role does not entitle him or her to do so, if a speaker violates recognised values or acts contradictory to norms. These problems are usually solved by pointing to other (unproblematic) standards and norms, referring to common experiences, citing relevant literature or authorities, etc.

The Language-Action Perspective

The broader context of the present work lies in the so-called Language-Action Perspective (LAP). LAP is based on Searle's and Habermas' theories and focuses on communication aspects in information systems. LAP was first introduced in the field of information systems (IS) in 1980 by Flores and Ludlow (1980), who argued that human beings are fundamentally linguistic beings and act through language. It was argued that language is not only used for exchanging information as in reports, statements, etc. but also to perform actions, e.g,. promises, orders, declarations, etc.

The conventional perspective on information systems stresses the contents of messages rather than the way they are exchanged (Lyytinen & Lehtinen, 1984). For example, data flow diagrams are used as primary design tools. Thus, the focus is on the form and structure of messages (Dignum & Dietz, 1997). In contrast, the Language-Action Perspective emphasises what people *do* while communicating, how language is used to create a common reality for all communication partners, and how their activities are coordinated through language. Here, the focus is on the pragmatic aspect of language, i.e., how language is used in particular contexts to achieve practical goals such as agreements or mutual understandings. This new approach argues that as social action is mediated through communication, the main role of an information system should be to support organisational communication (Schoop, 1998). LAP has since developed into a new paradigm for the design of computer systems.

There are a number of basic assumptions underlying LAP (Lyytinen, 1985; Verharen, 1997), e.g.:

- The basic unit of communication is a speech act.
- Natural language sentences correspond to the performance of speech acts.

- The meaning of sentences can be revealed by specifying the speech acts that have been performed.
- Speech acts obey socially determined rules.
- Cooperative work is coordinated by the performance of language actions which are speech acts.

The early work on LAP is based on Searle's Theory of Speech Acts (Searle, 1969). As a result of criticism of the shortcomings of Searle's theory (e.g., Dietz & Widdershoven, 1991; Suchman, 1994), Habermas' Theory of Communicative Action (Habermas, 1981) is nowadays used in combination with Searle's theory as the philosophical foundation of LAP.

Some Applications of the Language-Action Perspective

The Language-Action Perspective is not merely a philosophical framework but has stimulated the development of a number of methodologies and computer-based tools.

The first application of LAP was the Coordinator (Flores et al., 1988; Winograd & Flores, 1986). Developed by Winograd and Flores, it was motivated by the observation that the mere application of technology in an office did not necessarily lead to more efficient work structures; indeed it sometimes created more problems than it solved. Winograd and Flores argued that a theoretical basis for the design of new systems was necessary to support office work in an effective way. They claimed that LAP could provide this basis and argued that teaching people linguistic theory would make them aware of their communication structures. Winograd and Flores exemplified their ideas for the Coordinator as one system supporting conversations in an office setting.

SAMPO is an acronym for Speech-Act-based information-analysis-methodology with computer-aided tools and was developed around the same time as the Coordinator (Lyytinen & Lehtinen, 1984; Auramäki et al., 1988, 1992a, 1992b). Based on speech act theory, illocutionary logic, and discourse analysis, it is a tool for modelling organisational discourses in an information system (which is seen as a network of speech acts determining the structure of organisational transactions and resulting commitments). Lyytinen and Lehtinen (1984) present a new conceptual view of an information system as a medium for storing commitments and reporting on their fulfilments. This contrasts with the conventional view on IS paradigm as a "data storage paradigm," where the main emphasis is on the storage and processing of data and information.

DEMO stands for Dynamic Essential Modelling of Organizations and aims to provide a modelling method for effective business process redesign (Dietz, 1994a, 1994b; van Reijswoud, 1996). DEMO is based largely on Habermas' theory but also on Searle's theory. DEMO proposes to view an organisation as a social system in which individuals behave in certain ways and influence each other through communication (van der Rijst, 1997).

Current trends in the area of LAP can be distinguished into systems for communication support, formal foundations, and LAP approaches to current research topics such as e-commerce. For overviews of recent LAP approaches see Dignum and Dietz, 1997; Goldkuhl et al., 1998, 1999; Schoop and Quix, 2000.

Critiques of the Language-Action Perspective

The Language-Action Perspective has attracted much interest in the field of information system but also some critiques. We will present some important criticisms and will consider them in the remainder of this chapter.

LAP has been criticised from disciplines such as sociology, ethnography, philosophy, computer science, linguistics. Critiques often specifically concern Searle's theory but are also related to the more general use of the Language-Action Perspective for organisational communication.

There has been criticism from within the LAP community concerning the adequacy of Searle's theory for analysing human communication. As an example, Dietz and Widdershoven (1991) argue that Habermas' Theory of Communicative Action is superior. The critical points are illustrated using the Coordinator as an example of a system based solely on speech act theory; it is argued that the Coordinator has severe shortcomings due to the shortcomings of Searle's theory. The most significant drawback of Searle's theory is that it does not adequately consider what makes a speech act successful, i.e., Searle neglects validity claims. Consequently, the Coordinator is not able to state the success criteria for speech acts and it is not clear what mechanisms for communication and coordination the system supports. Moreover, since Searle does not consider a speaker's orientation, there is no distinction between directives based on validity claims and those based on power claims. Thus, strategic action cannot be distinguished from communication action.

Dietz and Widdershoven then go on to say that these problems can be overcome by using Habermas' theory as it provides the success criteria of speech acts in terms of criticisable validity claims. The consequences for the design of communication support systems are then obvious: There must be a facility to negotiate validity claims and to discuss problematic claims. The Coordinator is criticised for its aim to support coordination in stable environments with clear hierarchies where negotiation is not and should not be the priority.

One of the most prominent and challenging criticisms of LAP comes from Suchman (1994). She concentrates on speech act theory and the Coordinator as an exemplar of LAP applications. Her main argument is that using speech act theory for the development of computer-based communication systems enforces discipline and control and, therefore, oppresses the users. Suchman presents both LAP and especially the Coordinator as aiming to provide frameworks for representing and controlling normal communication practices.

Suchman comments that speech act theory proposes strict classifications that do not allow for individuality and creativity of communication partners and suggests that:

> Alternatively, we might embrace instead (…) an appreciation for and an engagement with the specificity, heterogeneity and practicality of organizational life. (Suchman, 1994, p.78)

The more concrete points she makes about the Coordinator are that, firstly, it concentrates on pairs of a speaker's utterance and a hearer's reaction rather than interactions between the two; secondly, that conversations are often indeterministic in that a speaker does not always know what (s)he means at the beginning of a dialogue but that the meaning and intentions emerge during the interactions with the hearer. This is not considered in the design of the Coordinator and, therefore, an unnatural structure is imposed. The intentions that are often implicit in normal interaction must be made explicit by the speakers in systems such as the Coordinator.

Suchman argues that the machine can be used to warn of potential breakdowns or to keep track of actions, a mechanism which can be used by organisations for control so that oppressive organisational structures are enforced rather than loosened:

> Rather than being a tool for the collaborative production of social action, in other words, THE COORDINATOR (...) is a tool for the reproduction of an established social order. (Suchman, 1994, p. 168)

Suchman (1987) argues that plans are not executable sets of actions but rather that actions are performed depending on circumstances in certain contexts and are only loosely related to any plans. Thus, if the application of speech act theory as in the Coordinator forces the user to act according to predefined plans it is oppressive and against natural behaviour.

A critical look at LAP from a linguistic perspective is provided by Allwood (1998). His conceptual criticism of Searle's and Habermas' theories has many facets. Firstly, he comments that the theories cannot account for the multifunctionality of speech acts. For example, the statement, "It is raining," could be a warning or an assertion, depending on the particular context. Furthermore, Allwood argues that Searle's speech act taxonomy does not consist of mutually exclusive categories. The speech act conditions that Searle proposes do not clearly separate what is general from what is particular for one act. For example, there are some conditions that make general statements about a class of acts, e.g., propositional content conditions, while others are valid for a particular act only, e.g., preparatory conditions. Finally, Allwood presents a perspectival criticism. He argues that the context is not sufficiently taken into account, especially any existing nonrational or non-intentional aspects of communication. Habermas does not deal with what he calls defective speech acts and Searle presupposes intentional conversations. Habermas makes no distinction between ethics and rationality, which leads to an insufficient treatment of ethics.

COOPERATIVE DOCUMENT MANAGEMENT IN HEALTHCARE

The aim of the present work is to exploit the potential of information technology to create a new generation of (computer-based) cooperative document management systems that can help to avoid breakdowns in communication and cooperation.

The approach taken in this work is as follows. The ethnographic studies showed that fundamental communication problems exist between doctors and nurses. Merely presenting data in different ways (e.g., in different interfaces for doctors and nurses in shared computer systems) according to the different viewpoints will not overcome these problems and thus not be a sufficient answer to the key findings. Rather, it is the author's conviction that the design of computer-based cooperative document management systems requires a fundamental overhaul, in particular that a rigorous theoretical foundation is required that draws on theories of communication and is anchored in empirical evidence. The qualitative analysis of communication patterns in healthcare discussed in previous sections showed which particular problems occurred and how they could be explained. These findings together with the theoretical basis provided by the Language-Action Perspective can be seen as indicating those features of multidisciplinary communication an ideal CDMS would need to facilitate.

To provide a basis for the design of cooperative document management systems, a means for defining and articulating communication and cooperation structures as the underlying basis for interactions via documents is then required. To specify requirements in these terms, a framework of features that need to be considered for the design of effective systems for cooperative document management will be presented. Therefore, a transition from the ethnography to an abstraction must take place. The development of such a conceptual design basis forms the focus for the remainder of this work. The concepts show the analysis of the problems observed in the fieldwork and the broader process of solving problems. Thus, they provide an abstraction from the richer environment of multidisciplinary healthcare onto general features of an ideal CDMS. The process of abstraction includes leaving behind some of the elements that the ethnographic studies identified. For example, the issue of power relations is only considered implicitly in this section. The conceptual elements for the design of effective document management systems are shown in Table 1.

The framework will now be introduced and illustrated using the following scenario:

A consultant asks a nurse to administer hypnotics and betablockers to a patient with hypertension.

Through the following presentation, the reader should bear in mind that the ultimate aim of the work is to use the framework as a basis for the design of cooperative document management systems. Much of the time the implications for design will be left implicit, although on occasion requirements will be made explicit and expressed with reference to an idealised CDMS.

Classification of Authors and Recipients

First of all, the possible actors in the cooperative document management system have to be specified. As mentioned before, the present work has

Table 1: Conceptual elements of the framework

Actors (authors and recipients)
Main task and primary interest of actors
Responsibilities and duties of actors
Domain specific illocutionary forces
Illocutionary forces for author-recipient combinations
Medical knowledge of actors and propositional content
Terminological correspondences
Propositional content conditions
Preconditions
Validity claims
Commitments of actors
Date of document entries
Interactions between document entries

concentrated on the professional groups of doctors and nurses as these are the main contributors to patient care. However, there are obviously many different subclasses of these groups and a more refined classification of possible authors and recipients is necessary in order to be able to specify the author and recipient of document entries in a detailed way. Table 2 shows some classes of these two groups of healthcare professionals.

In the example, the author is a consultant. The recipient is a senior staff nurse on day shift because only senior staff nurses are allowed to administer drugs, and hypnotics and betablockers are only administered during the day. Therefore, only this particular group of nurses is the recipient of the speech act; for all other groups of nurses it is irrelevant.

Main Task and Primary Interest

Two important concepts in the present approach deriving from the fieldwork are the professionals' main task and the primary interest. Each professional group has a main task, which determines the primary interest. A doctor's main task is to give the diagnosis and decide upon a treatment plan and, therefore, (s)he is primarily interested in the patients' presenting complaints, the past medical history, drug history, family history, etc. Nurses are primarily concerned with patients' needs while they are on the ward because their main task is caring for the patients. The main task and primary interest must be considered because they partly determine what the different professional groups will talk about when looking at the same patient, i.e., what can be said in the propositional content of their utterances.

Table 2: Some classes of nurses and doctors

Classes of Nurses	**Classes of Doctors**
Sister	Consultant
Charge Nurse	Senior Registrar
Senior Staff Nurse	Registrar
Staff Nurse	Senior House Officer
Nurse on Duty	Doctor Admitting Patient
Nurse on Day Shift	Doctor Prescribing Drugs
Nurse Doing Assessment	Doctor Doing Assessment
Nurse Giving IV Injections	Doctor Ordering Blood Test
Named Nurse	Doctor Ordering X-Ray
Nurse Preparing Discharge	Doctor Discharging Patient
District Nurse	Doctor Giving Diagnosis

For example, the consultant in the scenario might state that the patient suffers from hypertension, is obese, and has a family history of myocardial infarctions; whereas the nurse, looking at the same patient, might say that the patient is depressed, does not sleep well at night and needs assistance with washing and dressing because of breathlessness.

Responsibilities and Duties

Closely related to the main task are the responsibilities and duties of each professional group. The professional role indicates which obligations arise for different groups. This is an issue relevant to the set of possible illocutionary forces for each professional group.

A nurse, for example, is responsible for administering drugs, assessing the patient's activities of daily living, referring a patient to speech therapy, and preparing the patient's discharge; whereas a doctor is responsible for giving the diagnosis, prescribing drugs, assessing the patient's medical state, ordering blood tests, transferring a patient, etc. Therefore, "assess" is an illocutionary force that both groups use.

Classification of Illocutionary Forces

Searle's five categories of illocutionary forces are used for classifying forces in this work. However, a medically-oriented set of subcategories of illocutionary forces is necessary in order to be able to make statements about forces specific to healthcare. The forces observed to be used can be classified according to Searle's general framework as shown in Table 3. The following explains for some forces why they have been classified in that way and makes some general comments on the taxonomy.

Assertive Forces

Assertive illocutionary forces have the word-to-world fit, i.e., they reflect utterances intended to represent states of affairs in the real world. The

Table 3: Classification of illocutionary forces

Assertive	Commissive	Directive	Expressive	Declarative
assess diagnose evaluate identify needs inform observe record	evaluate investigate review set goal	investigate order refer request prescribe	query rule out suspect	admit discharge transfer

table lists seven such acts.

- Diagnose: Issuing a diagnosis means classifying and labelling the patient's disease. A diagnosis is a statement made by a healthcare professional who believes that the disease (s)he has given is actually the one the patient suffers from. However, a diagnosis does not change a patient's state of health and does not make the patient have the disease. Therefore, it is not a declarative speech act, which has the double direction of fit ("changing the world by saying so"), but an assertive act.
- Evaluate: Evaluating patient care and treatment implicitly includes two illocutionary forces, i.e., stating a patient's current state (assertive) and reviewing the planned interventions and goals and changing them if necessary (commissive). It appears in column one in the former sense.
- Identify needs: Nurses identify patients' needs during their assessment, i.e., they state the areas that are problematic and need to be considered in the daily care.
- Record: Recording statements (indirect communication) is telling someone else how things are (word-to-world fit).

Commissive Forces

Commissive forces have the world-to-word fit, i.e., they intend to change the world so that it reflects the utterance. The table lists four commissive forces.

- Evaluate: As mentioned, "evaluate" contains both an assertive and a commissive element.
- Investigate: In healthcare, "investigate" can be a commissive or a directive speech act, depending on the recipient. Investigating, for example, the cause of a patient's fall or the home circumstances commits either the same or a different professional group to carry out the relevant actions.
- Review: If a treatment or a prescription is reviewed, then the author is committed to consider the patient's actual state in order to decide about any necessary changes in the plan of care and treatment and to give reasons for the decision.
- Set goal: Nurses assess a patient's normal and altered states, identify the needs and then set appropriate goals they are committed to achieve while the patient is on the ward. Thus, setting a goal is committing nurses to ensure that the states described will be achieved.

Directive Forces

In addition to the general directive forces "order" (which indicates strategic action) and "request," there are three other specific directives for healthcare. We will discuss the forces of "refer" and "prescribe."

- Refer: Referring a patient to another specialty means issuing a commitment for a member of that specialty to assess the patient.
- Prescribe: The force of prescribing used by doctors is a request usually for a nurse and sometimes for a doctor to administer the drugs prescribed[4].

Expressive Forces

The process of classifying a patient's disease is usually one of exclusion (Hoffmann-La Roche and Urban & Schwarzenberg, 1987) and three expressive speech acts are involved. Possible diseases are queried and ruled out and the most likely disease is taken as a preliminary diagnosis. This process is represented by the phrases: "We query disease x," "Disease x cannot be ruled out," or "Disease x is suspected."

- Rule out: The phrase "cannot be ruled out" is often used in medical documents to indicate that, on the one hand, the professional is aware of the possibility that the patient might have a certain disease but, on the other hand, that the professional cannot decide yet whether this is really the case. Further actions such as tests or examinations are necessary; they are driven by the author's assumption that the patient is probably not suffering from the disease that is to be ruled out. Thus, uttering the phrase "ruling out" means implicitly making an expressive speech act, "It has to be investigated whether the patient has the disease or not, but I do not think it is likely."
- Suspect: A suspicion in the medical sense is a speech act in which the professional expresses uncertainty about the state of affairs, i.e., making a preliminary diagnosis means implicitly making the (expressive) speech act, "I suspect this disease but I am not certain whether the diagnosis is true." "Suspect" can be seen as the opposite of "ruling out." Here the author thinks that the patient is probably suffering from the suspected disease.
- Query: Querying a disease expresses even less certainty. Here, the professional has thought of the possibility of this disease but does not necessarily suspect it. "Query" is also used to put up a temporary list of possible alternative diagnoses. In this context, "query" represents a professional term in a specific context as described.

Many diseases can be suspected, ruled out, or queried during the process of specifying a diagnosis. In all three cases, the author does not believe that this is the disease the patient is suffering from. Therefore, these three illocutionary forces are classified not as assertive but as expressive speech acts.

Declarative Forces

The table shows three declarative forces.

- Admit: By admitting a patient to a ward, the patient is taken under the responsibility of the ward solely through the speech act of admission. A patient can even be admitted to a ward before (s)he physically arrives there.
- Discharge: Discharging a patient means being no longer responsible for the patient.
- Transfer: Transferring a patient to another ward or hospital means transferring the responsibility to someone else.

These three acts are not mere statements or commissives but change the world (the patient is now one of ward X; the patient is no longer one of ward X; the patient is now one of a different ward, Y) solely through their utterance.

Possible Forces for Author-Recipient Combinations

Table 3 shows a general classification of forces. However, some of these forces are only used by particular authors, which is again determined by their professional roles and associated pragmatics. For example, the "identification of needs" concerns nursing needs only and ism, therefore, specific to the nursing domain, whereas "rule out" is only used by doctors. Therefore, the set of all possible forces for each professional group has to be specified. For example, the set of illocutionary forces used by nurses (denoted by IF_{Nurse}) and the set of those forces that doctors use (denoted by IF_{Doctor}) can be specified as follows.

IF_{Nurse}= {assess, evaluate, identify needs, inform, observe, record, investigate, review, set goal, refer, request}

IF_{Doctor}= {assess, diagnose, evaluate, inform, observe, record, investigate, review, order, refer, request, prescribe, query, rule out, suspect, admit, discharge, transfer}

Furthermore, it must be made explicit which particular forces the professionals use in the context of certain recipients; this is again determined by the professional role. Table 4 shows some possible combinations of forces, authors, and recipients. For example, an evaluation carried out by a nurse will only be passed on to a nurse, whereas both doctor and nurse can be recipients of a request.

As in the example scenario, the author of an act of prescription is a doctor, the recipient is a nurse. The existing responsibilities and duties and power structures can be used to specify author-recipient combinations further. For example, only senior staff nurses are recipients of any act of prescription because only they are allowed to administer drugs; consultants can issue orders for (senior) registrars and SHOs but not vice versa.

Medical Knowledge and Propositional Content

The main task, primary interest, and professional role determine what knowledge each professional group has about a certain aspect of the care process. Doctors' knowledge and nurses' knowledge overlap but neither is a subset of the other. Such medical knowledge is embodied in the propositional content of speech acts, which in general describes what the act is about. Speech act theory and illocutionary logic treat the propositional content as a

Table 4: Combination of authors, illocutionary forces, and recipients

Author	Illocutionary Force	Recipient
doctor	assess	doctor, nurse
nurse	assess	nurse, doctor
doctor	diagnose	doctor, nurse
doctor	evaluate	doctor
nurse	evaluate	nurse
doctor	record	doctor, nurse
nurse	record	nurse, doctor
doctor	review	doctor
nurse	review	nurse
nurse	set goal	nurse
doctor	order	doctor, nurse
doctor	refer	doctor
nurse	refer	nurse
doctor	request	doctor, nurse
nurse	request	nurse, doctor
doctor	prescribe	senior staff nurse
doctor	rule out	doctor
doctor	suspect	doctor
doctor	admit	doctor, nurse

primitive (Searle & Vanderveken, 1985). However, formalisation of the propositional content is required in order to allow queries to be made about the contents of an utterance (e.g., "Has the patient had a chest x-ray?" or "What is the patient's medication?") and to enable basic comprehensibility problems to be addressed (see next section). This will also help to clarify questions such as, "What do nurses really mean when they speak about stroke?" and "What do doctors mean by this term?"

Terminological Correspondences

Comprehensibility problems can occur on two levels: that of unknown terms, where the utterance cannot be interpreted by the recipient, or that of misinterpretations, where the recipient's interpretation differs from the author's intended meaning. In routine interaction, comprehensibility problems are usually solved by rephrasing or translating. In written communication there is no possibility to employ these human problem-solving strategies and, therefore, even the most basic comprehensibility problems can lead to total breakdowns in communication and cooperation.

For example, if the nurse in the example scenario does not understand the term "hypnotics" and does not manage to find out what kind of drugs are meant, then she cannot do anything until she can communicate with the doctor and ask for clarification. There can be no guessing as healthcare is a sensitive area where communication and cooperation is necessary to ensure the best patient care.

In order to address these problems, it is clearly vital that a cooperative documentation system must provide mechanisms to support the translation of the propositional content according to each group's requirements if necessary in order to avoid breakdowns due to incomprehensibility. The need for such translation mechanisms is important given the prevalence of comprehensibility problems recorded by the empirical studies. These mechanisms will provide familiar terms of the recipient's own professional terminology rather than forcing cooperating participants to understand and use the terminology of their communication partners. The professional terminologies have been developed over time to fit each group's requirements; they are not necessarily useful for interaction between different professional groups. Therefore, it is argued here that the possibility of a basic translation process will enable the participants to express themselves in the best possible way (in their own terminology) and to understand the communication partner appropriately (by translating unfamiliar terms). The participants will thereby achieve greater autonomy and emancipation (Lyytinen & Hirschheim, 1989).

One possible point of criticism is that, in reality, comprehensibility problems are usually solved and such mechanisms will, therefore, not be necessary. This is true for experienced nurses and doctors who have learned over time to translate automatically when they talk to each other. In the interviews performed it was seen how the professionals switch their language (often subconsciously) when talking to the other group. Student nurses or staff nurses on the one hand and medical students or senior house officers on the other hand experience many comprehensibility problems. Therefore, it is argued that the possibility of translating basic terms or phrases can be helpful; in the end it is the professional who decides whether to use such support or not.

If translation is to be integral to a CDMS, it is vital that there are appropriate notational features for expressing such correspondences. However, translation between different (medical) terminologies is a major research topic in its own right and beyond the scope of this work. Furthermore, comprehensibility problems concern semantic issues, whereas the strategic emphasis of this work is on the metalinguistic and pragmatic level, where the validity claims of truth and appropriateness are based. A more limited aim of this work is thus adopted, namely to provide a simple notation for accommodating synonyms and characteristic phrases. Results from other areas will be accommodated as and when this work on translation matures. Some examples of translation work will be briefly described. Binsted et al. (1995) and Cawsey et al. (1995), for instance, report on work explaining parts of the medical patient record to patients, which includes translating from the medical terminology to that of the lay patients. Work within the GALEN project has included using a formal model of clinical terminology as an interlingua between different classification systems (Hardiker & Rector, 1998; Rector et al., 1998).

In the present approach, work has been carried out on the level of synonyms and characteristic phrases with different levels of detail where comprehensibility problems can be solved relatively easy. Examples include the following:

- MI (doctor) - heart attack (nurse)
- TIA (doctor) - mild stroke (nurse)
- fractured neck of femur (doctor) - broken hip (nurse)
- febrile (doctor) - pyrexial (nurse)
- analgesia (doctor) - painkiller (nurse)
- diuretic (doctor) - water tablets (nurse)
- decubitus (doctor) - pressure sore (nurse)
- myopic (doctor) - short-sighted (nurse)

In the example scenario the nurse might not understand the term "hypnotics," which is not part of the nursing terminology. She would use the nursing term "sleeping tablets."

Propositional Content Conditions

Speech act theory states that the illocutionary force imposes certain conditions on the propositional content (Searle & Vanderveken, 1985), e.g., a diagnosis is about medical issues. However, these conditions need to be refined for the present work because in many cases not only the force but also the author and recipient determine what can be expressed in the propositional content. For example, a report issued by a nurse for a nurse might contain medical, nursing, and social issues, whereas, if the recipient is a doctor, it might contain only medical and nursing issues.

Propositional content conditions are especially important to consider in relation to prestructured entries in a CDMS, rather than free text. The Coordinator, for example, consists of free text messages and structured illocutionary forces. It is possible to imagine other systems where content is entered using short phrases; propositional content conditions provide the basis for controlling what is entered and the composition of possible and sensible phrases which can be formed automatically into sentences. Examples for such systems can be found in the area of medical and nursing classifications.

In the example scenario of a prescription, propositional content conditions for such utterance restrict the contents to drugs.

Preconditions

Preconditions show the author's presuppositions when uttering a certain speech act, in this case making an entry in the cooperative document management system. Misunderstandings can be due to an author's (implicit) presuppositions if the recipient is not aware of them. Therefore, it is important to make preconditions explicit as the recipient might not agree with them and thus challenge their truth.

In the example, the consultant presupposes that the patient suffers from hypertension, a fact that the nurse might want to question.

Validity Claims

A key idea in the present approach is to incorporate validity claims as introduced by Habermas. They are critical to the success of speech acts. Only if the recipient of a speech act says implicitly "yes" to all the claims raised can the speech act be seen as successful. The consideration of validity claims allows fruitful discursive communication rather than a hierarchically-based issuance of orders and mere obedience of orders. In Habermas' words, communicative action that is oriented towards mutual agreement is enabled rather than concentrating only on strategic action oriented towards personal success. Nevertheless, these two types of action can be distinguished and strategic action can also be dealt with, e.g., in orders issued by doctors to nurses where no discussion is possible. Thus, both communicative and strategic action are supported equivalently.

To allow only sensible challenges, first of all the relations between the validity claims and the components of a speech act, i.e., the illocutionary force and the propositional content, need to be considered.

An utterance can be incomprehensible because the propositional content is not understood by the recipient. This is a common communication problem. However, it is also possible to challenge the comprehensibility of the illocutionary force used in a speech act. Illocutionary forces are not always specified in communicative interaction, which can lead to misunderstandings about which force the author meant to use when uttering a sentence. For example, a consultant in a case conference might utter the sentence, "We need to make a mental test with the patient," which was meant as a request (i.e., a directive) for the SHO to make the test; whereas, the SHO understands the utterance as a mere statement (i.e., an assertive). Therefore, the claim of comprehensibility is related to both the propositional content and the illocutionary force.

Questioning the truth of a statement means questioning whether the statement really represents a fact, a common experience, etc. It is not possible to challenge the truth of an illocutionary force because questioning whether the author's intentions indicated by the illocutionary force are sincere is questioning the author's truthfulness. Thus, "truth" is related to the propositional content only.

The challenge of truthfulness is only related to the illocutionary force since the recipient doubts whether the author is really committed to the illocutionary force used when truthfulness is questioned. Here, the ostensible nature of the speech act is questioned, e.g., what seems to be an assertive act is really an attempt to deceive.

Both the illocutionary force and the propositional content can be inappropriate. However, a challenge of appropriateness concerns more often the illocutionary force than the propositional content. The recipient challenges the appropriateness of the illocutionary force used by the author by questioning whether the author is entitled to use this force in this particular context. The author could have violated existing power relations, recognised norms, or professional standards. A propositional content can also be inappropriate. Here, the recipient questions whether the sentence fits a given normative context, i.e., whether it is legitimate to say so.

To summarise, the validity claim "truth" is related to the propositional content, whereas "truthfulness" concerns the illocutionary force only. Both "comprehensibility" and "appropriateness" can be challenged for the illocutionary force as well as for the propositional content.

Furthermore, the relations between particular speech acts and the validity claims must be examined (Schoop, 1997b; Schoop, 1998), e.g., a directive speech act can be incomprehensible or inappropriate but not false.

The relations between validity claims and the five types of speech acts used in this work are shown in Table 5, which also includes the relations to the particular component of the speech act as discussed before.[5] Table 5 can be explained as follows. Comprehensibility problems can occur in all utterances. Habermas argues that all claims can be criticised for all types of speech acts. The author does not agree with this notion as the claim of "truth" is not related to directive, commissive, expressive, and declarative speech acts themselves but to their presuppositions. Therefore, the validity claim of truth is taken to be only related to the propositional content of assertive speech acts.

The recipient can always challenge the author's sincerity and thereby question the truthfulness of an utterance. An author might not believe in the statement made (assertive), might not really promise something (commissive), might not want the recipient to carry out the action as directed (directive), might not express real feelings (expressive), or might not be sincere when declaring a new fact (declarative). Thus, "truthfulness" is relevant for the illocutionary force of all types of utterances.

Appropriateness is related to assertive, directive, expressive, and declarative speech acts. For example, a statement or an expression of feelings can be inappropriate if the utterance in that particular context is against certain social norms. It is argued here that appropriateness is not related to commissive speech acts because an author can always commit himself or herself to carry out a certain action. There are certain presuppositions attached to commissive acts. For example, a promise presupposes that the recipient wants the author to do as promised. Thus, a recipient can challenge the truth of these presuppositions but this is not a challenge of appropriateness.

In the example scenario, a consultant asks a nurse to administer betablockers and hypnotics, which is a directive speech act. Using the classification of Table 5, the following claims are relevant for this utterance: The utterance can be incomprehensible for the nurse as the recipient (i.e., challenge of comprehensibility), or the nurse can question whether the

Table 5: Relations between validity claims and types of speech act

	Assertive		Commissive		Directive		Expressive		Declarative	
Validity Claim	**PC**	**IF**	**PC**	**IF**	**PC**	**IF**	**PC**	**IF**	**PC**	**IF**
Comprehensibility	+	+	+	+	+	+	+	+	+	+
Truth	+									
Truthfulness		+		+		+		+		+
Appropriateness	+	+			+	+	+	+	+	+

consultant is really entitled to ask her to administer the drugs (which would be a challenge of appropriateness). The nurse would also be able to challenge the truthfulness. However, it has never been observed in the ethnographic studies that such a challenge was ever made. Therefore, it was decided not to deal with the claim of truthfulness. The nurse cannot challenge the truth of this utterance but the truth of the presupposition, namely that the patient suffers from hypertension.

Commitments

All utterances create commitments for author or recipient. As mentioned before, the most important forms of commitment occur in commissive and directive speech acts. Commissive and directive speech acts commit the author or recipient to carry out the action represented by the propositional content. However, the recipient has the possibility of explicitly accepting or rejecting such commitment. Only if the recipient accepts all claims raised in these types of speech acts can the related commitment be accepted. The rejection of a commitment is based on a challenge of an underlying validity claim. Therefore, it must be possible to express commitments used in a cooperative document management system to indicate whether each commitment has been accepted, rejected, or not yet dealt with. If a commitment is rejected then the claim that has been challenged and the component of the utterance concerned (i.e., illocutionary force or propositional content) must be specified. Thus, the CDMS must provide mechanisms to deal with commitments in that way.

Commitments can be used for several purposes, e.g., as a reminder (the patient has yet to be referred to district nurses), control by the users themselves (which commitments are not fulfilled yet?), discourse (where does the cooperation between ward nurses and district nurses break down, what could be changed?), and for coordination of cooperation (referral to district nurses means that the district nurses have to take up the patient's care within three days).

In the example, a commitment is created by the directive speech act. If the nurse as the recipient accepts all the claims raised then she will accept the commitment to administer betablockers and hypnotics.

Date

The date of the issuance of the speech act must be recorded in a (cooperative) document management system. Thus, the framework must accommodate dates and times. In addition to the date of utterance, commissives and directives have a review date (which is the date given by the author up to which the action should be completed) and a so-called achieved date (which is the date when the act was actually carried out and thus the commitment was fulfilled).

In the example, the date of the request will be documented. Furthermore, the consultant will enter a review date (in this case usually the day the directive was issued) and the nurse will enter the date when the drugs have been administered for the first time.

Interactions With Other Speech Acts

A speech act can trigger another act, it can be part of another speech act, or it can be a precondition for another act. These interactions with other speech acts need to be considered for particular speech acts. In general, explicit interactions can support the coordination of actions (e.g., a reminder that a particular speech act needs to be carried out as a result of another act), or they could be used for an automatic issuance of other acts.[6]

In the example, the directive act to administer the drugs is the precondition for another act, namely that of ordering these drugs from pharmacy (which is again a directive act, this time with the nurse as author and the pharmacist as recipient). It is not a trigger of that act because the drugs might be available on the ward in the required quantity,[7] in which case no drug order from pharmacy would have to be made.

Summary

In this chapter, the framework for cooperative documentation systems was introduced on a conceptual level. The elements that have to be considered for the design of useful CDMSs were introduced and it was discussed how they were informed by both the results of the ethnographic studies and the theoretical arguments of Searle's and Habermas' theories. It was shown how the two theories of communication can be combined for this work and necessary refinements for this work were introduced.

The classification of illocutionary forces does not produce a set of distinct classes. The force "evaluate" is classified both under assertive and commissive forces for reasons given above. Likewise, "investigate" is seen as either a commissive or a directive speech act, depending on the author's intention. It is felt that this is not a general problem of Searle's taxonomy but a specific problem of these forces. An evaluation consists really of two distinct (speech) acts, which is why this force is classified in that way. It would perhaps be more effective to divide the force into these two actions and classify each of them. However, it was decided to use the illocutionary forces as they are used in healthcare.

The framework goes beyond purely linguistic features. The qualitative research in multidisciplinary healthcare showed that, for example, the professional role, which determines the pragmatic concerns, can explain some communication problems (Schoop, 1998). These findings are reflected in the conceptual elements. The framework considers, for example, the different professional roles of the communication partners (described by responsibilities, duties, main tasks, etc.); their possible ways of communicating with each other, which also indicate different pragmatic concerns (described by the classification of possible forces for each author-recipient pair, possible contents of document entries); and the underlying organisational structures and power hierarchies (authorisations for discussions, initiations of discourses or their prohibitions in case of strategic actions).

The framework enables new types of access to data in a system, not only to contents of data entries but, for example, also to all requests made by Dr. Smith, all unfulfilled commitments, all speech acts concerning a certain patient, particular illocutionary forces, particular propositional contents, particular authors and recipients, commitments fulfilled so far, commitments rejected because of false propositional contents, commitments rejected because of inappropriate illocutionary forces, etc.

The general problem of Searle's theory is that it is author-focused. Suchman has criticised the Coordinator for having this characteristic. The present approach emphasises the interaction between author and recipient by incorporating Habermas' validity claims. This enables structured exchanges between two actors.

In the next section, we will present an evaluative discussion of the new approach to cooperative document management systems.

EVALUATIVE DISCUSSION

In this section, an empirical evaluation of the approach presented in the chapter will be given as follows. A cooperative document management system will be simulated on paper, and it will be shown how such a system could enhance document management and written communication in general between healthcare professionals. Three "example scenarios" will be considered for this purpose to show how real interactions would translate into the main conceptual categories as introduced before. These scenarios will illustrate interactions on a hypothetical healthcare environment based on the real hospital ward observed during the phase of qualitative research.

It will be shown that the new approach to document management in a multidisciplinary healthcare environment will contribute to enhanced interactions on the basis of shared documentation by providing the basis for better cooperative document management systems that promote effective written multidisciplinary communication.

First the conversational setting will be defined in terms of the elements of the framework as follows. In general, doctors and nurses are the principal actors in the system. The following three doctors and three nurses will be assumed to interact in the example scenarios (see Table 6). They are instances of the two general classes of actor and of the six specific groups of doctors and nurses. They act as authors and recipients of document entries.

To fulfil their main tasks, the different professionals are interested in certain information concerning the patient. As discussed in the previous chapter, these two elements are important for the possible contents of the medical utterances, i.e., together with the professional knowledge of each group of actors, they determine what the professionals will document with respect to the patient. The primary interests and main tasks of each actor are specified as shown in Table 7.

According to the professional procedures and standards, doctors and nurses are responsible for different acts. Table 8 shows some of them. Note that these are speech acts (e.g., prescribe drugs, assess incontinence state,

Table 6: Some actors in the CDMS

	Actors	**Instances**
Doctor	Consultant	Brigid May-Ringer
	Registrar	Joe Briggs
	SHO	Maria Mitchum
Nurse	Charge Nurse	David Green
	Senior Staff Nurse	Megan Lilley
	Staff Nurse	George Friend

Table 7: Primary interest and main tasks of the actors in the CDMS

Actor	Primary Interest	Main Task
Doctor	patient's presenting complaint past medical history family history drug history	give diagnosis decide on treatment
Nurse	patient's nursing needs family background social circumstances community care input	care for patient

refer to other professionals) as well as instrumental actions (e.g., administer drugs, take blood samples).

The actors interact in certain ways. This can be specified by the possible combinations of actors and illocutionary forces as shown in Table 4. The responsibilities and duties as shown in the previous table help to determine which forces can be used by certain actors. For example, in Table 8 it is stated that a doctor is responsible for assessing a patient's medical state and a nurse assesses a patient's continence state. Thus, both actors use the illocutionary force "assess." A doctor refers a patient to other doctors whereas a nurse is authorised to refer a patient to district nurses. Thus, a doctor is allowed to utter a speech act with the force "refer" to other doctors and a nurse is allowed to utter a referral to district nurses as shown in Table 9.

The illocutionary forces need to be classified according to the five categories of

Table 8: Some responsibilities and duties of the actors in the CDMS

Actor	Responsibilities, Duties
Doctor	prescribe drugs assess medical state take blood diagnose discharge refer to doctors inform other professionals
Nurse	administer drugs assess continence state send blood samples prepare discharge refer to district nurses set goals inform other professionals

Searle's theory in order to enable statements about classes of utterances. For this example, only three classes of illocutionary forces are relevant; see Table 10.

The classification of forces determines which of the validity claims are relevant for a particular utterance. Each class of forces in this example, i.e., assertive, directive and commissive forces, is related to certain claims. This is shown in Table 11, where "PC" stands for "propositional content," "IF" is used as an abbreviation for "illocutionary force," and "PR" represents "precondition."

To enable a translation process, a list of synonyms of terms and characteristic phrases needs to be specified. Some simple examples are shown in Table 12.

The author and recipient of a speech act and the illocutionary force used in it determine the propositional content conditions, i.e., these three elements limit the possible contents of utterances. For example, a nurse will inform another nurse of nursing interventions, medical or social issues but only pass on medical or nursing issues to a doctor. Some examples of propositional content conditions are shown in Table 13.

Table 9: Some possible combinations of actors in the CDMS and illocutionary forces

Author	**Illocutionary Force**	**Recipient**
Doctor	accept	Doctor, Nurse
Nurse	accept	Doctor, Nurse
Doctor	agree	Doctor, Nurse
Nurse	agree	Nurse, Doctor
Doctor	assess	Doctor, Nurse
Nurse	assess	Nurse, Doctor
Doctor	diagnose	Doctor, Nurse
Doctor	inform	Doctor, Nurse
Nurse	inform	Nurse, Doctor
Doctor	prescribe	Charge Nurse, Sister, Senior Staff Nurse
Doctor	refer	Doctor
Nurse	refer	District Nurse
Doctor	request	Doctor, Nurse
Nurse	request	Nurse, Doctor
Named Nurse	set goal	Nurse

Given these definitions, it will now be shown how the interactions would be orchestrated, i.e., how a computer-based CDMS based on the description language would mediate the conversations. The concrete form of this system is not specified, but the reader should

Table 10. Classification of some illocutionary forces

Assertive	**Directive**	**Commissive**
agree assess diagnose inform	prescribe refer request	accept set goal

Table 11. Relevant validity claims for different type of illocutionary forces

	agree assess diagnose inform			**prescribe refer request**			**accept set goal**		
Validity Claim	**PC**	**IF**	**PR**	**PC**	**IF**	**PR**	**PC**	**IF**	**PR**
Comprehensibility	+	+		+	+		+	+	
Truth	+		+			+			+
Appropriateness	+	+		+	+				

Table 12. Some synonyms used by the actors in the CDMS

Synonyms	
Phrase Used by Nurses	Phrase Used by Doctors
drug preventing blood clotting	anticoagulant
prompting	reminding to urinate or open bowels
sleeping tablets	hypnotics

Table 13. Some propositional content conditions

Author	**Illocutionary Force**	**Recipient**	**Propositional Content**
Doctor	prescribe	Nurse	drugs
Nurse	inform	Nurse	nursing interventions medical issues social issues
Nurse	inform	Doctor	medical issues nursing issues

imagine it being realised as a computerised online system perhaps with an interface similar to the format of present paper systems.

Scenario 1

Let us assume that the following interaction occurs.

Brigid May-Ringer uses the CDMS to request George Friend to arrange for a blood sample to be taken and sent to the lab regarding levels of anticoagulant within the next two days. George Friend indicates that he does not understand what anticoagulant means and asks the CDMS for clarification and receives it. George then agrees to do as requested. George asks Maria Mitchum to take the patient's blood within the next two days. Maria agrees and takes a blood sample the next day. George asks Megan Lilley to send the blood sample to the lab, which she does the same day the sample has been taken.

It will now be considered how and why these interactions are enabled by the CDMS. There are three speech acts in this interaction which will now be analysed.

The **first speech act** is a request made by Brigid May-Ringer to George Friend. Table 6 shows that Brigid is a doctor and more specifically a consultant; George is a staff nurse. The CDMS looks up the possible combinations of actors and forces in Table 9, where it states that a doctor can utter a request with a nurse as recipient. Therefore, the CDMS allows this act as valid. The illocutionary force used has been classified as a directive speech act (see Table 10), and the CDMS therefore allows George to consider the following validity claims. Comprehensibility and appropriateness are related to both parts of this utterance (i.e., illocutionary force and propositional content) and the claim of "truth" concerns the presupposition. Brigid will be required by the CDMS to make the presupposition explicit so that George can decide whether he agrees. In this case she presupposes that the patient suffers from TIA. The CDMS ensures the comprehensibility of the illocutionary force by making the force used explicit, i.e., request. Appropriateness of the force is likewise ensured by only allowing the speaker to use forces that have been specified beforehand (for this example in Table 9).

George now indicates to the CDMS that he cannot understand the term "anticoagulant" that Brigid has used. The CDMS allows this challenge of comprehensibility of the propositional content because it is valid for this type of utterance according to the definition in Table 11. The translation process provides the nursing phrase "drug preventing blood clotting" as a synonym; see Table 12. Now George understands the utterance and decides that he finds it appropriate. George thereby accepts the commitment to arrange for the sample to be taken and sent to the lab, which is classified as a commissive speech act (see Table 10). Brigid has been prompted to give the review date, which she specifies as four days later. The review date for George's commissive speech act would be the same date as Brigid's review date.

George now issues the second speech act. It is a request for Maria Mitchum to take the blood. Maria has been specified in the CDMS as an SHO (Table 6), and a request made by a nurse to a doctor is a valid act (specified in Table 9) and thus allowed by the CDMS. The validity claims associated with this type of speech act have been described above. Maria does not have any problems with this utterance and accepts the commitment to take the blood sample, which is a commissive speech act. George has recorded that the action needs to be carried out within two days. After Maria has taken the blood the day after George requested it (thus within the time limit he gave), she documents the achieved date in the CDMS.

Now the third speech act can commence. This is a request made by SN Friend to Megan Lilley to send the blood sample to the lab. The CDMS allows this request because Megan is a senior staff nurse (see Table 6), and requests by nurses to other nurses have been specified as authorised speech acts in Table 9. George needs to record the review date, which he gives as the current date. Megan accepts this commitment and sends the sample off straightaway. She records the achieved date. George can then record this date as the achieved date for the first speech act and thereby ends his commitment.

Scenario 2

The second example of the language in action is based on a previously-discussed scenario.

Joe Briggs prescribes hypnotics and betablockers for a patient with hypertension and wants a nurse to administer these drugs on the same day. He specifies the presupposition that the patient suffers from hypertension. Megan Lilley does not agree with this statement and indicates this to the CDMS, which presents this challenge to Joe. Joe explains why he wants Megan to administer the drugs and justifies the diagnosis of hypertension. Having read these explanations, Megan now agrees to do as requested.

Joe is a registrar on the ward (see Table 6). He is allowed to use the force "prescribe" with some nurses as hearers as indicated in Table 9. Originally, Joe wanted to ask George Friend to administer these drugs, but he is only allowed to choose between David Green or Megan Lilley because only sisters, charge nurses, or senior staff nurses are allowed to administer drugs and, therefore, only these actors are legitimate recipients of an act of prescription. Thus, the CDMS does not allow SN Friend to be the recipient for this request. With SSN Lilley as the recipient it is a valid act. The propositional content condition for an act of prescription limits the content to drugs as shown in Table 13. Joe as the recipient is prompted by the CDMS to make his presupposition explicit, which in this case is the diagnosis for the patient, i.e., that the patient suffers from hypertension.

In Table 10 it has been shown that the act of prescribing is a directive. The legitimate validity claims for directive speech acts are comprehensibility and appropriateness for both parts of the speech act (as specified in Table 11); both appropriateness and comprehensibility of the illocutionary force are automatically ensured by the CDMS. The claim of truth is not related to this type of act but truth is always related to the preconditions of any speech act. SSN Lilley can now consider whether the propositional content of the utterance is comprehensible and appropriate. Let us assume that the utterance as it stands is not comprehensible; comprehensibility must be achieved before the recipient can decide on the appropriateness of an utterance. The nurse wants to clarify the term "hypnotics," which nurses do not usually use, and asks the CDMS for clarification. The translation process in the CDMS then provides the nursing term "sleeping tablets." Now Megan indicates that she does not think that the patient suffers from hypertension. Thus, she challenges the truth of the presupposition made by the doctor, which is a valid challenge and therefore allowed by the CDMS.

She is prompted for her reasons, e.g., "The patient does not have high blood pressure. I have measured his bp for the last three days and it has always been normal." The CDMS will then present the challenge to Dr. Briggs, who has the option to accept the challenge or to rebut it. In this example, he does not agree with the nurse's statement and, therefore, answers with a rejoinder: "Patient suffers from hypertension, measured bp this morning 170/100, normal for last days only because he was on drugs, now change in drugs because they caused sleeplessness in interaction with other medication." This answer is presented to Megan, who now agrees and thus accepts the commitment to administer the drugs. Joe wants Megan to start with the course of drugs on the same day and thus records the current date as the review date. Megan administers the drugs later that day and records the achieved date.

Scenario 3

The last example is based on experiences on the real ward.

Brigid May-Ringer asks George Friend via the CDMS to make an incontinence assessment for a certain patient. Her presupposition is made explicit in the CDMS, namely that the patient is incontinent of faeces. George indicates to the CDMS that he does not agree. He states that the patient is not incontinent but needs prompting and suffers from diarrhoea. Brigid does not understand the word prompting and asks the CDMS for clarification. When she receives it she explains her statement that the patient suffers from incontinence. George then suggests an alternative course of action, namely to prescribe Loperamide and see whether this solves the problem, which Brigid accepts.

The two actors are again consultant Dr. Brigid May-Ringer and SN George Friend (as specified in Table 6). The first speech act is a request made by Brigid for George to assess the patient's state of continence. The classification of a request and the related validity claims have been discussed in the first scenario. In this example, the nurse challenges the truth of the doctor's presupposition that the patient is incontinent of faeces. The CDMS allows this challenge as a valid reply to the doctor's request, and George must specify the reasons: "I do not think the patient is incontinent. He only needs prompting. I think he has diarrhoea." Brigid is presented with this challenge by the CDMS. She wants to clarify the term "prompting" first, which will be translated into the medical phrase "reminded to urinate or open bowels." As she now understands George's reasons she replies by stating again that the patient is incontinent: "Patient suffers from stress incontinence, under control on ward because nurses remind the patient to go to the toilet." The CDMS will present this answer to George, who decides to suggest a compromise: "Why don't you write him up for Loperamide and see whether his loose stools become better. If this does not work we can make an assessment then." The CDMS presents this to Brigid, who now agrees on this new course of action and thus on the rejection of the original request. Therefore, the original request is marked as cancelled.

The second speech act is a new request with opposite roles of the actors, i.e., George as the author and Brigid as the recipient, which is allowed by the CDMS according to the predefined authorised interactions in Table 9. George is then required to give a review date, which would be the current date in this example. Brigid will record the achieved date if she accepts the related validity claims that George raises, which she does. Thus, she has committed herself to prescribe Loperamide.

Discussion

The first scenario in this section reconsiders a situation experienced during the fieldwork where it was an example for a complete cooperation breakdown due to existing problems (the doctor did not understand the nurse's document entry as a request for her to take the blood sample). These problems were only resolved in the face-to-face dialogue that took place after a considerable time. In the current practice, documentation is a purely passive medium prone to breakdowns which cannot easily be resolved. Note the contrast to the role of documentation as a true medium for communication/cooperation as proposed here. A CDMS based on the framework would avoid the breakdown by making the recipient of the speech act explicit, as shown in the first scenario in this section. This would make the doctor aware that (s)he was meant to take the blood.

The focus on validity claims is of particular importance as it enables the participants to enter discussions and negotiations towards mutual agreements. As demonstrated in the scenarios, CDMSs based on this approach would make challenges to validity claims explicit and indeed preempt them in the case of incomprehensible or inappropriate acts by making the illocutionary forces explicit and allowing only forces that have been defined as appropriate to be used by a particular author. Furthermore, a CDMS would make it possible for the communication partners to enter a discussion rather than having to wait until the communication partner is present, which is the current practice. If a challenge occurs, this means that a communication problem exists. However, the author is made aware of it and can react through the CDMS. Thus, cooperation is less likely to break down compared to the present situation.

A key difference between a new CDMS as discussed here and the current practice is that the whole process of the discussion is mediated and, therefore, recorded by the CDMS, which can help other professionals for their own decision making. For example, the history behind the agreements in Scenarios 2 and 3 could be seen by other professionals if required. Scenario 3 shows that the outcome of a discussion does not need to be the acceptance of the commitment intended by the author. In this case, the recipient did not agree and made a counteroffer which was then accepted by the author. Thus, the original request would be marked as rejected, but it would still exist in the system so that the professionals could access it if necessary. Scenario 1 shows that the mediation of conversations can be difficult due to the complexities of such interactions. For example, the three speech acts discussed in the scenario are all interrelated, and the system must recognise that they all belong to the same conversation even if there are other speech acts with the same author or recipient occurring in between the three utterances.

Whilst the benefits of the CDMS are clear, this is not to ignore the potential difficulties when it comes to implementing working CDMSs. The ethnographic work indicated that some communication problems were due to ambiguous speech acts. In applications based on the framework, certain features that were implicitly used before must be made explicit. By making communication more explicit (i.e., who is meant, which force is used, etc.), it is believed that many breakdowns in communication can be avoided. However, it is possible that a user might regard this as more disturbing than helpful. Therefore, a computer-based CDMS will have to have a carefully designed user interface to acquire the necessary data without requiring more effort of time and work for the user compared to existing systems. For example, it is possible to classify utterances automatically into the five classes (assertive, commissive, directive, expressive, declarative) through the illocutionary force used provided that the problem of multiple classifications has been solved.

Suchman (1994) has criticised the Coordinator for requiring users to make parts of an utterance explicit. She argued that this can be problematic because a speaker does not always know what (s)he means at the beginning of an interaction. I would argue that this might be the case in everyday interaction, but this is not very relevant for organisational communication in the case of multidisciplinary conversations in a healthcare setting. It has not been observed that the problems with implicit utterances concerned the speaker's problems of uttering what (s)he meant; rather, the speaker thought the utterance was clear for the listener, who did not understand it as was intended to, e.g., what was meant as a directive was understood as a mere statement.

It is a well-known claim for the development of computer-based systems that the advantages of existing paper-based systems should be retained while exploiting the benefits that computer-based systems can offer. Whilst this is a relevant consideration in this context, I would argue that not only should the advantages of paper and computer technology be combined, but paper should not necessarily be abandoned in favour of IT. For the context of multidisciplinary healthcare, it is not envisaged by this work to create a paperless hospital, not even to create paperless documentation. It is believed that paper documents will always play a role in cooperative work in healthcare. Even if documentation were completely computer-based, some paper documents would still exist. For example, most of the nurses observed during the fieldwork wrote on small pieces of paper what they wanted to remember, what they wanted to tell the other nurse during the handover, or what they wanted to document later on. Likewise, doctors sometimes wrote down results during an examination on some scrap paper before recording the results in the medical record.

It is also important to emphasise that it is not proposed to eliminate face-to-face communication which forms an important part of routine interaction. Nor is it proposed to force such types of communication into a documentation system. Rather, the aim is to use CDMSs to make written communication more effective, to strengthen the true role of documentation as a medium for supporting cooperative work through effective written communication.

Not all elements of the framework need to be implemented to have a positive impact on written communication. However, I would argue that even if all elements were implemented, the result would be less rigid compared to systems such as the Coordinator because this work addresses interactions between two actors rather than being focused on an author of an entry in the CDMS. Furthermore, through the incorporation of validity issues, discussion is encouraged and the recipient is given the possibility to criticise an utterance in a structured way. Finally, by including the possibility of a "free shot" through a charity relation which gives each actor the possibility to ask for a favour without being in the position to request it, it is acknowledged that there are situations that cannot or should not be structured but rather left to the actors to decide on an appropriate response. Another point worth mentioning is that this work presupposes the existing social structure in multidisciplinary healthcare. In this sense, the established social order is reproduced and the actors are forced to comply to this structure, a fact that both Suchman and Bowers have been critical about in their works. The author concedes that her goal was not to change the organisational structures but to enhance interactions within them. It is not believed that a system that dissolves the organisational and power structures would succeed in such a highly hierarchical domain as healthcare. However, this work could provide the possibility for social change. In this section, Table 9 showed a fixed definition of authorised illocutionary forces for each actor in the system. Another possibility would be to give and retract authorisations between communication partners dynamically (Verharen, 1997), i.e., the partners themselves could negotiate these authorisations. This could lead to the establishment of new social structures. For example, nurses could be allowed to prescribe certain drugs, doctors could relinquish their right to order nurses to perform actions, etc.

CONCLUSION

Summary

This chapter has introduced a Language-Action approach to cooperative document management systems. In particular, the development of a conceptual framework for the design of such systems to promote effective written communication in multidisciplinary healthcare has been proposed and discussed.

The approach taken for this work started with a general interest in how computer support could enhance multidisciplinary cooperation in healthcare, especially documentation for both doctors and nurses. To find out about general work practices, communication and cooperation patterns, documentation practices, and common causes of problems between doctors and nurses, ethnographic studies were carried out on a geriatric ward. At the end of these studies, which lasted for several months, it was decided to concentrate on providing a theoretical basis for the design of better cooperative document management systems that help to avoid communication and cooperation breakdowns. The reasons for this were threefold:

- It was found that for the cooperation between doctors and nurses, information technology could be helpful in non-copresence situations because in such situations, the existing problems were observed to have the potential for causing complete breakdowns in communication and cooperation. When the communication partners were copresent, problems occurred but could usually be solved in face-to-face dialogues. Documentation is the main form of a non-copresence situation and it plays an important role in healthcare.
- The cooperative aspect that is so important in multidisciplinary work is stressed in cooperative document management systems. The staff of the geriatric ward who developed the MDT system were enthusiastic about it, and it became apparent that the development of CDMSs would be a worthwhile form of computer-supported cooperative work.
- At the same time, it was observed that there were existing problems with this form of written communication which justified a new approach to the development of CDMSs. It was decided to exploit the potential of information technology to make CDMSs more effective.

The central phenomenon that threatened effective cooperation was problematic communication occurring between doctors and nurses. It was found that these problems needed to be solved first before a computer-based CDMS could be introduced for efficient cooperation. This finding prompted an examination of existing communication theories for developing a theoretical framework to explain the problems that had been observed in a structured way. Habermas' Theory of Communicative Action was looked at because his ideas have been quite influential in the area of information systems. Habermas' arguments of validity issues seemed like a revelation; it was found that the problems could indeed be classified according to the underlying validity challenges. However, there were problems of cooperation for which Habermas' theory did not seem sufficient. Here the researcher turned to Searle's Theory of Speech Acts and again found some useful concepts. The two theories were combined into a framework which was tested out in the field by recording communication scenarios and analysing them with the framework. It was established which concepts from both theories are relevant for the area of interest, i.e., multidisciplinary healthcare.

After establishing a classification of common communication and cooperation problems, the next step was to think about how breakdowns in written communication could be avoided, thus to think about features of an ideal CDMS. A framework for the design of such idealised CDMSs was developed that could accommodate these features and describe those aspects of multidisciplinary healthcare necessary to promote more effective document management. During this process, Searle's and Habermas' arguments were revisited and it was established that some of them needed refinement for the purposes of this work. For example, it was found that not only the illocutionary force but also the identity of the author and recipient of a certain speech act determined what could be expressed in the propositional content.

It has been illustrated how the framework could be used by simulating an operational CDMS based on the language. This initial evaluation used scenarios based on the ethnographic work to show how interaction would be enhanced by dealing with communication problems in a structured way and thereby preventing most breakdowns.

Revisiting the Key Findings of the Ethnographic Work

Earlier in the chapter, the key issues resulting from the ethnographic findings were discussed. It was argued that they need to be considered for the design of any computer-based systems supporting cooperative work, CDMSs in particular. In this section I will discuss how these issues were addressed in the present approach and will elaborate further implications as they arise. The issues are highlighted in italics.

The first finding was that *cooperative document management is important but breakdowns can occur.* The main philosophy behind this work is that cooperative document management is not only important but indeed vital for effective cooperation. However, cooperation does not always work. Cooperative document management systems must take into account potential breakdowns in communication and seek to ameliorate them. That is what this work is all about.

The *different pragmatic concerns* have influenced the development of the framework in many ways. The professional role has been considered through the specification of the main task, responsibilities, and duties of each professional group. The different pragmatics are also reflected in the utterances of professionals, which is the reason for including the medical knowledge in the language to enable a specification of what the professionals say or write to each other.

The *different linguistic styles* used by doctors and nurses and their *different professional terminologies* were the motivation for working towards a translation process to back up the interaction between doctors and nurses when they think it necessary. I have argued that for a CDMS to promote effective communication in multidisciplinary healthcare, the existing communication and cooperation problems have to be addressed in a theoretically rigorous way rather than attempting to address the different viewpoints of professionals by merely providing different presentations of patient data. Nevertheless, I would suggest that the latter approach can also be helpful once the theoretical basis for the design of CDMSs has been developed as in this work. Thus, different interfaces for the different professionals according to their requirements of access and data representation could address the different linguistic styles used by doctors and nurses, and provide the relevant information in their own professional terminologies.

The finding that *documentation plays a different role for doctors and nurses,* which also explains their *different attitudes toward document management,* is something that has not explicitly been addressed here. I believe that technology can never solve all existing problems between human actors. Some problems will remain, such as problems resulting from the different attitudes, and need to be addressed in a different way. If people do not want to cooperate then this cannot be enforced. Interpersonal relations must be dealt with elsewhere.

It is possible to implicitly address these problems, e.g., by making elements such as unfulfilled commitments explicit. For example, if doctors repeatedly fail to take blood samples although it had been requested by nurses, then this could initiate a different *mode of communication* such as discourse. The aim here is not to support this type of interaction by the system because it is not felt necessary and is best dealt with on a face-to-face basis. Documentation is mostly used for asynchronous processes, e.g., a nurse asks a doctor to look at a patient's pressure sores, which the doctor will usually not do at the same time the request is documented. However, one general advantage of computer-based systems, i.e., availability, can also be exploited for synchronous remote processes, e.g., a nurse documents a certain request in the cooperative document management system on the ward while a doctor looks at X-rays at the same time in the X-ray department and documents the diagnosis that the patient suffers from a fractured femur.

Future Work

Further work can be carried out in the following areas: evaluation, prototype design, and application to other domains. An initial evaluation of the framework was presented previously. Further work is required to perform a more rigorous evaluation. Further evaluation could be carried out through experiments in which nurses and doctors would be presented with hypothetical patient cases and asked to interact through the CDMS.

A natural continuation of the work will be to develop further the prototype of a computer-based cooperative document management system based on the framework to evaluate further how such an operational system would enhance written communication. A decision on candidate architectures will have to be made. The CDMS could be realised as a client-server architecture, where nurses and doctors access shared data resources that would be presented according to their different information requirements. To this end, alternative interfaces for nurses and doctors would have to be designed to represent these requirements with respect to presentation, access, and retrieval of information. Context would have to be represented according to the specific viewpoints, e.g., what information is relevant for present decisions, how are responsibilities handled, etc. This CDMS could either contain all features of the framework, it could contain some, or it could be implemented using the framework elements as an informal guide for considering important issues in multidisciplinary healthcare. The prototypical development of a CDMS based on the approach presented here is ongoing.

The present approach could be applied to other areas involving multidisciplinary work with documentation or indeed to other areas where the general findings could be helpful. For example, Te'eni and Schwartz (1998) have used the present work for their analysis of communication in an international cooperative work environment; Currel et al. (1998) have used the theoretical framework for analysing communication problems between doctors and nurses (Schoop, 1997a, 1997b) in their research into information use and information needs in nursing. The framework is currently being adapted to document management in an electronic commerce context.

There seems to be a trend toward more cooperative forms of document management in general. In healthcare, there is more and more cooperative documentation as we have observed over the last few years. A new initiative has recently been announced in which cooperative construction teams manage their documents as a group. Furthermore, we work in the area of e-commerce on document management, which is mainly contract management. As the contract is the result of a negotiation between two (or more) responsible partners, the contract is a cooperative document that needs to be managed by all parties involved.

Contributions

I would argue that the present research makes a number of specific contributions which are discussed below. The ethnographic work provides a good understanding of multidisciplinary work practices and group work. There has been hardly any study of doctor-nurse interaction; Fafchamps (1988) is an exception and reports on communication in a surgical intensive ward. Many studies in the area of healthcare have either concentrated on doctor-patient discourse or cooperation within one professional group; for example, Heath and Luff (1996) and Luff et al. (1992) talk about paper documentation to support cooperation between doctors. Multidisciplinary cooperation is at least as important as interaction within one group. In healthcare this kind of cooperation takes place mainly between doctors and nurses as the main contributors to patient care. Therefore, an ethnographic investigation into cooperation and its problems between doctors and nurses is a contribution in its own right.

Empirical studies using the Language-Action Perspective (LAP) have not frequently been done before. Although there has been much theoretical work in the LAP community, the practical modelling has usually not been based on empirical data. I would argue that by basing the approach on a solid empirical platform, many of the criticisms that have been made of LAP have been reassessed and overcome. Suchman's criticism that the categories and classifications of organisational behaviour are imposed from the outside rather than coming from the users of systems themselves (Suchman, 1994) is clearly avoided here. The classification of communication problems emerged during the ethnographic studies and was further refined using concepts from Searle's and Habermas' theories. The aim of ethnography is to present situations from the participants' own points of view rather than forcing the researcher's own categories on the data.

On the theoretical side, I have refined both Searle's and Habermas' theories for the present purposes. My notion of an illocutionary force is different from Searle's in that I have shown that the categories he presents are not only dependent on the force (as he argues) but also on the speaker or hearer of the utterance. Habermas' theory was slightly amended with respect to the relation between validity claims and certain types of utterances. I discussed my opinion that the claim of "truth" is not related to all utterances as Habermas argues.

Contrary to Dietz and Widdershoven (1991), I do not see the two theories as contradictory. Rather I would argue that they consider different aspects of speech. Searle describes different types of utterances and classifies them. Furthermore, general characteristics of a speech act are established and their different values are discussed for the different types of speech acts. Therefore, Searle describes conditions for ideal communication. Habermas, on the other hand, develops a framework for the process of achieving consensus through negotiating validity claims that are imminent in each utterance. He takes into account that communication problems can occur and describes the mechanism for achieving mutual agreements in human interaction. Therefore, the two theories can be integrated to provide a powerful framework for communication analysis.

The Language-Action paradigm focuses mainly on the pragmatic and metalinguistic level, which means that comprehensibility problems are often ignored. It has been argued in the present approach that comprehensibility problems need to be addressed in this context because they are the most common communication problem in doctor-nurse interactions. Therefore, the possibility of providing translation between different professional terminologies has been proposed. The aim is to bring in results from other approaches dealing with similar issues, e.g., explaining the medical record to patients or mapping between different medical classification systems. Thereby I aimed at drawing together the semantic level dealt with in these other approaches and the pragmatic level of the Language-Action Perspective.

The main contribution of this research is that it provides a systematic theoretical framework for the design of CDMSs. The categories introduced as elements of the framework show which features of multidisciplinary communication are salient and need to be considered for the design of CDMSs that will help to avoid breakdowns in communication and, therefore, enable better cooperation. It has never been claimed that this work could help to solve all communication problems but it is argued that most breakdowns can be avoided. This will make possible CDMSs that promote more effective multidisciplinary communication. Since the focus of the present work was interaction rather than one particular healthcare group, better systems will be enabled that are useful for and usable by all professionals involved. As cooperation problems are always to the disadvantage of the patient, this work is expected to contribute to improved patient care by making smooth cooperation easier. It is important to stress that this is not the only way to improve written communication. Another possibility could be to teach professionals to improve their communication skills.

The benefits of the Language-Action approach have been demonstrated for the example of multidisciplinary healthcare. It can also be expected that the framework developed here can be applied to other multiprofessional settings involving document management systems. The categories that have been introduced are not specific to the domain of healthcare but can be used to describe any communication setting by specifying:

- the possible actors in the system (classification of authors and recipients),
- their different professional roles (described by responsibilities, duties, main tasks, etc.),
- their possible ways of communicating with certain other actors (classification of possible forces for each author-recipient pair, possible contents of utterances),
- the underlying organisational structures and power hierarchies (authorisations for discussions, initiations of discourses or their prohibitions in case of strategic action), etc.

The issue of misunderstandings due to different professional terminologies (which is considered by the translation process) can be a general problem if professionals from different disciplines work together. Hence, the results of this work are expected to be generalisable.

To summarise, I have argued that this work will contribute to enhanced cooperation in healthcare by providing the basis for better CDMSs that promote effective written multidisciplinary communication.

ACKNOWLEDGEMENTS

The people without whom this work would not have been possible must, unfortunately, remain anonymous. I am indebted to the staff of the geriatric ward for all their help and support. Furthermore, I would like to thank Dr. David Wastell for his guidance, critical input, and incentive while I conducted the research reported on in this chapter.

REFERENCES

Allwood, J. (1998). A Critical Look at the Language Action Perspective in Communication Modelling. Invited Talk at the Third International Workshop on the Language-Action Perspective on Communication Modelling, LAP'98.

Auramäki, E., Hirschheim, R., and Lyytinen, K. (1992a). Modelling Offices Through Discourse Analysis: The SAMPO Approach. *The Computer Journal*, 35(4), 342-352.

Auramäki, E., Hirschheim, R., and Lyytinen, K. (1992b). Modelling Offices Through Discourse Analysis: A Comparison and Evaluation of SAMPO with OSSAD and ICN. *The Computer Journal*, 35(5):492-500.

Auramäki, E., Lehtinen, E., and Lyytinen, K. (1988). A Speech-Act-Based Office Modeling Approach. *ACM Transactions on Office Information Systems, Special Issue on the Language/Action Perspective*, 6(2): 126-152.

Bentley, R., Hughes, JA., Randall, D., Rodden, T., Sawyer, P., Shapiro, D. and Sommerville. I. (1992a). Ethnographically-Informed Systems Design for Air Traffic Control. In Turner and Kraut (1992), 123-129.

Bentley, R., Rodden, T., Sawyer, P., and Sommerville, I. (1992b). An Architecture for Tailoring Cooperative Multi-User Displays. In Turner and Kraut (1992), 187-194.

Binsted, K., Cawsey, A., and Jones, R. (1995). Generating Personalised Patient Information Using the Medical Record. In *Proceedings of Artificial Intelligence in Medicine Europe*, AIME '95.

Bowers, J. (1996). Hanging Around and Making Something of it: Ethnography. In J. Haworth, ed., *Psychological Research: Innovative Methods and Strategies*, 120-138. London: Routledge.

Bullock J. and Goble, C. (1998). TourisT: An Application of a Description Logic Based Semantic Hypermedia System for Tourism. In K. Gronbaek, E. Mulonas, and F.M. Shipman, eds., *Proceedings of the Ninth ACM Conference on Hypertext and Hypermedia*, Hypertext'98, 132-141, New York. ACM Press.

Burgess, R.G. (1984). *In the Field: An Introduction to Field Research.* London: Allen&Unwin.

Cawsey, A., Binsted, K., and Jones, R. (1995). An On-Line Explanation of the Medical Record to Patients via an Artificial Intelligence Approach. In B. Richards, H. de Glanville, and H. MacOwan, eds., *Proceedings of Current Perspectives in Healthcare Computing*, 269-275, Weybridge. BJHC Limited.

Currel, R., Gold G., Hardiker, N., Hoy, D., and Waiwright, P. (1998). Nursing Information Research Project, Final Report. NHS Centre for Coding and Classification.

Dietz, JLG . (1994a). Business Modelling for Business Redesign. In *Proceedings of the Twenty-Seventh Annual Hawaii International Conference on System Sciences*, HICSS'94, 723-732, Los Alamitos. IEEE Computer Society Press.

Dietz, JLG. (1994b). Modelling Business Processes for the Purpose of Redesign. In B.C. Glasson, I.T. Hawryszkiesycs, B.A. Underwood, and R.A. Weber, eds. *Proceedings of the IFIP TC8 Open Conference on Business Process Re-Engineering*, 233-242, North-Holland: Elsevier Science Publishers B.V.

Dietz, JLG, and Widdershoven, GAM. (1991). Speech Acts or Communicative Action? In L Bannon, M Robinson, and K Schmidt, eds., *Proceedings of the Second European Conference on Computer-Supported Cooperative Work*, ECSCW'91, pp 235-248, Dordrecht. Kluwer Academic Publishers.

Dignum, F., and Dietz, J., eds. (1997). Communication Modeling – The Language/Action Perspective; *Computing Science Reports* 97-09, Eindhoven. Eindhoven University of Technology.

Fafchamps, DL. (1988). Conventions and Strategies: a Framework for Understanding Communication in a Surgical Intensive Care Unit. PhD Thesis, Stanford University.

Flores, F., and Ludlow, JJ. (1980). Doing and Speaking in the Office. In G. Fick and R.H. Sprague Jr., eds., *Decision Support Systems: Issues and Challenges*, 95-118. Pergamon Press.

Glaser, B., and Strauss, A. (1967). *The Discovery of Grounded Theory.* Aldine.

Goldkuhl, G., Lind, M., and Seigerroth, U., eds. (1998). *Proceedings of the Third International Workshop on the Language Action Perspective on Communication Modelling*. Jönköping International Business School.

Goldkuhl, G., Lind, M., Seigerroth, U., and Ågerfalk, P., eds. (1999). *Proceedings of the Fourth International Workshop on the Language Action Perspective on Communication Modelling*. Jönköping International Business School.

Habermas, J. (1981). *Theorie des kommunikativen Handelns*, Teil 1: Handlungsrationalität und gesellschaftliche Rationalisierung. Suhrkamp, Frankfurt am Main.

Habermas, J. (1984). *The Theory of Communicative Action*, Volume 1: Reason and the Rationalisation of Society. London: Heinemann.

Hardiker, N.R., Heathfield, H.A., and Kirby J. (1995). Introducing Information Systems to Nursing Practice: the Professional and Cultural Barriers. In B. Richards, H. de Glanville, and H. MacOwan, eds., *Proceedings of Current Perspectives in Healthcare Computing*, 419-427, Weybridge. BJHC Limited.

Hardiker, N.R., and Rector, A.L. (1998). Modeling Nursing Terminology Using the GRAIL Representation Language. *Journal of the American Medical Informatics Association*, 5(1): 120-128.

Heath, C., and Luff, P. (1996). Documents and Professional Practice: 'Bad' Organisational Reasons for 'Good' Clinical Records. In M.S. Ackermann, ed. (1996), *Proceedings of the ACM 1996 Conference on Computer Supported Cooperative Work*, CSCW'96, 354-369, New York. ACM Press.

Heathfield, H., Kirby, J., Nowlan, A., and Rector, A. (1992). PEN&PAD (Geriatrics): A Collaborative Patient Record System for the Shared Care of the Elderly. In M.E. Frisse, ed., *Proceedings of the Sixteenth Annual Symposium on Computer Applications in Medical Care*, SCAMC'92, 147-150, New York: McGraw-Hill.

Heathfield, H.A., Hardiker, H., and Kirby, J. (1994). Using the PEN&PAD Information Model to Support Hospital-Based Clinical Care. In J.G. Ozbolt, ed., *Proceedings of the Eighteenth Annual Symposium on Computer Applications in Medical Care*, SCAMC'94, 452-456, Philadelphia: Hanley&Belfus Inc.

Hoffman-La Roche and Urban & Schwarzenberg, eds. (1987). *Roche Lexikon Medizin*. München: Urban & Schwarzenberg.

Hughes, J.A., Randall, D., and Shapiro, D. (1992). Faltering from Ethnography to Design. In Turner and Kraut (1992), 115-122.

Hughes, J.A., Randall, D., and Shapiro, D. (1993). From Ethnographic Record to System Design: Some Experiences from the Field. *Computer Supported Cooperative Work* (CSCW), 1:123-141.

Layton, A. (1993). Planning Individual Care with Protocols. *Nursing Standard*, 8(1):32-34.

Luff, P., Heath, C., and Greatbach, D. (1992). Tasks-In-Interaction: Paper and Screen Based Documentation in Collaborative Activity. In Turner and Kraut (1992), 163-170.

Lyytinen, K. (1985). Implications of Theories of Language for Information Systems. *MIS Quarterly*, pp 61-74.

Lyytinen, K. and Lehtinen, E. (1984). On Information Modelling Through Illocutionary Logic. In H. Kangassalo, ed., *Proceedings of Third Scandinavian Research Seminar on Information Modelling and Data Base Management*, 35-115, Tampere. Acta Universitatis Tamperensis, Ser. B, Vol, 22.

Lyytinen, K., and Klein, H.K. (1985). The Critical Theory of Jürgen Habermas as a Basis for a Theory of Information Systems. In E. Mumford, R. Hirschheim, G. Fitzgerald., A.T. Wood-Harper, eds., *Research Methods in Information Systems*, 19-236. Elsevier Science Publishers, Amsterdam.

Martin, D., Bowers, J., and Wastell, D.G. (1997). The Interactional Affordances of Technology: An Ethnography of Human-Computer Interaction in an

Ambulance Control Centre. In H. Thimbelby, B. O'Conaill, and P. Thomas, eds., *People and Computers XII: Proceedings of the Conference on Human-Computer Interaction*, HCI'97, 263-281, London. Springer Verlag.

Martin, D., Wastell, D.G., and Bowers, J. (1998). Ethnographically Informed System Design: The Development and Evaluation of an Internet-Based Electronic Banking Application. In WRJ Baets, ed., *Proceedings of the Sixth European Conference on Information Systems*, ECIS'98, 513-527. Euro-Arab Management School, Granada.

McCarthy, T. (1984). *The Critical Theory of Jürgen Habermas*. Cambridge: Polity Press.

Morgan, G. (1993). The Implications of Patient Focused Care. *Nursing Standard*, 7(52):37-39.

Newman, M.A. (1990). Towards an Integrative Model of Professional Practice. *Journal of Professional Nursing*, 6(3):167-173.

Plowman, L., Rogers, Y., and Ramage, M. (1995). What are Workplace Studies for? In H. Marmolin, Y. Sundbald, and K. Schmidt, eds., *Proceedings of the Fourth European Conference on Computer-Supported Cooperative Work*, ECSCW'95, 309-324, Dordrecht. Kluwer Academic Publishers.

Pycock, J., and Bowers, J. (1996). Getting Others to Get It Right: An Ethnography of Design Work in the Fashion Industry. In M.S. Ackermann, ed. (1996), *Proceedings of the ACM 1996 Conference on Computer Supported Cooperative Work*, CSCW'96, 219-228, New York. ACM Press.

Rouncefield, M., Hughes, J.A., Rodden, T., and Viller, S. (1994). Working with "Constant Interruption": CSCW and the Small Office. In R. Furuta and C. Neuwirth, eds., *Proceedings of the Conference on Computer Supported Cooperative Work*, CSCW'94, pp. 275-286, New York. ACM Press.

Schatzmann, L., and Strauss, A. (1973). *Field Research: Strategies for a Natural Sociology*. Prentice-Hall.

Schoop, M. (1997a). Describing Cooperative Documentation Systems in Healthcare: A Framework. In G. Büchele, D. Harder, and W. Gaus, eds., *Medizinische Informatik, Biometrie und Epidemiologie*, 203-208, München. MMV Medizin Verlag.

Schoop, M. (1997b). Habermas and Searle in Hospital: A Description Language for Cooperative Documentation Systems in Healthcare. In Dignum and Dietz (1997), 117-132.

Schoop, M. (1998). Towards Effective Multidisciplinary Communication: A Language-Action Approach to Cooperative Documentation Systems. PhD

Thesis, University of Manchester.

Schoop, M., and Wastell, D.G. (1998). A Language-Action Approach to Cooperative Documentation Systems. In WRJ Baets, ed., *Proceedings of the Sixth European Conference on Information Systems*, ECIS'98, 984-997. Euro-Arab Management School, Granada.

Schoop, M., and Wastell, D.G. (1999). Effective Multidisciplinary Communication in Healthcare: Cooperative Documentation Systems. *Methods of Information in Medicine*, 38(4-5):265-273.

Schoop, M., and Quix, C., eds. (2000). *Proceedings of the Fifth International Workshop on the Language Action Perspective on Communication Modelling*. Aachener Informatik Berichte, RWTH Aachen.

Searle, J.R. (1969). *Speech Acts: An Essay in the Philosophy of Language*. Cambridge: Cambridge University Press.

Searle, J.R. and Vanderveken, D. (1985). *Foundations of Illocutionary Logic*. Cambridge: Cambridge University Press.

Suchman, L. (1983). Office Procedure as Practical Action: Models of Work and System Design. *ACM Transaction on Office Information Systems*, 1(4):320-328.

Suchman, L. (1987). *Plans and Situated Actions: The Problem of Human Machine Communication*. Cambridge University Press.

Suchman, L. (1994). Do Categories Have Politics? The Language/Action Perspective Reconsidered. *Computer Supported Cooperative Work*, 2(3): 177-190.

Te'eni, D., and Schwartz, D.G. (1998). Rich Communication for International Cooperation. In R. Traunmüller, ed., *Telecooperation - Proceedings of XV IFIP World Computer Congress*, 343-357, Vienna. Austrian Computer Society.

Turner, J., and Kraut, R., eds. (1992). *Proceedings of the Conference on Computer-Supported Cooperative Work*, CSCW'92. ACM Press, New York.

van Reijswoud, V.E. (1996). The Structure of Business Communication, PhD Thesis, Delft University of Technology.

van der Rijst, NBJ. Analysis and Design of Emerging Network Organizations. In Dignum and Dietz (1997), 1-12.

Verharen, E.M. (1997). A Language-Action Perspective on the Design of Cooperative Information Agents. PhD Thesis, Katholieke Universiteit Brabant, Tilburg.

Winograd, T. (1988). A Language/Action Perspective on the Design of Cooperative Work. In I. Greif, ed., *Computer-Supported Cooperative Work: A Book of Readings*, 623-653. San Mateo: Morgan Kaufman.

Winograd, T., and Flores, F. (1986). *Understanding Computers and Cognition: A New Foundation for Design*. Norwood: Ablex.

ENDNOTES

1 Patient-identifiable data has been changed. The documents show direct transcripts of the original entries.

2 The MDT had been changed during my ethnographic studies. This example shows the new forms that were used for this patient.

3 Although both Searle and Habermas talk about "speaker" and "hearer," their theories can be applied to written communication as well.

4 Note that this is specific to secondary healthcare. In primary healthcare, a prescription made by a doctor does not usually involve a nurse. In the ethnographic studies it was observed that nurses are allowed to administer all drugs. Thus, in the present work the force of prescription is taken as a directive made by a doctor to a nurse.

5 PC stands for "Propositional Content"; IF stands for "Illocutionary Force."

6 However, it is the author's opinion that the responsibilities should always remain with the human individual because this professional will be accountable for the actions in case of problems.

7 Some drugs are stored on the ward. These are usually drugs that are used very often such as Paracetamol, Frusemide, or Senokot.

Chapter VIII

Supporting Access to Information Created in Interorganizational Processes

Virpi Lyytikäinen, Pasi Tiitinen, Airi Salminen
University of Jyväskylä, Finland

INTRODUCTION

Text databases available on the Internet serve as massive information resources. To a person needing a piece of information, finding the piece however is often quite problematic. The databases are organized in different ways, their content is written in different languages, and their retrieval techniques vary. The text databases containing legal information on the Internet offer a typical example. A recent trend towards electronic government (e-government) has tremendously increased the amount of public information available to citizens and organizations on the Internet. In Europe, due to the development towards European integration, this information is increasingly needed also regarding foreign European legal systems and the European Union itself. Differences in legal systems aggravate the problems of information retrieval. Similarly, on the intranets and extranets of organizations, information resources are often scattered in heterogeneous repositories. In paper machine manufacturing, for example, the amount of cooperating organizations and documents involved is always immense, and the information related to the manufacturing process is more and more often stored on documents available via intranets and extranets.

To be able to find relevant documents and to be able to interpret the content of the documents correctly, people often need information about the context where the documents have been created. This contextual metadata may be hard to find. In this chapter, we introduce a method for improving the retrieval of documents created in interorganizational processes by collecting metadata about the context of documents. The metadata is visualized to the users by graphical models. These models offer information about the context through viewpoints of processes, actors, and information sources and facilitate the retrieval of documents from different databases. The solution is demonstrated by a case of retrieving information from distributed European legal text databases.

The rest of the chapter is organized as follows. In the next section we discuss the background of the study with references to previous literature. Then the next section describes legal information in Europe as a case and demonstrates the challenges related to information retrieval in the case. We then introduce the retrieval interfaces for finding information and accessing documents related to legal information from European legal databases. Finally, the last section discusses future trends related to the need for visualization of metadata.

BACKGROUND

In order to assist users who need to retrieve documents originating from multiple organizations, the documents should be associated with metadata describing the context where documents were created. This kind of contextual metadata should contain information concerning the production processes, organizations involved, and relationships between different document types produced (e.g., Bearman, 1995). Information models provided by document analysis offer a useful tool for gathering metadata about the context where documents are created.

Document Analysis

In the project called RASKE (Rakenteisten AsiakirjaStandardien KEhittäminen, meaning development of standards for structured documents), methods for *document analysis* have been developed (Salminen, Lehtovaara & Kauppinen, 1996; Salminen, Kauppinen & Lehtovaara, 1997; Salminen, 2000; Salminen, Lyytikäinen & Tiitinen, 2000). The document analysis methodology includes methods and techniques to be used to study and describe electronic document management (EDM) environments (Figure

1) and to plan improvements to the environments. An EDM environment is modeled by the central notions of Information Control Nets (ICNs): *activities* and *resources* (Ellis, 1979). Information in an EDM environment is produced and used in activities. The resources are information repositories where information produced can be stored or from where information can be taken. The resources are divided into three types: documents, systems, and actors. *Documents* consist of the recorded data intended for human perception. A document can be identified and handled as a unit in the activities, and it is intended to be understood as information pertaining to a topic. *Systems* consist of devices, software, and data used to support the performance of activities. *Actors* are people and organizations performing activities and using documents as well as systems in the activities.

The RASKE methodology was originally developed for the purposes of document standardization. In the document analysis phase of the standardization process, current documents and document management practices are studied and described, and new document structures and document management practices are proposed. Later we realized that document analysis and descriptions provided during the analysis are important and useful also in developing improved retrieval capabilities for existing document repositories. Figure 2 shows the phases of a document analysis.

The analysis starts with *specifying the domain* to be analyzed. The domain is an activity like Creation of the Legal Sources in European Union or Paper Machine Manufacturing. The phase includes the identification of the major organizational actors of the activity. After the specification of the domain, three phases are started in parallel: process modeling, document modeling, and role modeling. *Process modeling* is used as a means to identify smaller activities and their interrelationships within the domain, the organizations responsible for those activities, and the documents created or used. *Document modeling* covers the description of document types, their lifecycles, contents, and relationships to each other. In *role modeling,* the key users of

Figure 1. Electronic Document Management Environment

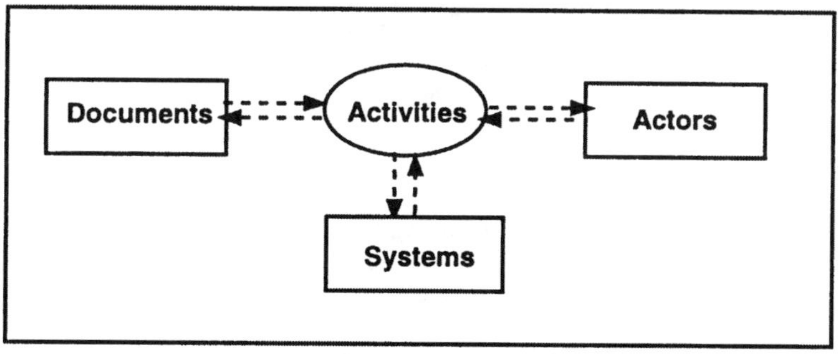

documents are identified and their document management activities are described. *User needs analysis* studies the problems in current document management and the needs for the future as identified by document users. *Collecting the analysis report* takes place at the end of the analysis. The report is collected on the basis of the descriptions and models produced in the earlier phases. The report includes suggestions and specifications for EDM of the future. The analysis methodology is described in detail in Salminen, Lehtovaara and Kauppinen (1996), Salminen, Kauppinen and Lehtovaara (1997), Salminen (2000), Salminen, Lyytikäinen and Tiitinen (2000), Tiitinen, Lyytikäinen, Päivärinta and Salminen (2000).

Modeling Techniques in Document Analysis

The modeling techniques of document analysis are intended for describing documents, activities where documents are created and manipulated, and actors in the activities. While developing and testing suitable modeling techniques the following requirements were identified (Salminen, Lyytikäinen & Tiitinen, 2000):

Figure 2. Phases of Document Analysis

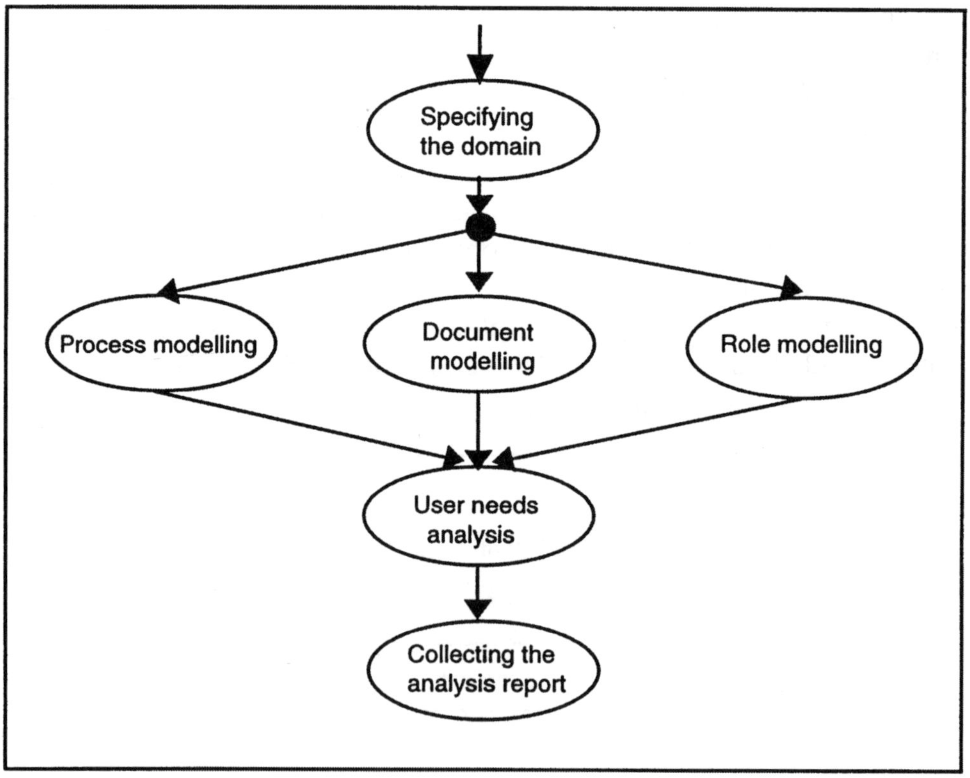

1. The models are intended *for human readers* to support communication and understanding. The models need not show all special cases; they have to allow human judgments in determining the detailed meaning in special cases.
2. The models have to be *graphical*, as *clear* as possible having *few notions and symbols*, supporting intuitive understanding. The major purpose of the models is to support the understanding of the domain and communication between people.
3. To avoid too many models in one communication situation, process models must allow showing the most important entities in the same model: activities, actors, and documents. Process models are not intended for process automation but to show how work is actually done. Thus they have to be *descriptive*, not prescriptive. The capability for separating the control and data flow is important to depict the creation and use of documents in business processes. Separate description of data and control flow also allows the use of the same symbols to describe control flow between activities only or data flow only when needed.

The most important origins of the modeling techniques chosen for document analysis are in the object-based modeling methodology of Shlaer and Mellor (1992), in Information Control Nets (Ellis, 1979), and in the document structure specification methods of SGML standard and elm graphs (Goldfarb, 1990; Maler & Andaloussi, 1996). The domain is described by an *organizational framework model* using the ICN notations. Quite the same result could be achieved by using notations from data flow diagrams of structured analysis and design (Yourdon, 1989). In the process modeling phase, the ICN diagrams are used for the *document output models* and *document input models*. The document output model shows the document types produced in each of the activities by performing actors, while the document input model shows the document types used during the activities. During the document modeling phase, the relationships of different document types with each other are described by a *document-relationship diagram* corresponding to the information structure diagram of OOA, or the entity-relationship diagram. The hierarchic structure of document types is described by elm graphs (Maler & Andaloussi, 1996) and SGML or XML DTDs or schemas (Goldfarb, 1990). The dynamic behavior of each document type is described by *state transition diagrams* originating from OOA modeling methodology. The role modeling phase includes the identification of different uses of documents by actors. The role is an abstraction of the document management needs, tasks and responsibilities of groups of people. A textual description of each of the roles is written and the relationships between the roles and document types are described in tables.

The important feature distinguishing Information Control Nets from many other process modeling methods is the clear separation of the control flow and information flow. The same kind of separation is also applied in the UML's action-object flow relationship diagram, a variation of the basic action diagram (UML-1.1, 1997; Booch, Rumbaugh, & Jacobson, 1999). In the UML's action-object diagram, however, the control flow and information flow can be combined if one activity produced output which in turn serves as input to the next activity.

Information Visualization

The models created during the document analysis can be seen as visualizations of contextual metadata. *Information visualization* is an emerging discipline which aims at transforming data, information and knowledge into visual form to exploit humans' natural visual capabilities (Gershon, Eick & Card, 1998). Visualization of organizational structures, processes and the information created and used in them is common in many areas. *Graphical models* are familiar tools, for example, in software engineering (e.g., UML; Booch, Rumbaugh & Jacobson, 1999) and in business process redesign (Abeysinghe & Phalp, 1997), where the visualizations are used by the experts who are doing the design work. In office information systems, work-flow management systems (Ellis, 1983), and computer-supported cooperative work systems (Sarin, Abbott & McCarthy, 1991), graphical models are used in the user interfaces, which in turn are used in everyday work tasks. Such has also been the case in the visualization of organizational processes and roles for use, e.g., in organizational learning (Käkölä, 1995) and for the management of multiple roles and related documents in the workplace (Plaisant & Shneiderman, 1995). Dourish, Bentley, Jones and MacLean (1999) have discussed the visualization of the history of one document instance within the work-flow description.

The visualizations we propose in this chapter add a new perspective for the above-mentioned uses of visual presentations. Our solution for visualizing contextual metadata by graphical models is intended to be used as a retrieval interface for distributed document repositories. The visualized metadata is designed to help the users of the document repositories in coping with the complex interorganizational environment.

LEGAL INFORMATION AS A CASE

Distributed legal databases in Europe offer an interesting and important example of information created in interorganizational processes. The case was studied in a project called EULEGIS (European User Views to Legislative Information in Structured Form) belonging to the Telematics Application Programme of the European Commission. The main practical intent of the EULEGIS project was to offer a single point Web access to European legal information created in different legal systems and at different levels—European Union, a country, a region, or a municipality—through a unified interface.

Documents created in the legislative processes in different European countries contain information important to all people and organizations in Europe. Some decades ago, people rarely needed other legal information except information created in their own country and own local area. Nowadays legal information from foreign countries and from the European Commission is often required in the activities of European people and organizations. The retrieval of European legal information, however, causes problems even for experts of legal matters. The problems are mainly related to three different areas: differences of the legal systems in different countries, heterogeneity of the databases, and heterogeneity of the users of the information (Lyytikäinen, Tiitinen & Salminen, 2000).

In all European countries, the legal rules are created in processes that are quite different in detail, although they may bear some resemblance to each other. When the legislation and the role of the courts are examined in different countries, two main traditions can be distinguished: a common law and a civil law (e.g., Gallagher, Laver & Mair, 1995). Within Europe, the United Kingdom and Ireland have a common law tradition. Most European countries belong to the civil law tradition, where the role of case law has much less significance.

Another major difference in the producing of legal rules in different countries is in the role of regions. In some countries (e.g., Germany, Austria and Belgium), legislative power has been decentralized so that several power centers have their own legal systems. On the other hand, there are countries, such as Finland, which only have minor legislative power at the regional level. A certain amount of regulative power has often also been left with, e.g., provinces or municipalities.

The various types of legal documents and their significance vary in different countries. However, three major groups of legal documents can be identified: normative documents including acts and decrees, preparatory works, and court judgments. The types of documents, their structures, and the languages used in them are, however, different. Even if the same language were used in two countries, the terminology can vary considerably.

The number of legal information providers on the Internet has been growing rapidly. The dissemination of normative and preparative documents on the Internet free-of-charge has become policy in many countries (e.g., in Finland, http://finlex.edita.fi; Sweden, http://www.riksdagen.se/debatt/; or Norway, http://www.lovdata.no). In addition, many fee-based services offer national legal information. Legal information concerning the European Union is also available at many Web sites, for example, CELEX (http:/ europa.eu.int/celex).

Legal Web sites in Europe usually contain documents from one country or region only. Some databases specialize in one or more subject areas or contain only selected types of legal rules. Also, temporal coverage may vary among databases; some contain only recently published rules, while others may include legal norms dating back to the 18th century.

A Web site can offer several ways of accessing the legal information it contains. Legal rules may be accessed by date of publication, type of document, the organization which originated the document, or subject. However, subject classification methods differ between Web sites. In addition, the functionality and presentation offered to the users of these databases vary, and even the most frequently used functions may have been implemented in different ways. Moreover, different fonts, colors, and layout make the casual use of multiple databases problematic.

All people need legal information but there are several particular user groups to whom foreign and EU legal information seems to be especially important. A problem in designing retrieval capabilities is that the experience and expertise of the users varies widely. User needs interviews related to legal information were carried out as part of the EULEGIS and RASKE projects. In-depth interviews were arranged in Finland and revealed that several groups of people regarded the accessibility of foreign legal information and EU legal information as important (Tiitinen, Lyytikäinen, Päivärinta & Salminen, 2000). Examples of these groups are people involved in national legislative processes, working in international and large companies, law firms, small and medium-sized companies doing business with foreign partners, law institutions, and the mass media, as well as researchers and public administrators in general. The groups include both those highly expert in legal information retrieval as well as laymen. Legal information is also becoming increasingly important for ordinary citizens, who may, e.g., be changing their country of residence or buying property or goods from another EU state.

In spite of the differences in the interviewed user groups, in several of them similar needs were identified. The differences in various legal systems of Europe were mentioned as a major problem by the interviewed people. These differences often hindered both the search and the use of foreign legal information. Even where the access to the relevant documents had been gained, the utilization of the documents was difficult without sufficient knowledge of the particular legal system. This was a common problem especially for information specialists working in libraries and other public services whose clients regularly ask about legal situations in various European countries.

VISUALIZATION OF THE CONTEXTUAL METADATA

To support the users in coping with the challenges in retrieving information from complex interorganizational domain, as for example the legal domain in Europe, we suggest different models created during the document analysis to be used as visualizations of information. The models can be used as a retrieval interface to access documents stored in distributed repositories. We have used three different models to represent three different views to information (Lyytikäinen, Tiitinen, Salminen, Mercier & Vidick, 2000): the *actor view* describes the most significant actors in the domain, the *information source view* shows the different kinds of documents and their relationships, and the *process view* describes activities related to the information production process. In order to enable querying the document databases, links from each element of the view to the query form of the database can be defined. Also, additional information concerning the element visualized in the views is offered to the users.

The views have been implemented in the prototype version in the demonstrator built during the EULEGIS project. The feedback from the users has been encouraging. The views have been seen as a good tool to become acquainted with a previously unfamiliar legal system and to limit the scope of a query statement. In the following, the actor view, information source view, and process view will be discussed in more detail.

Actor View

The actor view describes the most significant actors that create information in a given domain. The actors are shown in graphical form, and their roles are concisely described. The graphical model is the same model that in the document analysis was called organizational framework model. Figure 3 shows an example of the actor view, where producers of the legal sources in Finland are described. The circle in the middle of the actor view graph represents the domain whose information is created by these actors. The actors in turn are depicted by rectangles connected by arrows to the domain

Figure 3. Actor View of Finnish Legal System

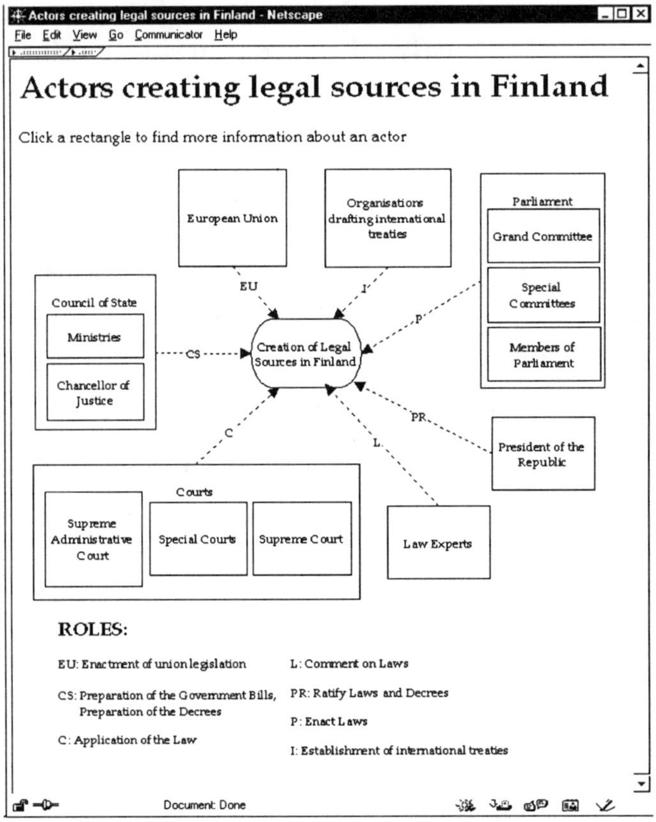

circle. Actors can be put into subgroups, which are shown graphically by nested rectangles.

The actors belonging to an actor group may be part of a larger organization (e.g., Parliament) or may otherwise have similar roles in the creation of the information in question (e.g., different courts). The broken arrows are labeled by identifiers, with phrases in the bottom part briefly describing the tasks of the actors or actor groups of the graph.

By clicking the name of an actor, the user can obtain more information

Figure 4. Information About Supreme Court

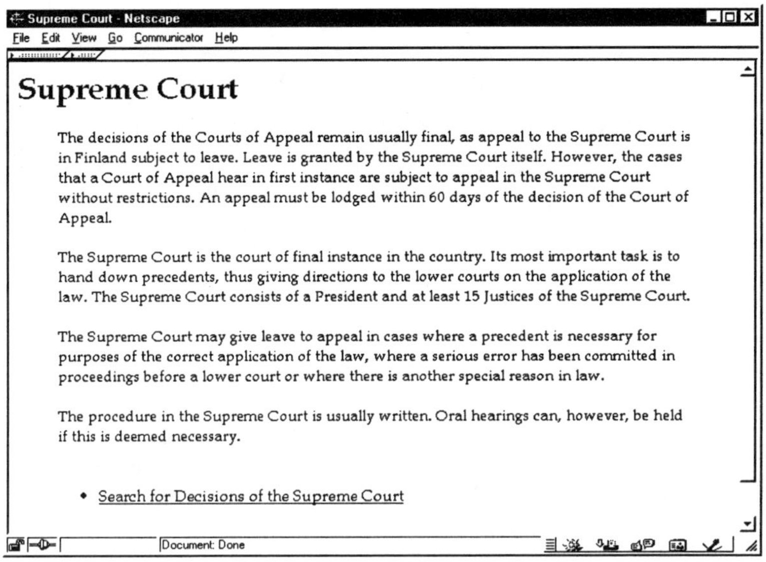

about the role of that actor. From this additional information, a link leads to a search form by which the user can search for the documents that originate from the selected actor (Figure 4).

Information Source View

The information source view shows the most significant documents in a given domain and their relationships to each other. The graphical representation shows the document types, document type groups, and hierarchy connectors. The representation is a modified form of a document-relationship diagram used in the document modeling phase of the document analysis.

Figure 5 describes the legal information sources of the Finnish legal system as an example. National legal documents are categorized into five categories that exist in almost every country: preparatory works, normative documents, court judgments, legal literature, and miscellaneous parliamentary documents, including, for example, parliamentary questions and minutes of plenary sessions. The hierarchical relations of the constitution, act, decree, and administrative act are represented by their vertical relation to each other and by the line connecting them. As a reminder to the user, the significance of the related international legal documents is emphasized by referring to them in a separate box above the national legal documents.

As in the actor view, additional information about the document types can be offered to users. From the information page related to a document type, a hypertext link leads to a search form allowing the user to target to the selected document type.

Process View

The process view gives a graphical overview of the most significant activities related to the creation of information sources in a given domain. It contains information about the order of activities, the actors responsible for performing the activities and the documents created by those activities. The form and semantics of the graph are similar to those of ICNs (Ellis, 1979),

Figure 5. Legal Information Source View of Finland

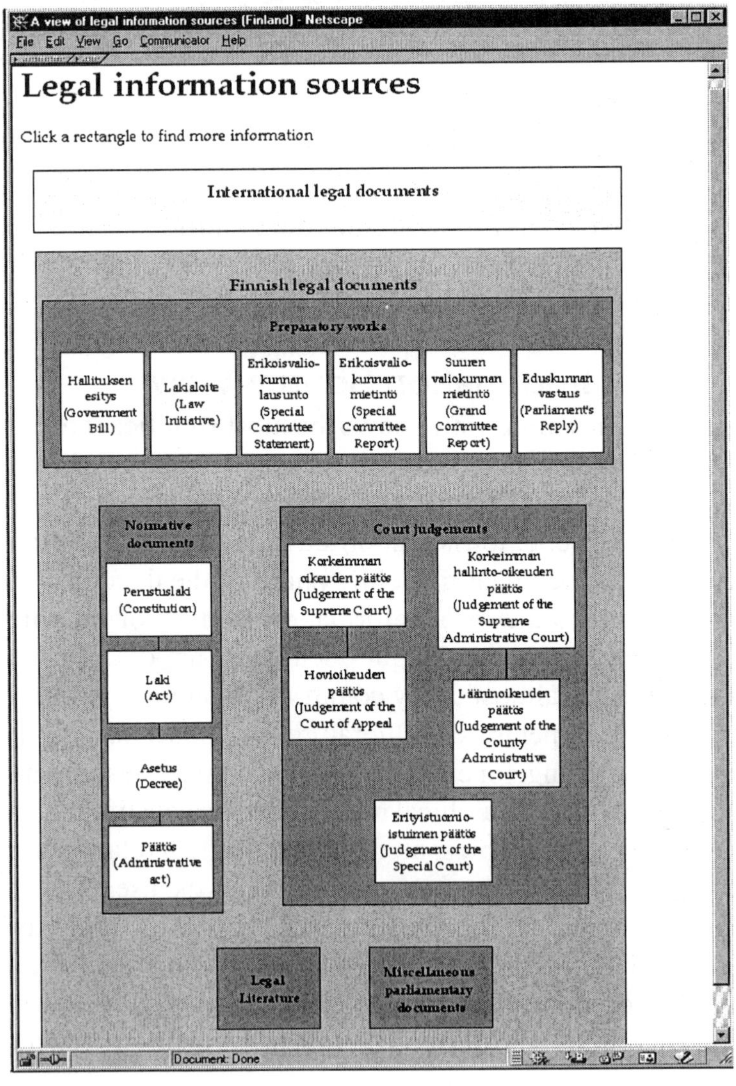

which were used in the process modeling phase of the document analysis. The difference between our process models and ICNs is in the notion of control flow. We regard the control flow between successive activities A and B as *weak*, meaning that activity B begins after A has begun (Salminen, Lyytikäinen & Tiitinen, 2000). In our descriptive models there has been no need to constrain the relationship between the ending and beginning of successive activities. As an example of the process view, the Finnish national legal system is presented in Figure 6.

Figure 6. Process View of the Finnish National Legal System

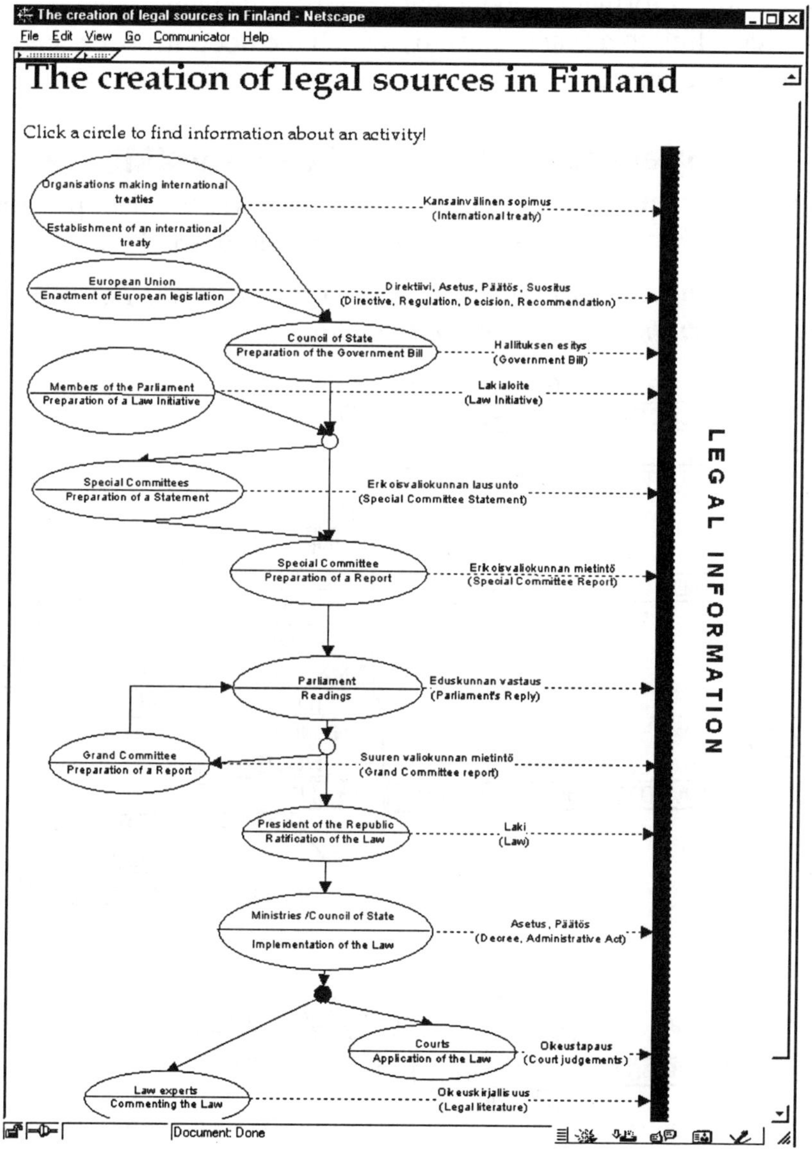

The main activities of the modeled process are depicted by circles. Each circle shows both the name(s) of the activity and the actor(s) performing that activity. The actors in the view should be the same as those presented in the actor view. The order of activities is expressed by unbroken arrows. The direction of the arrow refers to the order in which the activities start. Thus, several activities can actually be performed in parallel. A black dot preceding two or more activities indicates that the activities may start at the same time or in any order. Alternative control flows are indicated by a hollow dot.

As with the other views, additional information can be linked to the components of the process view. When the user clicks an activity symbol in the graph, more information about that activity will appear. That information will provide a link to a search form by which the documents created by that activity can be queried.

Specification of the Views by XML

For the dynamic generation of graphical views, the data pertaining to those views has to be formally defined. For this purpose, we used XML

Figure 7. Graphical Representation of the XML DTD For Describing Metadata For an Interorganizational Domain

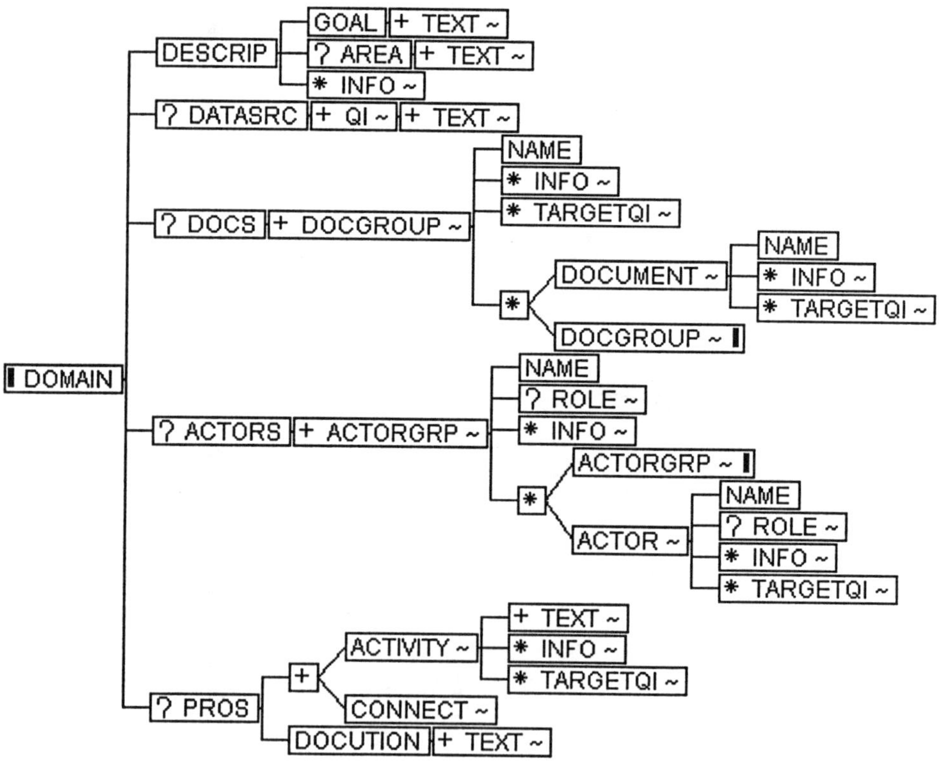

(eXtensible Markup Language), which has been developed especially for specifying document standards for use in Web information systems (Bray, Paoli & Sperberg-McQueen, 1998). We have designed an XML document type definition by which a domain and the different views to it can be described. The document type definition for defining the data is presented in Figure 7 in a graphical form created by Near & Far Designer 3.0.

With this DTD all three separate views—actor view, information source view, and process view—can be described. In the DTD, the data sources, documents, actors, and processes of a certain domain are defined together with their relationships to each other. The DTD is also designed in a way that enables the models to be described in many languages.

The first element in the DTD describes the domain in general terms. The domain has some *goal* (e.g., creation of the legal sources in Finland), and it covers some *area* (e.g., Finland). Both area and goal can be described in several languages. With the *info* element, more detailed textual description about the domain can be inserted.

The document repositories of the domain are defined as query interfaces (*qis*). Each query interface needs to have at least a *name* and some identification, which is defined as an attribute. *Docs*, *actors*, and *pros* elements are each used to describe the corresponding views. The *targetqi* element is used to link query interfaces of original repositories to elements in the view description.

An advantage of the XML solution is in its capability to express multiple models in multiple languages. Since slightly different versions of models are needed, conversion from one basic model is useful. XML files are also easy to transfer in the network environment since XML solutions are system and vendor independent. This also enables long-term archiving of the data.

FUTURE TRENDS

In global and organizational networks, documents are ever more commonly created in interorganizational processes. The improved authoring and communication technology also tends to increase document production. In Europe, the expansion of the European Union within the past years and in the future is creating a situation where organizations and citizens all over Europe have a need for legal information not only concerning their own country but also related to foreign countries and European Union in general. The similar trend can also be seen in the business world where corporations operate in global markets and information related to a business process is produced in different countries. To assure the accessibility of information created in complicated processes, different kinds of new techniques and support for information retrieval are needed. One approach is to associate documents with metadata about the context where the documents were created.

In the activities toward e-government one goal is to offer governmental information on the Web to all citizens. All citizens are expected to be users of the governmental information repositories. Intuitive and informative user interfaces are important, for example, in the e-Government services of the future intended for heterogeneous groups of users. The graphical presentation of the metadata described above is intended for such an interface. Usability studies, however, are needed to evaluate the solutions.

The contextual metadata offered to the user at the time of information access has to be transmitted between collaborative partners and updated occasionally. At the time when organizational networks are extending and reshaping all the time, maintaining the currency and accuracy of the metadata is a challenge. Therefore the graphical representation should be automatically generated from a form which is easy to maintain in a metadata database and also easy to transmit on the Web. The XML format of the metadata has these benefits. Further research is, however, required in order to solve problems related to the automatic generation of the graphical presentation from the XML form.

CONCLUSION

The information needed by people, more and more, is available in Web repositories. Lack of the knowledge about the repositories, differences in the organization of the repositories and in their user interfaces, and lack of knowledge about the context where the information is created hinder the use of the repositories. In this chapter, we suggested collecting metadata concerning the context of the document in the repositories. This contextual metadata can be visualized as an interface with three views to information produced in interorganizational processes. Graphical information models were used to visualize document types, their relationships to each other, actors, and activities in the documentation creation process. In order to formally define the models, an XML schema was designed. The graphical interface has been tested in the EULEGIS project. The test users regarded the interface as a valuable tool for retrieving information from foreign legal systems. More systematic user testing is an important area of future research.

REFERENCES

Abeysinghe, G., & Phalp, K. (1997). Combining process modelling methods. *Information and Software Technology 39*, 107-124.

Bearman, D. (1995). Towards a reference model for business acceptable communications. In *The Recordkeeping Functional Requirements Project at the University of Pittsburgh; A Second Progress Report, March.* Retrieved January 14, 2000 from the World Wide Web: http://www.lis.pitt.edu/~nhprc/tab.html.

Booch, G., Rumbaugh, J., & Jacobson, I. (1999). *The Unified Modeling Language User Guide*. Reading, MA: Addison-Wesley.

Bray, T., Paoli, J., & Sperberg-McQueen, C. M. (Eds.). (1998). Extensible Markup Language (XML) 1.0. W3C Recommendation February 10. Retrieved March 31,1999 from the World Wide Web: http://www.w3.org/TR/REC-xml.

Dourish, P., Bentley, R., Jones, R., & MacLean, A. (1999). Getting some perspective: Using process descriptions to index document history. *Proceedings of the International ACM SIGGROUP Conference on Supporting Group Work*, New York: ACM Press, 375-384.

Ellis, C. A. (1979). Information Control Nets: A mathematical model of office information flow. *Proceedings of the Conference on Simulation, Measurement and Modeling of Computer Systems, ACM SIGMETRICS Performance Evaluation Review*, 8(3), 225-238.

Ellis, C. A. (1983). Formal and informal models of office activity. R. E. A. Mason (Ed.), *Proceedings of the IFIP 9th World Computer Congress,* Paris, France, September 19-23. New York: North-Holland, 11-22.

Gallagher, M., Laver, M., & Mair, P. (1995). *Representative Government in Modern Europe*. New York: McGraw-Hill.

Gershon, N., Eick, S.G., & Card, S. (1998). Information visualization. *Interactions 5*(2), 9-15.

Goldfarb, C.F. (1990). *The SGML Handbook.* Y. Rubinsky (Ed.), Oxford, UK: Oxford University Press.

Käkölä, T. (1995). Fostering organizational learning with embedded application systems: The XTEND2 prototype. J. F. Nunamaker and R. H. Sprague (Eds.), *Proceedings of the 28th Annual Hawaii International Conference on System Sciences*, Los Alamitos, CA: IEEE Computer Society Press, 199-208.

Lyytikäinen, V., Tiitinen, P., & Salminen, A. (2000). Challenges for European legal information retrieval. F. Galindo and G. Quirchmayer (Eds.), *Proceedings of the IFIP 8.5 Working Conference on Advances in Elec-*

tronic Government, Zaragoza: Seminario de Informática y Derecho, Universidad de Zaragoza, 121-132.

Lyytikäinen, V., Tiitinen, P., Salminen, A., Mercier, L., & Vidick, J-L. (2000). Visualizing legal systems for information retrieval. In M. Khosrowpour (Ed.) *Challenges of Information Technology Management in the 21st Century, Proceedings of 2000 Information Resources Management Association International Conference*, 245-249, Hershey, PA: Idea Group Publishing.

Maler, E., & El Andaloussi, J. (1996). *Developing SGML DTDs. From text to model to markup*. Upper Saddle River, NJ: Prentice Hall.

Plaisant, C. & Shneiderman, B. (1995). Organization overviews and role management: inspiration for future desktop environments. *IEEE Proceedings 4th Workshop on Enabling Technologies: Infrastructure for Collaborative Enterprises*, Berkeley Springs, *WV, April 20-22,* 14-22.

Salminen, A. (2000). Methodology for document analysis. In A. Kent (Ed.), *Encyclopedia of Library and Information Science,* 67(30). New York: Marcel Dekker, Inc, 299-320.

Salminen, A., Kauppinen, K., & Lehtovaara, M. (1997). Towards a methodology for document analysis. *Journal of the American Society for Information Science, 48*(7), 644-655.

Salminen, A., Lehtovaara, M., & Kauppinen, K. (1996). Standardization of digital legislative documents, a case study. M. S. Lynn (Ed.), *Proceedings of the 29th Annual Hawaii International Conference on System Sciences*, Los Alamitos, CA: IEEE Computer Society Press, 72-81.

Salminen, A., Lyytikäinen, V., & Tiitinen, P. (2000). Putting documents into their work context in document analysis. *Information Processing & Management 36*(4), 623-641.

Sarin, S.K., Abbott, K.R., & McCarthy, D.R. (1991). A process model and system for supporting collaborative work. *Conference on Organizational Computing Systems, SIGOIS Bulletin 12*(2,3), 213-224.

Shlaer, S., & Mellor, S.J. (1992). *Object Lifecycles: Modeling the World in States*. Englewood Cliffs, NJ: Yourdon Press.

Tiitinen, P., Lyytikäinen, V., Päivärinta, T., & Salminen, A. (2000). User needs for electronic document management in public administration: a study of two cases. H.R. Hansen, M. Bichler & H. Mahler (Eds.), *Proceedings of the 8th European Conference on Information Systems, Volume 2,* Vienna University of Economics and Business Administration, Wien: Wirtschaftsuniversität Wien, 1144-1151.

UML-1.1 (1997). UML Notation Guide. Version 1.1, September 1. Retrieved March 31, 1999 from the World Wide Web: http://www.rational.com/uml/resources/documentation/notation/index.jtmpl.

Yourdon, E. (1989). *Modern Structured Analysis.* Englewood Cliffs, NJ: Prentice Hall.

About the Authors

Amita Goyal Chin

Dr. Amita Goyal Chin is an associate professor in the Information Systems Department at Virginia Commonwealth University. She received her BS in Computer Science and MS and PhD in Information Systems all from the University of Maryland at College Park. Her research focuses primarily on database technology and its applications in information systems. She has been investigating new approaches in data models for text representation and document databases, hoping this area will contribute to information delivery vehicles beyond the World Wide Web. Additionally, she is pursuing new answers to managing data quality in database systems. Dr. Chin has combined her information technology experience with her classroom skills to experiment with new teaching technologies and methodologies.

***

Maria Fernanda Caropreso

Maria Fernanda Caropreso received an MsC in computer science at the University of Buenos Aires in 2000. In 2000 she was a visiting scientist at the Department of Computer Science of the University of Ottawa, and in 2001 she has been a visiting scientist at the Italian National Council of Research in Pisa. Her research interests are in indexing techniques for automated text categorization and information retrieval.

Ingrid Fisher

Ingrid E. Fisher is a CPA with 17 years experience in private practice. Currently a full-time member of the State University of New York at Albany faculty in the Department of Accounting and Law, she teaches courses primarily in accounting information systems and auditing.

Jagdish Gangolly

Jagdish Gangolly is an associate professor of Accounting and of Management Science and Information Systems at the State University of New York at Albany. He is also a senior program faculty member of the doctoral program in Information Science at the School of Information Science and Policy. He has published papers in various journals in accounting, auditing, operations research and expert systems. He is an associate editor of the *E-Services Journal* and serves on the editorial board of the journal *Issues in Accounting Education.*

Wendy Lucas

Wendy Lucas is an assistant professor in the Department of Computer Information Systems at Bentley College in Waltham, MA. She received her B.S. in Electrical Engineering from Tufts University, her M.S. in Management from the Sloan School of Management at MIT., and her Ph.D. from the Electrical Engineering and Computer Science Department at Tufts University, where her dissertation topic was a visual approach to querying and presenting multimedia data. Her research interests include Internet search engines, customizable user interfaces, and Web technology.

Virpi Lyytikäinen

Virpi Lyytikäinen is a Ph.D. student at the University of Jyväskylä, Department of Computer Science and Information Systems, in Finland. For four years she has been active in research and development projects in public administration, where methods for electronic document management have been developed. Currently she participates in a project studying usability of structure document repositories containing industrial documentation. Her research interests include structured documents and methods for electronic document management.

Stan Matwin

Stan Matwin is a professor of information technology and engineering and the director of the Graduate Certificate on Electronic Commerce at the University of Ottawa. He is the former Head of the Canadian Society for Computational Studies of Intelligence and of IFIP WG 12.2 (Machine Learning). His research interests are in Data and Text Mining and Knowledge-based Systems. He has authored and co-authored around 100 research papers in refereed conferences and journals. Stan is particularly interested in applied research which tackles practical problems in need of a solution.

Fabrizio Sebastiani

Fabrizio Sebastiani has been a researcher of the Italian National Council of Research since 1988 and contract professor at the Department of Computer Science of the University of Pisa since 1998. He has published several papers in international journals and conferences in the fields of natural language processing, knowledge representation, and information retrieval. His current area of research is the automated categorization of written and spoken text by means of machine learning techniques. He is the guest editor (with Thorsten Joachims) of the forthcoming Special Issue on Automated Text Categorization of the *Journal of Intelligent Information Systems* (Kluwer).

Lisa D. Murphy

Lisa D. Murphy is an assistant professor in the Information Systems and Decision Sciences Department at the Ourso College of Business Administration at Louisiana State University in Baton Rouge, LA. Before earning her doctorate at Indiana University, she was a systems developer and manager in industry for more than a decade. Her research interests include digital documents in organizations, geographic information systems, and environmental systems.

Airi Salminen

Airi Salminen is professor at the University of Jyväskylä, Department of Computer Science and Information Systems, in Finland. She received her Ph.D. in Computer Science from the University of Tampere in 1989. She was responsible for planning a new master's program in Digital Media at the University of Jyväskylä and has headed the program from its beginning in 1995. She has been the leader of several projects where research has been tied to document management development efforts in major Finnish companies or public sector organizations. Her current research interests include document management, structured documents, user interfaces, and software environments.

Mareike Schoop

Mareike Schoop is assistant professor in the Information Systems Group (Informatik V) at Aachen University of Technology, Germany. She obtained her Ph.D. in Computer Science from the University of Manchester, UK. The topic of her research was cooperative document management. Her thesis entitled "Towards Effective Multidisciplinary Communication: A Language-Action Approach to Cooperative Documentation Systems" was ranked among the top five in the 1999 ICIS Doctoral Dissertation Award, a worldwide contest of theses in information systems. Dr. Schoop works on cooperative document management; multidisciplinary communication and cooperation support, especially negotiation support in electronic commerce; and logical semantics for communication models. She has published 20 refereed articles in international conference proceedings and journals.

Arijit Sengupta

Dr. Arijit Sengupta is an assistant professor in the Department of Computer Information Systems at Georgia State University. He received his Ph.D. in Computer Science from Indiana University in 1997 and worked as the director of educational development and assistant professor in Indiana University before joining Georgia State University in 1999. His research interests are primarily in database systems and, in particular, database systems for structured documents. He has published several papers in leading conferences and journals and has led the development of the research prototype Docbase, a query processing software for SGML and XML documents.

Pasi Tiitinen

Pasi Tiitinen is a Ph.D. student at the University of Jyväskylä, Department of Computer Science and Information Systems, in Finland. Since 1996 he has participated in research and development projects in public administration, where methods for electronic document management have been developed. At the moment he participates in a project studying usability of structured document repositories containing industrial documentation. His research interests include user needs analysis and usability engineering in document management projects, and structured documents.

Index